W9-CCO-983

WITHDRAWN

PUBLIC LIBRARY
DANVILLE, ILLINOIS

Praise for *Spiritual Delights and Delusions*

"Steve Posner has painted for us a brilliant picture of spirituality-in-action. This book shows how active, awakened spiritual realism can make a difference."

—Louise Diamond, author of *The Peace Book* and *The Courage for Peace*

"Posner's intriguing story of self-realization includes timeless, universal esoteric gems that hold the keys to the awakening of higher consciousness."

—Bob Waxman, author of *Kabbalah Simply Stated*

"With grace and a keen wit, Steve Posner has the courage to remove delusion and move his readers into spiritual reality."

—John English, author of *The Shift: An Awakening*

"A book that I've been waiting for that obliterates the oxymoron 'Spiritual Realism' and converts it into wisdom that will help everyone find their path."

—Warren Bennis, Distinguished Professor of Business, University of Southern California, and author of *On Becoming a Leader*

"Steve Posner shows why achieving our spiritual goals requires an approach that stays with us long after the initial excitement about the next big thing in self-development begins to fade. *Spiritual Delights and Delusions* is a down-to-earth manual that uplifts the reader and reveals a technique for spiritual success that is available to us right now."

—Debra Poneman, founder of Yes to Success! and author of *Chicken Soup for the American Idol Soul*

"With lucidity and genuine intimacy, *Spiritual Delights and Delusions* shows me how inner peace, far from dulling outer awareness, can help us respond more compassionately to injustice."

—Alex Raksin, winner of the 2002 Pulitzer Prize for Editorial Writing

"A much needed book. Learning how to combine spirituality with everyday life is an essential skill, too much neglected in modern life."

—Dr. Yehuda Stolov, Executive Director, Interfaith Encounter Association, Jerusalem

"The combination of spiritual concepts along with a deep knowledge of politics and world events makes this book quite unique."

—Sharon Janis, author of *Secrets of Happiness* and *Spirituality for Dummies*

"In *Spiritual Delights and Delusions*, Steve shares his belief in 'spiritual realism,' which insists that we must never close our eyes to the horrors of the world, yet suggests that there is a way to find stillness amidst it all."

—Denise Linn, author of *The Soul Loves the Truth*

"As a person who was born and lives in a country that is in a continuous conflict and war, I find *Spiritual Delights and Delusions* important and honest. It is my blessing that this book will serve its purpose in the world."

—Rabbi Ohad Ezrahi, author of *Worlds of Doubt*,
Two are the Cherubs, and *Who's Afraid of Lilith*

"Steve Posner avoids the Western cultural misunderstandings about Islam, which so often inform our thinking and beliefs. He shows us its sweetness and provides a new way of dealing with conflict."

—Dr. J. Shams Prinzivalli,
Center for Healing and Conflict Resolution,
New York and Jerusalem

"Amidst a world of stark contrasts, between absolutes of spirituality and secular rationality, Steve manages to fuse the best of these worlds together into 'spiritual realism,' articulating wonderfully what so many of us have been feeling in our guts. May this new addition to the Torah of life spread forth and take root all over the world."

—Jacob Ner-David, Managing Partner, Jerusalem Capital, Co-founder of
Delta Three, NomadIQ, Ambient, and Double Fusion

"One directly feels that this book is written with the heart, as a living witness of a search for peace which depends on an inner disposition and not on a political project. Posner has given us a precious gift."

—Sheikh Abdul Hadi Palazzi,
Secretary-general, the Italian Muslim Assembly,
Director, the Cultural Institute of the Italian
Muslim Community in Rome

"A book of hope, one that seeks to apply the fruits of spiritual practice to the violent and compassionate reality that is our world."

—Sonia Linebaugh, author of *At the Feet of Mother Meera*

SPIRITUAL DELIGHTS
AND DELUSIONS

*How to Bridge the Gap between Spiritual
Fulfillment and Emotional Realities*

STEVE POSNER

John Wiley & Sons, Inc.

Copyright © 2008 by Steve Posner. All rights reserved

Published by John Wiley & Sons, Inc., Hoboken, New Jersey
Published simultaneously in Canada

No part of this publication may be reproduced, stored in a retrieval system, or transmitted in any form or by any means, electronic, mechanical, photocopying, recording, scanning, or otherwise, except as permitted under Section 107 or 108 of the 1976 United States Copyright Act, without either the prior written permission of the Publisher, or authorization through payment of the appropriate per-copy fee to the Copyright Clearance Center, 222 Rosewood Drive, Danvers, MA 01923, (978) 750-8400, fax (978) 646-8600, or on the web at www.copyright.com. Requests to the Publisher for permission should be addressed to the Permissions Department, John Wiley & Sons, Inc., 111 River Street, Hoboken, NJ 07030, (201) 748-6011, fax (201) 748-6008, or online at http://www.wiley.com/go/permissions.

Limit of Liability/Disclaimer of Warranty: While the publisher and the author have used their best efforts in preparing this book, they make no representations or warranties with respect to the accuracy or completeness of the contents of this book and specifically disclaim any implied warranties of merchantability or fitness for a particular purpose. No warranty may be created or extended by sales representatives or written sales materials. The advice and strategies contained herein may not be suitable for your situation. You should consult with a professional where appropriate. Neither the publisher nor the author shall be liable for any loss of profit or any other commercial damages, including but not limited to special, incidental, consequential, or other damages.

For general information about our other products and services, please contact our Customer Care Department within the United States at (800) 762-2974, outside the United States at (317) 572-3993 or fax (317) 572-4002.

Wiley also publishes its books in a variety of electronic formats. Some content that appears in print may not be available in electronic books. For more information about Wiley products, visit our web site at www.wiley.com.

ISBN: 978-0-471-69825-8

Printed in the United States of America

10 9 8 7 6 5 4 3 2 1

2045
po
c/s !

To my wife, a pure soul who helps all souls feel at home
To my children, for the wisdom and warmth they give to this world
To my brother, a loyal friend who serves with insight and caring
To my mother, whose loving presence is what I wish for every child

And for my father, my first, last, and highest teacher,
forever my beloved satguru

PUBLIC LIBRARY
DANVILLE, ILLINOIS

CONTENTS

INTRODUCTION

Spiritual fantasies make us wonder whether we can ever become who we want to be. We may think we are not high enough, not pure enough, not good enough to become enlightened, and that only the saints are in a state of perfection. We might have had a flashy experience of a higher state of consciousness now and then, but it never seems to last. So we figure that we are just ordinary people destined to a lifetime of yearning for a small taste of nirvana. Is there anything more self-limiting?

Spiritual realism releases us from the delusion that we are not yet capable of finding fulfillment in our everyday lives. Spiritual realism frees us from the fantasy of having to develop a perfect personality in order to consider ourselves enlightened. Only silence is perfect.

A realistic spirituality enables us to make peace with the world's imperfections—and our own. We can stop chasing spiritual illusions and instead experience the spiritual delights that are already available to us.

Our obsession with achieving a far-off state of consciousness where we become perfect human beings, always satisfied and capable of doing the right thing, distracts us from what we can achieve now.

When we drop our spiritual delusions, we may become disillusioned. Our daily reality might seem so much less rewarding than our fantasies about enlightenment. All the world's cruelties—blood-soaked wars, rapes, genital mutilations, unrelenting mass starvations, the brutal persistence of child slavery, ravaging diseases like AIDS and malaria that kill millions every single year—make us naturally cry out for a future consciousness that will lift us out of the grip of such horrors and somehow deliver us into a liberating realm of ceaseless joy. Yet this spiritual utopia remains beyond our grasp, year after year. And it remains elusive for a reason. Not because we are spiritual failures, but because we are spiritually unrealistic.

Understandably, finding constant bliss in a world of continuous conflict is the spiritual aim of most seekers. The search for perpetual happiness is the reason most of us began our spiritual seeking. So the eventual acceptance of the impossibility of this goal, the letting go of our spiritual delusions, may be too shattering to face. Yet it is this letting go of spiritual fantasy that actually frees us.

Spiritual delusions lure us into thinking that if we could just integrate true spirituality into daily life, then our emotions would always be calm. We would no longer bounce between happiness and sorrow. Even when we fail to achieve this imaginary state, we keep focusing on a future spiritual utopia because we assume that our emotional upheavals merely prove that we are not where we should be. If only I were more spiritually advanced, then surely I would be freed from the sufferings of the body and the tug of my emotions. But what if this notion of spirituality is unrealistic? What if enlightenment enables us to make peace with our difficult emotions but not eliminate them?

Spiritual realism allows us to make peace with the world as it is, not with how we wish it to be. No longer distracted by our obsession with who we need to become, we can enjoy who we are. By letting go of our fixation on an unrealistic future, we can experience the presence of a soothing silence that is within us right now.

If we can accept the volatile shifting of our thoughts, ideas, and feelings, then we can truly be set free. When we stop resisting change, we can make peace with it. If we don't waste our energy trying to pursue a state of consciousness that doesn't exist, then we can finally achieve a more realistic state of enlightenment.

Getting in touch with the peaceful quiet within is something we can all do. A first step is to close our eyes and listen. We can all awaken to the silence between every sound and every breath. When we become familiar with the quiet that resides in every pause, its calming presence can be experienced even when our eyes are open. We can feel the silent center on the inside, even if there is noise on the outside. Our awareness of the underlying stillness that lingers in a world of constant change steadies us, enlightens us.

Our inner silence calms us in the midst of conflict. Personal, social, and emotional difficulties—all of which are natural in a world of contradiction, competition, and constant uncertainty—are soothed by the unchanging comfort of inner stillness. Even the fears of our post-9/11 world and the pain of physical illness are eased by the simplicity of silence.

All of us can center ourselves in silence. It need not be a struggle. Spiritual practice is not only about chanting, praying, meditating, studying scripture, and reading self-help books. These may help to turn us inward so that we can eventually feel the presence of silence, but our opening to the quiet within is not a prize to be awarded at the end of a long and arduous journey. We can all experience it right now. Seek, and ye shall find. Listen, and you will hear. Silence abounds.

Chapter 1

THE REWARDS OF SPIRITUAL
REALISM

Does spiritual realism expand us or limit us?

Sundaram, a kind and devoted American disciple of the Indian sage Paramahansa Yogananda, cautioned, "Let us be spiritually realistic, yes, but let's not encourage people to be satisfied with less than their unlimited divine potential."

An inspiring belief in our boundless potential is essential, motivating us to expand our minds and our hearts so that we might hope to one day heal ourselves and the world.

Alan Wallace, a dedicated Buddhist scholar, emphasizes that traditional beliefs in future states of spiritual perfection should not be dismissed. "Many of the great men and women of the past have transformed the world in meaningful ways by striving for ideals that others dismissed as 'unrealistic.' Who is the final arbiter of realism and fantasy?"

Our vision of distant possibilities is shaped by our faith, not by our experience. Yet faith in an ideal future can transform us, creating new experiences.

Of course, spiritual beliefs differ from one person to the next. Cynthia Lane, a dear friend and a seasoned spiritual teacher, reminds us of a favorite saying by Maharishi Mahesh Yogi: the world is as we are. "Our interpretation of our third-dimensional reality is a function of our perception, the flavors of consciousness that color our worldview," she observed. "A million souls will see the world a million ways and who is to say with absolute authority what is truth and what is illusion?"

Every spiritual seeker chooses his or her own vision of enlightenment. But like sleep, silence is the same for everyone. It is a present reality that we can all agree on.

It took me three decades to abandon my own original concept of enlightenment. When I finally dropped my yearning for a future personality that had no anger, disappointment, and desire, I was able to relax into the immediate spiritual calm of my own inner silence.

But is silence the essence of spirituality?

"Silence cannot be equated with spirituality. That is simply not true," insisted Michael Kagan, a Jerusalem teacher who takes a holistic approach to Judaism. The experience of the quiet stillness within is just one of many spiritual practices that serves as a gateway to the divine, Kagan explains. "Silence is not in itself spiritual," he said. "Experiencing the presence of God is spiritual. Silence simply opens us to this experience."

Inner silence can be its own spiritual reward or the door to a variety of religious experiences.

"The Father uttered one Word," wrote St. John of the Cross, the sixteenth-century Christian mystic. "That Word is His Son, and he utters Him for ever in everlasting silence; and in silence the soul has to hear it."

Depending on one's own spiritual beliefs, silence may be experienced as a spiritual gift to humanity or a divine blessing from God.

"When Lord Buddha speaks about Nirvana, let us think only of silence," the Hindu guru Sri Chinmoy taught. "This silence that the Buddhists speak of is nothing other than God, for inside silence we see the whole creation."

Whether the experience of inner silence alone is the essence of spirituality or a gateway to the God realization of rabbis, monks, and gurus, the path to fulfillment remains the same: our awareness of the quiet within leads to a profound awakening. This spiritual awakening gives us inner peace. And it gives birth to wisdom.

Adin Steinsaltz, a renowned expert on the mystical teachings of the Kabbalah, described how insight emerges from silence. "Often cited in the literature of Chabad Hassidism, is the case of a person struggling with an extremely difficult concept," he wrote. "At first, the concept is completely elusive, the mind an utter blank," Steinsaltz explained. "Then, suddenly, there comes in a flash the sense that 'Eureka! I got it!' If, at this point, we were to stop this person and ask him, 'What did you get? What have you understood?' he would be unable to explain anything to us, except that he has grasped the concept."

When we accept the blankness within, welcome it, relax into it, and enjoy it, then knowledge dawns. And eureka! We experience a silent moment of insight that is beyond words. What follows this revelation can be analyzed, categorized, and described in different ways. It is the presence of God, says one seeker. It is the unfolding of the true Self, another explains. It is the experience of Unity, others declare. Yet what is common to all of these descriptions is the uplifting experience of the blank stillness within.

The silent eureka moment can be accessed by all of us—the devout and the faithless, the believer and the skeptic, the inspired and the disillusioned. Some of us still long for a far-off state of nirvana where ecstasy constantly flows. Whether this goal is spiritually realistic or not, the inner stillness needed to attain this state is available to all of us, here and now. As Sri Chinmoy observed, "Perhaps only one person out of a million or a billion will know what Nirvana is. But everybody knows what silence is."

The search for a distant spiritual goal can propel us past what is already possible. We wind up getting trapped by our belief in an exotic state of consciousness, which we assume is capable of turning our daily ups and downs into a lifetime of steady, unalterable bliss. We become ensnared by the future's promise, when the present is all we need.

There is no shame in having chased the implausible and no contempt for those who still do. A spiritual journey is just that: a movement from one revelation to another. We trade our illusions for insights as we make our way along the path. Let us honor the noble people who seek perfection, who courageously strive for absolute virtue and a ceaseless harmonious future. Yet may the silence of the present also bring them peace.

My own experience is not the godlike stuff of legendary yogis and mythical sages, but rather the simple awareness of peaceful inner quiet. Absolute virtue and unwavering serenity still elude. Emotions rise and fall, fading in and out. Passions and obsessions emerge, dissolve, reappear, and disappear. Fears grip, release, return, and vanish. Thoughts change—questioning, clarifying, and questioning once again. Spiritual ecstasy comes, but it also goes. Yet a deep, stabilizing stillness endures.

The eighteenth-century mystical poet William Blake observed, "Men are admitted into Heaven not because they have curbed and governed their passions or have no passions, but because they have cultivated their understandings." We can understand that it is the heavenly reality of silence, which hovers beneath our conflicting emotions, that keeps us from falling into hellish despair.

Inner silence offers salvation because its timeless presence cushions our daily sufferings. Silence is eternal, so it is ever ready to comfort us. Silence has no end, just as it has no beginning. In the beginning was the Word, but before the beginning, before all words, there was nothing. Only silence. What will there be long after the beginning, after the end has come? Only silence. What is left when our thinking and feelings subside? Inner silence.

We can become aware of our own inner silence any time, anywhere. Silence never disappears. It is the grace that has been bestowed upon every one of us. We don't have to invent silence, manipulate it, or worship it. Silence has been given freely to each of us. All we need to do is put our attention on it.

Chapter 2

THE WISDOM OF FEELING GOOD
ABOUT FEELING BAD

For years, I ignored the silence in everyday life.

Instead of looking toward the present stillness within, I focused on descriptions of a higher consciousness that was yet to come. I tried to guess when and where I might finally reach enlightenment—or what I imagined enlightenment to be. I busily meditated for weeks, months, and decades, which served me well. I sampled this and that path, picking through different spiritual philosophies, which deepened my understanding. Yet I was determined to reach a state of awareness that would permanently eliminate all obstacles once and forever, solve all of life's mysteries, and end all of my sufferings. It was a mistake to expect all these things from spiritual enlightenment.

Even into my forties, I still clung to spiritual dreams of perpetual emotional pleasure and total knowledge of life's cosmic purpose.

Finally, at my wit's end, I accepted my mental bewilderment, my emotional passions, and I surrendered. I surrendered to the quiet silence that lies beyond thoughts and feelings.

St. Paul wrote, "When I was a child, I spoke as a child, and reasoned as a child, and thought as a child: now that I am a man, I am through with childish things." Discovering the powerful silence of the present made me spiritually mature. I had uncovered the peaceful inner stillness that can be experienced in daily life, regardless of what I am thinking or feeling at any given moment. My frustrating childish delusions gave way to a more spiritually realistic and subtle delight. I continued to be thrilled one day, frustrated the next, but my soothing inner silence diminished the impact of these emotions, allowing me to make peace with them.

Yet even with inner silence at our side, peace can be difficult to find when life's unexpected changes turn us upside down. At one point in my marriage, my wife, Mona, became ill, then anxious, and decided to move in with her mother. Her condition could have lasted for years; there was no telling when she would return home. We had been married for more than twenty-five years. Suddenly, I found myself alone, and lonely, with no clear promise of when it would end. I was not quite single, yet we were no longer living as husband and wife. My future was uncertain, my security shaken. What if she didn't recover? What if she was unable to live with me again?

I became increasingly filled with self-doubt. I struggled with the notion that somehow, in some way, it was my responsibility to cure her—and if I couldn't, I would be failing her as a husband. I'd be a failure as a man. Wasn't it my job to rescue my beloved in distress? Hokey, yet this question gnawed at me. As evolved as I thought I had become, as much as I believed my politically correct consciousness had been raised, the age-old male chest-pounding snuck up on me, heaving me into a fierce determination to save her, which gradually reduced me to gasping frustration. I'd get fired up again by raging testosterone and renewed commitment. As time wore on without success, I found myself ensnared in a tangle of useless agonizing, impotent self-recrimination, and, mostly, sorrow.

Still I wondered, Wasn't I beyond the grip of such unenlightened sufferings? I was a devoted meditator and a faithful seeker, and I had come to believe that I was a spiritually informed being who had already dispelled the last shadowy remnants of my lowly earthly struggles and ignorant childish anguish. I had learned my high spiritual lessons and now was beyond all that, or so I assumed.

I figured that I had already traveled the path described by St. John of the Cross in his *Dark Night of the Soul*, where the Spanish monk wrote that the "many blessings of the dark night" eventually "cleanse the soul and purify it from all these imperfections." Hadn't I already experienced my own dark night? Didn't I spend decades purifying my soul through earnest spiritual practices so that I could detach myself from such base imperfections as loneliness, anxiety, and insecurity?

Surely, my spiritual journey had given me the understanding that whining about loneliness and chastened masculinity were the foolish cries of a spiritually naive child. I was a spiritual grown-up. I was not like the baby who wakes up crying as if he had been abandoned, even though his parents are in the next room. Pain and suffering were not real. They were merely the false imaginings of those who did not yet know the reality of spiritual enlightenment. I knew better than to cry about my own loneliness when my spiritually elevated insights should be enough of a comfort to keep me warm and happy with whatever came along. Yet if I was so high, why did I feel so low?

There is a story about John Lennon when he suddenly decided to leave Maharishi's ashram in India. Stunned by the rejection, Maharishi asked, "Why are you leaving?" Lennon laughed, "If you're so cosmic, you tell me!" So there I was, overwhelmed by sudden loneliness, longing for my married life in America's suburbia, wondering, If I'm so cosmic, why am I in such worldly pain? Like the disciple who thinks that his guru should know everything, I had succumbed to the lure of a spiritual absurdity, sinking deeper into my childish delusion that enlightened hearts never ache, and the enlightened do not weep.

Regressing into the tantalizing fantasy of a nirvana without tears, I struggled to hang on to my conviction that a spiritual awakening is like alchemy, capable of turning every pain into pleasure, every misfortune into a blessing. I wanted to find a way into that state of consciousness where I would soon realize that everything is as it should be. "It's all good," would become my spiritual motto. It would be the cosmic truth that could quell my painful emotions. So what if Mona never recovered or returned? Her spirit endures, connecting us to each other through the same energy that connects us to all things. So why should I moan about her physical absence? If I could just expand my spiritual awareness, I would realize that there was no reason to cry, no reason to hurt. This stupidity was a symptom of my spiritual adolescence.

In my bewildering despair and wild hope, I stubbornly clung to my swiftly evaporating delusion that if I could truly awaken from my soul's dark night, the divine light would help me see that all is well in this world and in the next. I would then experience perfect joy at all times, in every circumstance, whether or not my wife would ever recover and return to me, whether the news of the day was inspiring or tragic, whether drowning lives were lost or rescued, or children starved, or cancers thrived, and nations warred. It's all good, isn't it? Part of the divine plan, a perfect creation that only the spiritually blind fail to see, and the ignorant dare to protest.

Yet in the here and now, the emotional serenity of such cosmic complacency was nowhere to be found. The days lingered, my mood flattened. I aimlessly moved through unfamiliar grocery aisles, sorted mail that was rarely addressed to me, and plotted when to call her, when to give her space, and whether my love should be tougher, more manly. Should I push Mona harder so that she might heal more quickly?

I took long walks along sagebrush trails through the hills surrounding my cookie-cutter suburban home, which no longer felt so staid and reassuring. I avoided neighbors and passersby, as if they might detect my embarrassing, self-conscious loneliness. I listlessly soaked in scalding hot baths, absent-mindedly scooping up the soapy green bubble-bath foam to remind me of better days. I had bathed in warm tubs overflowing with the same distinctive lime scent in small rooms across Europe, during those long promising months of meditation when I was just nineteen years old.

Disoriented by the uninvited solitude, I somehow hoped that I could sweat the despair out of me. Gently moving in that soundless womb of water, I managed to steal moments of calm. Now and then I succeeded in creating periods of optimism. But mostly, I was unable to keep them from slipping away. The heartache kept pulling me under.

Desperate and exhausted, I eventually remembered to return to silence. It was all I had left. And it turned out to be everything I needed.

In my darkest nights, when even my dreams were depressing, I stared into the glistening blackness and managed to discover my inner silence. Falling asleep, face up and all alone on my side of the bed, I was comforted by the enveloping stillness. I kept returning to that quiet presence with each passing day. I allowed my awareness to expand, uncovering the silence beneath the torrent of my obsessive thinking and choking heartache. The sleeping silence within had spiritually awakened me, and each night, as I slid deeper into slumber, its whisper called me back to the quiet source of peace.

This silent presence had been patiently waiting for my return, ready to take me into the center of my authentic self. The transcendent quiet hovering beneath the noise of passion and pain seemed to rise, lifting me out of my weary worldliness. I rested upon its silent calm, like a baby quietly sleeping against his mother's breast. Yet from time to time I became restless as my mind grappled with the paradox of spiritual stillness dwelling alongside emotional turmoil. How could my inner world differ so much from the outer one? Silence did not unravel this mystery, yet, eventually, it enabled me to make peace with it.

Despite our unanswered questions and confusion, we can find solace in our return to silence. The majesty of this return makes us humble. Even in our weakness and our ignorance, silence sustains us. And for this, we are thankful.

Silence is liberation. It frees us from our need to dominate our surroundings. It helps us to let go of the belief that we can control our lives and protect ourselves from the unknown. In silence, we learn that the unknown can never be thwarted and that the mystery of life can only be answered by silence.

One certain fate shared by all human beings also cannot be avoided. The reality common to all living things is that they will one day die. There is no defense against death in a world of fragile survival and mutual destruction. "The universe wants to kill us," noted the Harvard-trained physicist Neil deGrasse Tyson. Black holes and galactic explosions and terrifying earthquakes and animal predators and toxic viral mutations conspire with the rest of nature to keep the cycle of creation and destruction churning. But silence cannot be destroyed. It needs no protection.

The enduring power of inner silence can help to shield us from our greed, jealousy, hostility, and resentment, which stem from our desperate desire to find emotional safety in an unsafe world. We are reassured once we realize that the safest place for us is found in our silent center, which even the conflicts of this world can never kill. So the need to rely on our egos to bolster our defenses becomes moot. In the security of inner silence we are empowered to love freely, which is the natural state of those at peace. Even a tortured soul can be calmed and rehabilitated by the stillness within. As light comes in, darkness recedes.

During my own tortuous time, in the midst of the shadow of a faltering marriage, my silent light returned. Despite my despair, my love grew stronger. Silence became my most trustworthy friend. I continued to take my early evening strolls through the sagebrush, a husband still not quite married, a man still unable to fix what only nature could heal. Yet this time, I would stop and share the stoic silence of my favorite willow. I could see how we both were rooted in a stillness that can serve others, offering shelter from rain, shading us from pain. As I stood before that silent tree, sharing the stillness, the twilight seemed to gently push away my stale spiritual delusions, making way for a renewed inner delight.

With inner silence as my steadfast companion, nothing could stop me from loving. You might not love me, and my heart may ache, but I can still love you. Neither pleasure nor pain, happiness nor unhappiness, can keep any of us from loving. A quiet stillness within sustains us. And like silence, our ability to love never leaves us.

A few weeks later, unexpectedly, my wife recovered. She returned to me and was welcomed back in silence, and with love.

Chapter 3

THE ILLUSION OF A PERFECT
PERSONALITY

I once believed that peaceful inner silence could only be experienced while I was meditating, sitting still, back straight, for several minutes and frequently several hours at a time. I continued with this belief until a teacher told me to simply open my eyes and become aware of the same silence that I experienced in meditation.

Meditation was indeed a wondrous tool that introduced me to the presence of inner silence. If someone had asked me what inner silence was before I began meditating, I would have been confused. I would have thought, Isn't inner silence the same as outer silence? If a room is quiet, then there is silence. If people are talking or the television is on or cars are honking and lawn mowers are cutting, then there is no silence. What other type of silence exists, other than the kind that we experience when there is simply no noise?

Only when I closed my eyes, letting the outside noise pass as I turned inward, did I grasp a different type of silence. One that exists regardless of the sounds that might be clanging around me.

People choose a variety of ways to tap into their inner silence, including a range of different meditation techniques. After doggedly pursuing transcendental silence through years of practicing my chosen brand of meditation, I was surprised that just a few words by a new spiritual teacher could make me aware of the persistent presence of silence outside of meditation. After I became aware of its omnipresence, whenever I found myself talking about stillness or reading about it, I was reminded to put my attention on it.

The right words at the right time can change us. Certain words, such as the unspoken mantras mentally repeated in meditation, can lead us into stillness. When enlightening words stop, we are pointed to the quiet that lies at the end of every sentence. When my new teacher's words stopped, she watched as I looked back at her. I felt the same spiritual silence that she was experiencing, the silence I had so frequently encountered during my years of meditation. But this time, I experienced it with my eyes open.

This instance was not the only occasion when a spiritual teacher's words pointed me in a direction that I unknowingly sought. Decades ago, a lecture about higher levels of consciousness first put me on the road to awakening. This spiritual initiation had nothing to do with miraculous healings or magical manifestations of holy ash and sacred trinkets.

Just a few words at the right time, some spoken, others read, can lead us inward.

Vague hints of enlightened states offered by my first guru's words were enough to put me on the spiritual path. His descriptions seemed fantastic. I had never heard anything like them before. A state of consciousness other than the usual ones that exist when we are sleeping, dreaming, or awake? Sure, I had already experienced altered states of consciousness through mind-expanding drugs. But an enlightened awareness where we recognize the expanse of infinite silence that transcends all other ordinary states of consciousness? This was something new. I wasn't completely clear about what "enlightened awareness" actually meant or how it might feel even if it happened to me. Yet enlightenment became my goal long before I knew what it really was. Somehow, luckily, I understood its promise.

That first guru's talk inspired me. His words changed me. They prompted me to turn away from my futile attempts to escape from sadness and focus instead on the charm of transcendent silence. Better to flee toward something than away from something.

Thus, when I was seventeen years old, a guru put me on a new spiritual path. My brother Mitch had told me to go and get myself a word. Just one powerful word. The same guru who had inspired me had told him that a word was all that was needed to attain perfect happiness. And so I got one. One of the guru's followers whispered a single syllable, a mantra, into my ear. It was a Sanskrit word that had no meaning to me at all. I was told to sit, close my eyes, and silently repeat it. Effortlessly, it would lead me to my inner silence. And it did. About a year later, another syllable was added, and then another, and several others more, each of them equally incomprehensible to me. But their repetition during my meditations gradually empowered me by helping me to uncover the expansive stillness within me. I felt as if I were returning home.

The sounds of certain phrases, like the words of a lullaby sung to an infant too young to understand them, are enough to soothe us, enlighten us. Such is the power of a few chosen words, even those that have no meaning to us.

My meditation teacher had told me to just experience the sound of the mantra, to gently think it with my eyes closed. Sitting comfortably, twice a day, I silently repeated it, not controlling my mind, unconcerned with its meaning, letting my awareness fall effortlessly upon it until there was nothing left but a faint impulse, more the vague idea of the mantra than the actual sound of it. Whenever I became aware that I had forgotten the mantra completely, I easily came back to it.

And so began my quest to attain infinite cosmic joy, using words to discover the knowledge of all things. I expected to one day enter a kingdom of heaven within, where divine bliss would overflow without interruption. I continued meditating like this for thirty years. Along the way, I became deluded by my imaginings of a faraway spiritual utopia. Instead of appreciating the transcendent silence of the moment, I became preoccupied with the notion of a supreme level of consciousness that awaited me, to be reached after just a few more weeks or months or years of repeating mantras, a mystical state where I would finally attain constant confidence and endless happiness. Now I recognize this longing as spiritual silliness, yet it was very seductive at the time. Sometimes a dream is preferable to no dream at all.

I had been told that the conflicts and despair of this world were mere illusions. I believed it and preached it. As the enlightened masters supposedly taught, all suffering is due to maya, which veils the truth that life is always good because God is always good. And eternal joy is the natural state of an enlightened man. Once I reached enlightenment, there would be no more unfulfilled desires. No physical pain. No mental confusion. No more anger. Just a life of all-knowing tranquility, punctuated by the carefree laughter of my liberated soul. So I kept faithfully repeating my mantra, hoping that the more I repeated it, the closer I would get to that higher level of unending emotional bliss. Perfect health, perfect wisdom, perfect happiness. Enough to keep one meditating for decades. That's what I did.

I was not alone in my search for overwhelming emotional gratification. Most of my spiritual friends were seeking the same thing. My quest was not merely a typical teenage craving for unrelenting pleasure. Many of my fellow travelers were longtime spiritual seekers, some in their forties, others in their fifties, a few in their sixties, seventies, and older. After all, as the American philosopher William James put it, "How to gain, how to keep, how to recover happiness, is in fact for most men at all times the secret motive of all they do, and of all they are willing to endure." Yet the likelihood of its achievement depends on the meaning of the word *happiness*. The spiritual happiness that I sought was compelling but ridiculous.

There I sat with my Sanskrit sounds, year after year, sometimes meditating for fourteen hours straight, for months at a time, looking forward to yet another advanced technique, an additional mantra, an esoteric insight, working and expecting and hoping for a dramatic spiritual experience that would at last make me happy all the time. A worthy goal, if only it were humanly possible.

Over the next three decades, I meditated at round-the-clock spiritual gatherings across Italy, Spain, France, and Switzerland; in primitive mud huts beneath India's Himalayan peaks; atop crumbling thousand-year-old Buddhist hillside shrines in the remote corners of Burma; and inside Israel's sacred sites. I made pilgrimages to the ancient desert caves of Qumran on the northwest shore of the Dead Sea, journeying to the holy churches and mosques in Bethlehem to touch the birth spot of Jesus and listen to prayers from the Koran. I stood beside the remnants of the Western Wall of King Solomon's temple in Jerusalem, laying my hands upon the stone bricks so that I might absorb their ancient mystical energy. I walked alongside the al-Aqsa Mosque to caress the holy sacrificial rock where Abraham's sword almost slew Isaac. I climbed down into the dank crevices of the Great Pyramid of Giza, crouching low to immerse myself in the fabled metaphysical vibrations that resonated in the Egyptian darkness. In each and every place I inwardly begged for a wondrous light of perpetual spiritual joy to burst open within me.

I followed the masters of the East, its yogis and monks, and studied with venerated academic scholars, even attending graduate school at Harvard to see where centuries of Western wisdom might take me. I perused best-selling self-help books, analyzed hallowed scriptures, pondered over political magazines and religious journals, searched newspapers, wrote poetry, sang chants, seeking and thinking, reciting mantras and reading more and more words. I was looking for just one more word, a single penetrating notion that might make sense of this worldly struggle and catapult me onto a higher spiritual plane where I would find the infinite joy that I had been told was my birthright. My search was both dramatically alluring and fanciful.

Like many other boomers from the sixties, I was still riding the metaphysical wave that arose during that troubled transition between two distinct eras, when the greatest generation borne of depression's poverty and fascism's bloody struggle receded, and freewheeling hippies rushed in. Adventurous beatniks had led the way. The flower children swore off war and renounced money. They turned on, tuned in, and dropped acid. Altered states became their preoccupation. Revelation, not revolution, was their maxim. Insights, not possessions, were the goal. As the celebrated beat writer Jack Kerouac described in *On the Road*: "We were on the roof of America and all we could do was yell, I guess—across the night, eastward over the Plains, where somewhere an old man with white hair was probably walking toward us with the Word, and would arrive any minute and make us silent."

I met an old man with white hair and a long beard. More than one. Young ones with dark hair, too. Spiritual masters who promised perfect wisdom. And women who called themselves Divine Mothers, teaching about supernatural love and compassion. The road to human perfection seemed clear. A new era was dawning, old ways were dying. Yesterday's narrow skeptics had had their chance; it was time for wiser minds to rule the day.

Many masters did walk toward me with the Word. And several did make me silent. But my journey didn't end in silence. Instead of focusing on the silent presence that had been available to me right from the start, I kept pushing myself out of it, hustling toward a far-off spiritual utopia, nursing dreams of a distant enlightenment that could deliver a cosmic gift of endless emotional pleasure. My goals were both optimistic and frustrating.

I longed to have a perfect personality, where I would never experience fear and always make the right choices. I imagined that in this perfected state, my days and nights would be buoyed by a staggering appreciation of every facet of life. Infinite love would enable me to have an absolutely equal affection for every single living thing in creation. Predator or victim, it wouldn't matter. Revulsion was too judgmental, intolerant, spiritually ignorant. I would see that everything in the world was equally good, in perfect harmony. When the plan is divine, all is divine. I would never be upset with the world's negativity because I would accurately perceive all things as being ultimately positive, instruments in service of a greater good. Suffering would be revealed as attachment to illusion, pain as the mirage of the unenlightened.

Such airy delusions led me away from the concrete gifts of the now. In mad pursuit of an enticing heavenly payoff, I accumulated more and more spiritual techniques as if I were playing a lottery—as if buying more tickets would increase my odds of winning. Eventually, I just stopped. I'd had enough. I calmed down. Went blank. Got real. I had finally heard that one powerful Word. The Word was *now*. And it made me silent.

My path became less dramatic. I became more humble. Less delusional, more content. I traded my illusions of human perfection for the experience of perfect silence. Sometimes I suddenly stopped reading for a moment and noticed the ink on the surrounding whiteness of a page. I paused, experienced the stillness, then continued to read the words of each sentence, watching them slowly unfold, one after another, until another moment of silence unexpectedly emerged. The words might even have triggered doubts, impatience, anxious anticipation. Regardless, I spontaneously slipped back into the silent gap between each word, soothed by the surprising spiritual quiet inside. I felt surprised because my eyes were open, yet the silence did not fade. And there was no place I needed to go to find more of it.

My restless mind can still drown out the silence, as it churns out opinions, plans my next move, judges the value of what I am doing, pulls me out of my inner quiet. But then I return to it, remembering that the stillness in between thought and emotion is a tunnel that can take me deep into my peaceful center. I let myself fall freely into that tunnel, letting go of my attachment to unattainable perfection. Instead, I plunge into a deep, expansive silence. I feel the unwavering presence of a perfect stillness that can be experienced even while my troubled thoughts and worries flow. I rediscover the awareness that total knowledge of this infinite universe and the absence of unpleasant emotions are not the hallmarks of spiritual happiness.

When we let go of our spiritual fantasies, we discover that the seeker's path is shorter than we think. Silence needs nothing but our attention. We don't have to create it, since it can't be created. It doesn't have to be found, since it can never be lost. All we need do is put our awareness on the silent self. No doubt, my meditations took me deep and often enough into silence so that I was able to recognize it once I was told it was time to open my eyes and feel it. But the experience of silence is immediate, there for the knowing.

Spiritual realism showed me that the transcendent silence that brings us peace is not found at the end of the journey. It is with us from the beginning. And it is present at this very moment because silence is always here for us.

If we can let go of our obsession with one day attaining the unremitting emotional gratification of some imagined state of hyperconsciousness, we might finally relax into the spiritual silence that exists right now.

Silence offers us a peace that is unattached to our changing emotions. Silence is indifferent to them because it doesn't depend on them. The presence of inner silence comforts us despite the flurry of feelings, good and bad, that persist as we naturally react to pleasant and unpleasant events on the outside. It stabilizes us, giving us the confidence to grow, reflect, learn from mistakes, and overcome obstacles, making us more able to love in our weakness and our strength. We become content without being complacent. Knowing that we will never reach perfection, we still realize that perfect silence helps us to become more perfect. Spiritual realism teaches us that although the goal is worthy, our failure to ever fully reach it does not make us unworthy. Living in the now will give us greater power to love tomorrow.

It took decades for me to realize that this powerful spiritual silence had been available to me right from the beginning, with my eyes open or closed. It was available the first instant that I began riding mantras into the center of my consciousness so many years ago, when I experienced the faintest glimmers of my subsequent flashes of awakening to the stillness of this very moment. This peaceful inner silence is here for all of us right now. It is here for you.

Chapter 4

AN ENLIGHTENED WEEPING

Experiencing inner silence while engaged in normal activities, outside of meditation with our eyes open, is not an elusive metaphysical state reserved for only the most advanced souls among us. And although this awareness does not eliminate all suffering, it does yield tangible results that make daily life more peaceful.

A few years ago, I fractured a vertebra. I didn't fall, wasn't pushed, and hadn't been doing any heavy lifting. Actually, I was sitting cross-legged on my lawn, back straight, eyes closed, enjoying the inner silence, feeling the energy run through my spine, and wiggling occasionally with delight. I was quite pleased with all things. Until the pain hit. Dull at first, then intensifying, and, by evening, excruciating. I figured I would tough it out so there I lay bedridden for days, barely able to move, waiting to heal. Waiting and waiting. And waiting. I had watched my wife go through labor twice, and it seemed as if I were going through something

PUBLIC LIBRARY
DANVILLE, ILLINOIS

similar. Except that there was no rhythm to the contractions, no subsiding of the pain. Just an ongoing, piercing ache with no letup.

Hours passed, days slipped into one another, and the lonely isolating blackness of nighttime agony slowly rolled into dawning daylight and speechless afternoons. Each passing moment was a timeless warp of paralyzing hurt. One might reasonably wonder, What about the silence that underlies all things? Couldn't a clear experience of the silent spiritual presence within, which transcends the distorting prism of the physical body, completely transform my deluded hurting? Couldn't the powerful reality of an expanded consciousness lift me out of suffering's depth, carrying me up to a higher plane of truth and cosmic bliss? Not a chance.

Bodily pain is as real as the blood that pours from any open wound. As Shakespeare observed, "If you prick us, do we not bleed? If you tickle us, do we not laugh? If you poison us, do we not die?" All of us can be injured, all of us can be killed. We are human beings in human bodies. Although the essence of our spirituality is an awareness of the inner world of silence, we live in the midst of an external material world of sensations, painful and pleasing.

The silence within us cannot be crushed, yet if our legs are cut, our bodies will fall. Silence is immortal, but we who experience silence are not. Silence cannot be slain, but the brain that becomes aware of it can be. Silence is comforting, but we will not always be comfortable. Although the stillness within gave me solace, the fractured vertebra in my spine still ached.

Attuning ourselves to the spiritual silence within does not immunize us from all of life's ills. Our minds may experience a powerful and peaceful quiet, but our bodies remain vulnerable to whatever nature might bring us. Rational links between physical cause and effect do not vanish. Enlightened men and women still freeze from too much cold and sweat from too much heat. Though the enlightened know the deep mystical silence that is beyond reason, enlightenment is not unreasonable.

If the potential for suffering persists, then what is the value of inner silence? When measured against the pangs of hunger or cracking spines, what use is there in contacting the silent mind-space within? If spiritual liberation is incapable of satisfying all of our material needs, why bother chasing it at all? Where's the deliverance in pursuing an elevated consciousness in which we can still be taunted by the threat of sickened lungs and aging bones? Many prophets throughout the ages have predicted that we will be forever granted physical protection by the saving grace of enlightenment. If they were mistaken, then what's the difference whether we are rooted in spiritual silence or not? Either way, we're screwed.

The Christian novelist C. S. Lewis once observed, "So much mercy, yet still there is Hell." Despite our light, darkness and death are everywhere, always. Heaven doesn't replace hell. It exists alongside of it. A vertebral compression fracture does hurt like hell. All the nerves converge in the spine, and an injury to the vertebra sends excruciating signals to the brain. Still, if the only truth we know is hellish torment, then our suffering can be even worse.

Lewis also observed, "Part of every misery is, so to speak, the misery's shadow or reflection: the fact that you don't merely suffer but have to keep on thinking about the fact that you suffer." If your mind is preoccupied only with pain and suffering, then indeed there is little relief. We become overwhelmed by our misery. There is no inner mindspace in which to rest. All we can think of is our own pain, instead of also being aware of the quiet presence within that can give us some relief.

We are not always able to maintain an awareness of inner silence when we are sick. We are often distracted by the physical discomfort. Yet once we become aware of the distraction, we can return to silence. As long as we are awake and not unconscious, we can keep moving into our inner mindspace, which is filled with nothing but a vast empty silence. It is inside this infinite stillness that we discover the spiritual peace that can coexist with physical pain. Just as there are pockets of peace even in the midst of war, there is a spiritual solace to be had in the midst of our suffering.

Shifting in and out of silence eventually results in our being able to experience it for longer periods. We become more familiar with it, more able to recognize that despite our pain, silence is always present, available to us whenever we remember to put our attention on it. Continuously opening ourselves up to the stillness within, even as we wait for the body's agony to pass, keeps a bit of heaven in place when the torments of hell are flailing.

As for my own bout with hellish hurt, after days of steady deterioration, I was rushed by ambulance into the emergency room. Gripped by such searing pain that I could not even speak, I was unable to describe my condition to the doctor leaning over me. Yet the awareness of inner silence managed to stay with me, lively and palpable. I was somehow able to still remain linked to that quiet inner mindspace, which steadied me amid the rhythmic moans of nearby patients and the hushed tones of rushing nurses. My mind was anchored in its silent spiritual stillness, keeping me from falling into self-pity over my undeserved misery or being overwhelmed by the fear of irreversible spinal damage. Inexplicably, I managed to make peace with my own helplessness. After I was wheeled into intensive care, a doctor told me that a cracked vertebra fully heals on its own, like a broken arm. So I relaxed into the silence and the pain, and waited.

Some people must wait longer than others for pain to pass. Not everyone heals so easily or completely. Spiritual realists do not confuse the spirituality of the silent present with the certain arrival of miraculous cures. Spiritual silence may help to produce miracles of healing or it might not. But the peace that emerges from the experience of inner silence does not depend on the miraculous. We need not believe that all pain can be healed or that the suffering that cannot be cured is either an illusion or the righteous result of the laws of karma. Enlightenment does not require complacency in order for us to make peace with fate.

Spiritual maturity is about holding the peaceful silence of this moment while being able to confront, not deny or dismiss, the reality of our own suffering.

We may find inner peace, yet may still recoil at our physical and emotional pain. We are human, so this is natural. And although the spiritually awakened experience a transcendent calm, acknowledging the real suffering of others is what characterizes the peaceful compassion of the enlightened.

I still choke over the sufferings of my father, a man of innocence struck down as if he were guilty of a crime he did not commit. In 1954, when he was just twenty-nine years old, he came home from work with an awful headache. A few days later he was rushed into a respirator called an iron lung. He'd been stricken with polio and was paralyzed from the neck down, unable to breathe on his own. For months, he struggled to regain his strength, tediously exercising and straining to take a single breath outside of his respirator. This ordeal made him feel as if he were about to suffocate, as if concrete bricks had been piled high onto his chest. My father finally emerged from that machine. More relentless physical therapy added up to a total of two years in the hospital. When he did return home, he was confined to a wheelchair, able to move his upper body but unable to stand or walk.

I was a nine-month-old toddler when my father was taken to the hospital. After he got back, I often stared up at him tentatively or peered out from my bedroom as he sat in his scary chrome wheelchair watching television in the living room. I was three years old and afraid of that strange man whom I vaguely recalled as being my dad. I wondered how anyone who had to drag himself in and out of bed, who had to pull lifeless, atrophied legs on and off the toilet, could possibly ever be happy. Even at that young age, I sensed the frustration in our home, the humiliation at being unable to do what other fathers and husbands could. Maybe I didn't really sense the sadness at the time; perhaps I just thought that I did or should have. Something was terribly wrong with the world, that much I always knew from the moment he came home.

Was it bad karma that struck my father down? This notion is just a desperate attempt to make sense of things. There were tiny blameless infants lying crippled alongside my grown-up father in those polio wards, lined up row upon row, only their tiny heads sticking out of those huge cylindrical iron lungs. A just plight stemming from the sins of their past lives? I dare not accuse those babies of that. To label their paralysis just is to blaspheme against justice itself. Have we not already been shown how the innocent are crucified along with the guilty?

The French author and philosopher Voltaire fiercely rejected the notion that the immense suffering that is too often visited upon the innocent is somehow to be accepted as a just fate in service of a higher cause. On November 1, 1755, an immense earthquake shook Lisbon, killing nearly sixty thousand people and injuring thousands of others. Within a few weeks, Voltaire composed a powerful poem expressing his reaction, which my daughter, Mia, translated from the French in honor of the admirable conscience of an honest soul:

> Those deluded philosophers who cry, "All is well."
> Approach, consider these ghastly ruins,
> This debris, these scraps, this sorrowful cinder,
> These women, these children, both piled upon one another
> Their limbs dispersed underneath this broken marble,
> These thousand unfortunate beings that the earth devours
> Whom, bloody, torn, and palpitating still,
> Are buried under their roofs, dying without assistance,
> In the horror of affliction their lamentable days!
> To these half-formed cries of their faint voices,
> At the terrifying spectacle of their smoking ashes,
> Will you say, "This is the effect of eternal laws
> Which are of a liberated God and are necessitated by good
> choice"?

> Will you say, in seeing these stacks of victims,
> "Vengeance is God's, their death is the price of their crimes"?

Voltaire scorned the facile explanations of people who attempted to explain away inexplicable pain by promoting the belief in a righteous cosmic scheme that justified the slaughter of sixty thousand helpless men, women, and children and the maiming of thousands more, their horrible suffering dutifully inflicted by some unseen divine wrath in service of a flawless, godly machine.

The authentic human response to the suffering of innocents is anguish—pure, honest, and caring. We need not try to cultivate a false equanimity by pretending that suffering is just the price of unholiness. The Old Testament shows us how pain can afflict even the most holy among us. "Man's life is a prison; he is sentenced to pain and grief," cried Job, who was known for his devotion to God. "Each day I live seems endless, and I suffer through endless nights." Who among us has not at least tasted a bit of Job's same tears or at times felt his clinging despair? If not, have we not known anyone who has? "When I lie down, I long for morning," Job wailed. "When I get up, I long for evening; all day I toss and turn." Should we dismiss Job's lament in order to bolster the belief in a utopian, tragic-free enlightenment? Or is our embrace of spiritual fulfillment strong enough to keep it from being weakened by Job's harsh biblical plight and the fate of others like him?

We do not have to cloak ourselves in spiritual denial in order to protect our spirituality. We are capable of finding spiritual solace in this world as we know it to be. Refusing to recognize the injustice of pain and suffering, spun as a grander holistic knowledge of the just balance of good and bad governed by a higher force, is not spiritual. It is not the enlightenment of detached equanimity; it is the spiritual delusion that nurtures a misplaced callousness. Be still inside, stay centered in silence, be at peace within, but care and cry over catastrophes everywhere. When all is not good, proclaim that it is not.

The experience of spiritual silence does not require that we refrain from speaking out against the curse of physical suffering. We do not have to rationalize the sad realities of atrophied muscles and lifeless limbs or the anguish of cancer patients or the victims of nature's terrifying destruction. There is no good reason for the suffering. It attacks indiscriminately, targeting the young and the saintly, as well as the hateful. Their suffering is nothing that a compassionate human being can justify. Our inner peace is speechless, but the outer world often cries out at us. Hear the silence, and also hear the cries.

Spiritual realism offers us a way out of the paradox of internal peace and external torment. We push the positive to fight the negative. Our spiritual silence allows us to make peace with both, and our inner peaceful energy moves outward to bring peace to others. Though Job wailed against his worldly sufferings, he never abandoned the promise of an authentic spiritual life infused with love and compassion. And neither did my father.

Whether slouching in his wheelchair or lying with his paralyzed legs stretched limply across his bed, you could see him absorbed in his own private silence, and you could sense that his spiritual love was always expanding.

My father never talked about spirituality, about inner stillness. I suspect that months of lying flat, unable to move while locked inside an iron cylinder, took him naturally into a silent place beyond tears and comprehension. Whatever we call it or however we uncover it, inner silence remains indifferent to conviction and impervious to philosophy, psychology, and theology. Unimpeded by the intellectual's skepticism, unhindered by the scholar's disdain, silence cannot be denied. Despite our egotistical preening, silence is willing to serve us. Imponderable yet palpable, silence exists and proves it whenever we open ourselves to it.

Spiritual believers might insist that for silence to arise within us, it needs a proper invocation. Religious ceremonies have been performed throughout the ages to invoke the silent presence. There are rituals in Sanskrit, Latin, Chinese, Hebrew, and Arabic, each of them calling for the arrival of a divine silent knowing, each a prayerful entreaty for an encounter with a mute but enlightening holy spirit. Generations of devout men and women preached that communion with transcendental silence is achieved through prayer, through penance, through reverent contemplation, in traditional meditation, or in some of these or all of them and more. Nearly all religions embrace the single truth that we need to awaken to a profound inner presence. It is an experience upon which religious revelations rely.

Inner silence can emerge alone or in a crowd, alongside priests and mullahs and gurus and rabbis and their worshippers, or without any of them. Whether we are in pews and shrines or in wheelchairs and hospital rooms, with fractured bones or paralyzed ones, with scriptures at our bedsides and prayers on our tongues, silence will come toward us if awareness welcomes it. Our experience of the silent presence within may be facilitated by religion and ritual. But our experience of it is not dependent on either of them.

Whichever way you choose to get there, whatever you want to name it, eternal silence will embrace and envelop you, giving you inner peace anywhere and everywhere, at any time, including this very moment.

In *The Purpose Driven Life*, the popular preacher Rick Warren wrote, "Real security can only be found in that which can never be taken from you." In the reverend's view, what can never be stolen is our relationship with God, which for him means a personal connection to Jesus Christ. Is this a relationship where Jesus appears to you in a vision and speaks directly to you? Or might it be a Christlike consciousness of a silent divine presence, a relationship with a merciful inner stillness that comforts us, now and forever? The deep silence within does seem to save us, making us feel as if we were truly born again, in communion with an immortal truth. Our relationship to this silent inner presence can never be taken away from us. Even when we ignore it or choose to turn away from it like a wayward prodigal son dismissive of its value, silence patiently waits for our return. We do not need to believe in its divinity or call it the revelation of Jesus or Krishna, Allah or YHWH, Buddha or the Tao.

The loving kindness that our inner quiet releases has the power to transform, whether in worship, in science, or in politics. Our search for spiritual silence can produce periods of quiet reflection, unleashing an extraordinary powerful insight and a loving force that is not only capable of transforming us, but one that is able to dramatically lessen the troubling social ills and improve the political realities around us.

After President John F. Kennedy was assassinated, Robert Kennedy quietly withdrew into himself to rediscover his life's purpose and the meaning of his brother's death. Political observers reported that when he emerged, those who previously labeled him a ruthless politico now found him to be gentler, less aggressive, more giving. This transformation proved itself one evening nearly five years after his brother's murder. Robert Kennedy had been elected to the Senate and had declared his own candidacy for president. That night, the senator found himself having to personally pass along tragic news to a group of African Americans who had assembled to hear one of his campaign speeches. He had to tell them that Martin Luther King Jr. had just been assassinated.

In those tense moments following the news of King's murder, Kennedy somberly climbed onto a platform along the volatile inner city street in Indianapolis. "For those of you who are black and are tempted to be filled with hatred and distrust at the injustice of such an act, against all white people, I can only say that I feel in my own breast the same kind of feeling," he said softly. "I had a member of my family killed, but he was killed by a white man." Kennedy then quoted Aeschylus, an ancient Greek writer and his favorite poet. "'In our sleep, pain which we cannot forget falls drop by drop upon the heart until, in our own despair, against our will, comes wisdom through the awful grace of God,'" he recited, looking out across the gathering of his fellow Americans, carefully pausing to let the silence in between his words comfort the shocked and grieving crowd.

Without posturing or preparation, Kennedy had gone deep into the moment, unrushed and unrehearsed, drawing upon the compassion that was released during his long period of quiet reflection and mourning. He spontaneously tapped into the gentle love that resides in our silent, wounded hearts, the quiet spot where resentment, revenge, and forgiveness converge, giving way to a wordless insight that helps us find a silent peace in ourselves and lets us make peace with the world. And helps us bring peace to others. There, in that quiet space within, in the midst of deafening heartache, tenderly and without effort an unbounded spiritual compassion can arise. And it arose that evening, during a political rally, from a politician's heart.

"What we need in the United States is not hatred," Kennedy said, speaking from his passion, not from a speechwriter's notes. "What we need in the United States is not violence and lawlessness, but love and wisdom, and compassion toward one another." Rarely does a politician speak of love during a political speech. Robert Kennedy was able to console by celebrating mercy on that murderous night, offering up a simple plea to the weeping crowd. "Let us dedicate ourselves to what the Greeks wrote so many years ago," he urged, "to tame the savageness of man and make gentle the life of this world. Let us dedicate ourselves to that, and say a prayer for our country, and for our people."

That night, race riots broke out in more than a thousand places across America. The rage over King's murder turned to violence as fires were lit by angry African American mobs and buildings burned in the inner cities. But not in Indianapolis, where Kennedy had spoken. There, mourners, both black and white, peacefully returned to their homes and said their prayers.

Two months after Martin Luther King was killed, Robert Kennedy was also assassinated.

Political upheaval and national tragedy can be as shattering as personal pain. Pearl Harbor, Auschwitz, the killings of King and the two Kennedys, the Indonesian tsunami, 9/11—the tragic march of history rolls on. But so does the inner silence and the powerful spiritual peace that it sustains. Even political love is nourished by a quiet presence. As I lay flattened by my own shattering spinal pain, clutching the rails of the hospital bed to keep from moving and to contain the hurt, it was the quiet peace that radiates outward from the silent stillness within that managed to tame my own despair.

My awareness of silence was not able to change the laws of nature and remove the pain of a fractured back, just as the silent presence could not protect King and the Kennedys from a determined assassin's gun or rescue the World Trade Center's workers from suicidal hate or make my paralyzed father walk again. The tragic laws that govern bullets and bodies, unchecked viruses and disease, gravity and fragile bones cannot be altered. Neither can the healing laws of love, which all of us can willingly obey.

My father never discussed silence, inner or otherwise, yet he honored the rules of love. He had found his own peace and was determined to help others find theirs. This was the law of compassion that he obeyed. He distrusted religion, was skeptical of gurus, and was unimpressed by philosophy. Perhaps his desperate months in that polio ward or the decades of struggle after he left it, when he was confined by a body too crippled to crawl away from his despair—maybe they had led him to that silent place where his spirit could enjoy total freedom even though his legs remained unable to carry him. Maybe he found his own way to that quiet peaceful spot within, which activated his extraordinary wisdom and compassionate love and which later became so obvious to anyone who knew him. I do not know. Every spiritual path is unique.

Luckily, for most of us, paralysis and assassination are not the kind of prerequisites needed to prompt us into searching for a path into silence. Yet our general unease, which can often turn deeply sorrowful, can push us onto the spiritual journey to stillness. "If we did not feel that there was something wrong," the Catholic monk Thomas Merton wrote, "we would do nothing to change our condition." To change his condition, Merton spent years sitting still in silent contemplation.

The human condition improves not only because more wealth is created or new bridges are built, but because the rich become more generous and bridge builders become more creative. Spiritual silence helps to bring this about. It is as practical a means of change as the cures that heal us or the inventions that serve us. There is a reason why the greatest and most practical among us, visionaries like Jonas Salk and Albert Einstein, were also spiritual men.

Even Einstein, a genius among men, sat quietly before the mystery of our unending universe, transfixed by its awesome silent vastness. "The fairest thing we can experience is the mysterious," the great physicist concluded. "A knowledge of the existence of something we cannot penetrate, of the manifestations of the profoundest reason and the most radiant beauty, which are only accessible to our reason in their most elementary forms—it is this knowledge and this emotion that constitute the truly religious attitude," Einstein wrote. "In this sense, and in this alone, I am a deeply religious man." The silent mystery brings us into reverential awe. And although our contact with silence can be a transforming religious experience, our awareness of its existence is the essence of a universal spirituality that is independent of any one particular religion.

Salk was a young doctor who developed the polio vaccine and studied microbes and viruses under his laboratory microscope while babies and vigorous fathers collapsed. He proclaimed that "the most highly evolved form of existence is seen in the human mind, in human consciousness." This consciousness, Salk explained, "is expressed in its highest form in those who are the most enlightened and the most developed with respect to their awareness of themselves and with respect to their relationship with all else in the cosmos, near and far." What connects all of us to each other and to the infinite cosmos around us? The same silence that exists everywhere, in every place, in every age, for all people. It can inspire a noble effort to change the world, leading to discoveries that eliminate diseases and solutions that help us to live longer and easier.

Great men, like Einstein and Salk, know that we cannot completely change the world, even though they ceaselessly try to positively influence world events. Life can still break backs, disease can still cripple, the good die young while others live long, wars are won and lost, galaxies expand, and stars implode. The universe and its infinite energies unfold in accordance with a power too magnificent to fully comprehend.

Nature rules the world. Yet it is in our nature to change how we experience the world. A century ago, the Vedic master Swami Vivekananda said, "The note of hope is: I have no control of the external world, but that which is in me and nearer unto me, my own world, is in my control." Each of us can draw nearer to the peaceful inner world of silent stillness. We can prove this by doing it now, by feeling the quiet presence of this moment.

As we move closer to our inner silence and then out of silence and again back into silence, we begin to recognize that the inability of our enlightened consciousness to right all wrongs and heal all ills is not our fault. Neither Einstein nor Salk could do it, and neither can we. This inability is not a mark of spiritual failure. Be humble. Although you can begin to feel the silent presence of the Creator, you never become the Creator. Humility is not only refusing to take credit for the blessings in our lives. It is also not taking the blame for the ills of this world. Let God do what He does, and let us do what we can do.

God rules according to His whim, not yours. And the Creator is not obliged to justify His intentions to any of us. So, like scientists and healers, politicians and priests, we can only remain mystified by our mix of virtuous desires and unsuccessful attempts to fulfill them, puzzled by the presence of the great joy that can exist along-side great sorrow, baffled by the peace that can reside in a pained and fractured body, dazzled by a handicapped man's compassion for the able-bodied. This confusing spiritual reality cannot be changed or fully comprehended. The Creator is a jealous God, so don't even think about challenging Him, of trying to learn what only He can know and do what only He can do. Remember the high price that was paid for taking just one small bite of the apple.

Omniscience and omnipotence do not belong to us. The Creator keeps them for Himself. He will not give them to us. He will not tell us why bones and hearts must break. When Moses asked the Lord merely for His name, he was flatly told, "I am what I am." How can you respond to that? What can you say or think after hearing such words? Nothing. Not quite humiliated because we know that His very breath is what gave us life, we are still humbled before the unfathomable face of God. To know God is to be struck by silence.

Yet in that humbling silence, we can surrender to the spiritual reality that without total knowledge of creation's purpose, we can never always feel the right feelings, think the right thoughts, do the right thing, fix all that is broken, and understand everything that others know. We can realize that there is nothing much that we can always do except love one another. I will lose family and friends, energy and health, and sometimes I will lose confidence, but I know that no one can ever take my loving kindness away. I, too, am what I am. I am the ability to love. And so are you.

Chapter 5

YOUR FEARS NEED NOT

FRIGHTEN YOU

There is a common belief among spiritual aspirants that raising one's consciousness perfects the personality, finally freeing us from all of our fears. But what if a car careens out of control and sideswipes an enlightened man at an intersection? Would it be reasonable for him to feel a sudden jolt of adrenaline, maybe even several minutes of fright until he was safe from further harm? Sure. To expect someone, however highly evolved, to be indifferent to danger, to be as cool tempered whether sleeping under a roof or falling off one, is fanciful. Spirituality is realistic. The goal is to become fully human, not superhuman.

The average person already has the qualities necessary to deal calmly with emotional fears and psychological anxieties. There is no need to speculate about a distant future where some fantastic state of hyperconsciousness dissipates every twinge of concern and mental discomfort. Almost always, there is a way to stay poised while experiencing fear at the same time. It is not a contradiction. Rather, it's an integration—an integration between a reliable inner calm and a sometimes tough external reality.

We can develop a balanced response to the real challenges and threats of daily life, which will enable us to react proportionately to them. It is possible to experience instances of fright in the face of reasonable dangers without slipping into a disproportionate state of prolonged anxiety. If a danger is overwhelming, such as the specter of imminent violence, then we will naturally get fully absorbed in the fear—and protect ourselves accordingly. Once the danger has passed, our mission is to recover from the fear, to quickly pull ourselves out of it and return to our spiritual inner calm.

The Indian teacher Jiddu Krishnamurti didn't even consider the intensity triggered by danger to be actual moments of fear. To him, a frightful reaction following a car crash is simply the unleashing of a smart survival instinct, prompting us to do what is necessary to get away from a life-threatening situation. "When you see a wild animal, a snake, to withdraw, is that fear? Or is it intelligence?" Krishnamurti asked. "When you see a snake, you jump. That is not fear, because that is the natural reaction of the body," he explained. "When you see a precipice, you do not walk just blindly along. That is not fear." Of course not; it is prudence.

Since most people in the industrialized world are not forced to hike through untamed jungles or climb up dangerous narrow switchbacks, few of us will confront the prospect of being killed by wild animals or falling off towering cliffs. Human violence is also not an imminent threat. Civil wars are not raging around us, pitting neighbor against neighbor; looters and roaming militias do not make our visits to the corner grocery a death-defying trek. We do have to take reasonable precautions to reduce the chances of being mugged if we walk through a high-crime urban alleyway. But most of us do not spend our days afraid of being killed. Instead, we may worry about paying the bills, be nervous about getting fired at work, or feel anxious about a failing romance.

Our own fears might not involve matters of life and death, but we can still feel threatened. These everyday fears are linked to powerful emotions that rattle our sense of well-being, often leaving us with uneasy stomachs, restless nights, tense confrontations, and irritable moods. We can't attribute all of them to unenlightened hallucinations. These emotions feel real, so they are real. Sometimes they are rational, other times they are exaggerated or even unfounded. But we cannot break free of them by trying to dismiss them as an impediment to spiritual advancement that must be denied, ignored, or disguised. Posturing as someone who has moved beyond negative emotions, while they are still percolating under the surface, is spiritual pretense.

Conflict will never cease as long as we are living in a world of duality, where opposites both attract and repel. The world is a roller coaster of relative change, which keeps us from feeling absolute tranquility. Shifting energies coincide, and they collide. We naturally enjoy energies that harmonize and flinch at those that divide. This constant seesawing between positive and negative often pushes us off our emotional center. We may overact or react proportionately. But not to react at all, to insist that true spirituality requires that we remain indifferent, whether we feel emotionally supported or threatened, is damaging to our personal growth. We wind up trying to maintain or chase an impossible equanimity, instead of feeling the normal ebb and flow of emotions while also accessing the underlying steady, calming stillness within that transcends all emotions.

Only this stillness is impervious to the conflicting feelings that arise from our living in a relative world of constant change. Opening up to this empowering silence gives us the confidence we need to identify which threats are serious, which are minor, and how best to deal with both varieties.

Rather than repressing our intensely negative emotional reactions, we can watch them dissipate naturally as we become less attached to them and more attached to peaceful inner silence. Loyalty and betrayal, aggression and acceptance, hope and disillusion: these opposite energies can make us depressed, weary, hot tempered, passive aggressive, rebellious, meek, and unstable. Wishing it were otherwise will not make it so. But our silent center helps us to recover our emotional balance, keeping us from giving in to instinctive overreactions, disproportionate belligerence, and unhelpful defensiveness. Spiritual realism means accepting that we cannot eliminate all negative feelings. It also means returning to the quiet stillness within us that diminishes their intensity. If we return to inner silence when extreme emotions push us off center, it makes us more resilient and better able to quickly recover from them. We don't feel the need to rashly act on them.

"Let your inner spiritual revelation become deep enough to include the whole world of time and space," advised Adyashanti, a former Zen monk and a spiritual teacher. "If your spiritual revelation is only big enough to go beyond the relative world but not include it, then you will continue to experience a duality and therefore a struggle with the relative world." Just as our ignorance of inner silence prevents us from fully experiencing the totality of life, so does ignoring the realities of relative existence. Integrating both is the aim of spiritual realism.

We are often shaken out of our experience of silence by cries of suffering and pain from the relative world. It may be our own pain or someone else's. Suffering that is primal or that stems from childhood insecurities is especially difficult to bear. Aside from the more obvious traumas, such as an abusive parent or a sexual molestation, even mundane insecurities can take root in our personalities and play themselves out years later. Will the clique of popular girls shun me? Will the schoolyard bully beat me up? There are the constant childhood contests to be the smartest, the cutest, the best athlete, the teacher's favorite. The pressure to excel continues into adulthood: in the workplace where we compete, at parties where we flirt, and during the constant comparisons between who we think the other person is and who we think we should be. We are incessantly grading and measuring ourselves and scheming to fit in with friends, family, colleagues, neighbors—and lovers.

Some of the fears that can be traced back to childhood are like anxieties brought on by phantom visions of monsters looming in dark bedroom corners, angling to attack as we hide under the blankets and struggle to fall asleep. A higher state of consciousness or, more likely, just the normal process of growing up clarifies our present situation, enabling us to separate real dangers from fictitious ones. But then there are the lasting childhood fears that hover over us throughout our adult lives.

The Buddhist teacher Stephen Batchelor harkens back to those first few moments of worldly life to illustrate the primal reality that can make life so fearful. "I was forced from my mother's uterus to emerge bloodied and screaming, gasping for air in an alien world," he wrote. "To be thrown into existence is painful and shocking." We arrive expecting immediate pleasure. It's our nature. Instead, we are thrust into classroom grading, playground jealousies, schoolyard cruelties, and stinging rejections. Poorly equipped to free ourselves from these traps, we construct personality traits to defend ourselves: preemptive confrontation and preemptive avoidance, attention-grabbing gregariousness and attention-avoiding shyness. We defend weakness by feigning strength; we refuse to get stronger by pretending to be weak.

"I project self-assurance, but feel as though I'm wearing a mask; I present a cheerful exterior, but inwardly suffer a quiet desperation; I affirm my singularity, but suspect that I am a jumbled collection of roles," Batchelor explained. "I appear to be self-sufficient, but crave to be loved and recognized by others." Without the spiritual reality of inner silence, the genuine tool that can give us authentic protection from our real fears, it is a surprise that everyone doesn't wind up depressed.

My own early fears revolved around the daily threats that sprung up from the tense underside of the low-income Bronx housing projects where I lived. There was a rumor that a dead guy had been found slumped over the bushes with a knife in his back, right behind the corner bus stop where I used to wait. I could hardly focus on the street long enough not to miss the bus because I kept looking at the bushes behind me, worried that I'd be stabbed. An imaginary fear about unproved rumors or a vigilant step worth taking? You decide.

Then there was the young tough whom I saw prancing around the playground in front of my building one day. He hit a pregnant woman with his fully clenched fist, knocking her to the ground while he towered over her spitting taunts and insults. Stunned mothers sat and stared helplessly, as they held their frightened kids tightly against their skirts. Just a bit of teenage bravado that was bound to pass? Or a signal that that there were no rules, no restraint; that if pregnant women were targets for brutality, then I would certainly not be exempt, however young I was and however much older the assailant. It was a constant gymnastic challenge for me to keep from falling off the monkey bars while watching out for hair-triggered teens in the playground who might single me out because of a perceived slight or their own frustrated rage. Paranoia or precaution? I wasn't sure. I'm still not sure.

Early on, I recognized that on those Bronx streets I would have to make a crucial decision—to either stand at perilous bus stops despite the fear or vow never to go near them. To hate those street thugs who preyed on helpless mothers or try and love them—or at least not despise them. Maybe I could learn how to draw blood and bruises and inflict swift damage on my attackers, by using my hands if I was bigger or a nearby broken bottle if I was not. Or perhaps I could somehow cleverly manage to avoid them without surrendering my will, without being cowed by my aversion to violence. Discretion, not cowardice, and cleverness, not weakness, would have to be the method if I were to stay gentle, free, and loving. Without access to inner silence, my panic often made me excessively aggressive or pitiful and cowardly or brashly foolish and willing to take too many risks. I was too young to understand anything about inner silence. There are no excuses now.

The world can still be dangerous and unpredictable. I have not served in the military, so I have been able to avoid greater dangers, and I appreciate people who face them in order to protect the rest of us from them. But I have been shaken down by thieves in Shanghai and confronted by Middle Eastern terrorist supporters on the West Bank. Scared and intimidated, I usually tried to defend myself with a combination of a prudent sensitivity to external dangers and an awareness of the spiritual power of inner silence. I was frequently able to juggle reasonable retreat and courageous advance, justifiable acquiescence and a just persistence. Yet facing down a brutish thief from Mongolia or sipping tea with a Palestinian boasting about the latest suicide bomber is not necessarily fearlessness bolstered by the calm of inner silence. It could be simple carelessness, a stupid disregard of the useful fears that serve us during times of serious danger.

Memories of childhood traumas and constant vigilance about current dangers may trigger needless angst, or they can prompt us into taking useful precautions. In either case, the influences of a troubled past and the stress of an uneasy present do not disappear just because we chant, pray, meditate—or fantasize about a future life of happiness with all things. The experience of silence is not enough to make all of our fears disappear once and forever. Yet our repeated return to the underlying silence within does restore a calming clarity that enables us to parse the fright into pieces and separate the credible from the habitual.

During our confident moments of reassuring silence, we may discover that some of our lifelong concerns are shadowing our enlightenment. Even with silence as our comfort, we may at times react negatively to the primal fears that stalk us and the new ones that trap us. Enlightenment does not completely cut us off from our past.

Nor does a spiritual awakening give us a perfect connection to the future. We cannot always know what we should ignore and what we should protect. This perplexity happens because the information we process is always changing. What seems like a perfect response to present circumstances might have consequences that are far from perfect. This unpredictability has nothing to do with the limits of an unenlightened consciousness. The uncertainty is an ineluctable characteristic of nature. Our enlightenment cannot stop events from unfolding in ways that are surprising, or even mystifying, to us. Even the enlightened must acquiesce to life's ambiguities: "Let thy will be done, as it is in heaven, and on earth."

The saints of centuries past who were revered for having attained the highest levels of consciousness did not predict the realities of this era. They did not write about the modern wonders of lifesaving kidney transplants or the horrors of nuclear bombs. Which of these should be embraced and which should be resisted is obvious to each of us. Yet just a few generations ago, atomic research was encouraged and the removal of organs from live human beings was not. At the time, could anyone have had the perfect judgment capable of deciding which activity to support and which to oppose? Would an enlightened teacher, supposedly possessing perfect judgment, have made the same decision that a similarly enlightened person would make today? The information we process is always changing, so the wise choice of today can be the foolish one of tomorrow.

We accept our imperfect judgments so that we can stay focused on improving them, without being clouded by self-recrimination. Acceptance of our limits makes us humble, but it need not discourage us from the effort to exceed them, which makes us noble. Both converge in a spiritual realism that gives us peace.

The drive for a perfect personality can even create the greatest anxiety since it is a futile ambition. One person's appealing talent might be considered an irritating eccentricity by another. Some laugh at the jokester; others find the jokes offensive. Even a helping hand might turn out to be one that handicaps. Warren Buffett, whose net worth of more than $40 billion in 2006 made him second only to the Microsoft founder Bill Gates as the world's richest man, once observed, "A very rich person should leave his kids enough to do anything, but not enough to do nothing." An indulging parent who lavishes money on a child might support an ambitious goal or instead rob him of all ambition. Our intention may be to do the right thing, but acting on it may not always turn out right. Nobody's perfect.

We can see the quandary of unintentional consequences in the Old Testament. Moses leads his people to the Promised Land, but not before leaving them unsupervised at Mount Sinai. While he was busy climbing upward to make contact with a divine presence, his followers descended into debauchery and idolatry below. Should the great seer have taken better precautions to ensure that while he was gone, his chosen people would choose correctly in his absence?

The Hebrews were stuck in the middle of the Sinai wilderness with nothing but one another to make the waiting less tedious. Surely, any competent leader could have predicted that relying on the self-discipline of an unruly bunch of wanderers for forty days and forty nights would turn out to be a stupid blunder. Who could not foresee that once the tribal leader was no longer brandishing his holy staff demanding strict obedience, his fawning followers would gradually become emboldened, rise up, and loosen up. We concede that no one could have guessed that they might wind up building a golden calf to dance around in delirious worship. Still, whether one is the head of a clan or the CEO of a Fortune 500 company, effective leaders know that if authority is not properly delegated, it eventually breaks down when the primary authority is unavailable. A failure of foresight led Moses to make a crucial mistake. He left no second-in-command. An icon of enlightenment, he was not able to foresee that if he was not around, his disciples would likely falter in their search for liberation.

It is silly to criticize Moses for not having anticipated every circumstance. Rabbi Adin Steinsaltz, a noted expert on the Tanya and other mystical Hebrew texts, explained that even for an enlightened Jewish mystic, a tzaddik, not every judgment turns out to have the desired effect. "Situations arise in which perfection is not possible, in which the very structure of reality and the relations between a person, the world and God are such that no perfect solution exists," he wrote. "In such a situation, even a tzaddik can reach an erroneous decision."

So nobody knows everything. Not Moses, not the enlightened gurus and saints or the exalted spiritual masters whom their followers believe are avatars, divine incarnations that appear when God Himself takes a human body. Whether they are people who have raised their consciousness up to become one with God or are gods who have brought their consciousness down to earth to serve people, they are still living as human beings on a planet inhabited by men and women of free will, whose unexpected decisions produce unpredictable events. So mistakes are made. As we are told in Ecclesiastes, "There is not one good man on earth who does what is best and doesn't err."

In our unsettling uncertainty, we yearn for an infallible teacher whom we can follow, someone who can explain everything in the world and bring some predictability to it. We may consult psychics, astrologers, numerologists, and clairvoyants. They may know a lot more than us but not everything. The enlightened may rarely screw up, but not everything they do meets with success.

When I first learned Transcendental Meditation (TM), Maharishi predicted that those who practiced his technique just twice a day for twenty minutes would become enlightened. He approximated that it would take somewhere between five and eight years. I began TM on April 18, 1971, but I didn't start meditating regularly until January 1, 1972. After that, I almost never missed my twice-a-day meditation. And if I did, I usually managed to meditate at least once that day. I stopped using the technique sometime in 2000, nearly twenty years past the maximum eight-year prediction.

TM did introduce me to the notion of transcending thought, enabling me to experience the inner silence. Did its regular practice for more than three decades deepen my ability to more easily repeat the experience? Undoubtedly. Do I consider Maharishi to be one of my most important spiritual teachers? Without question. I am grateful for the techniques of transcending that he taught me and for the knowledge that he so clearly articulated, which to this day continues to inform me in almost everything that I do. I respect his impressive insight and will always have a deep love for him. Yet did the regular practice of TM bring me or anyone else I know to enlightenment within five to eight years? I can only speak for myself. No.

The TM organization estimates that over the last fifty years, at least six million people were taught the technique. Even if only 1 percent of them continued meditating regularly during the five- to eight-year period, then about sixty thousand people should have attained enlightenment within that time. Perhaps I just hadn't met any of them, or none of them wanted to talk about their enlightenment. Maybe I wasn't able to recognize enlightened people then and still cannot.

"Transcendental Meditation develops full potential," was the speech I was told to deliver to potential meditators during my teacher training course in 1972. "Use full potential to eliminate suffering." And that is what I taught.

During one of his earliest public appearances, Maharishi described his view of enlightenment, which I came to share, and which millions of others who follow various spiritual teachers around the world still do. "Nothing from outside can stop a man from enjoying lasting peace and permanent joy in life," Maharishi said during a talk delivered at a 1955 spiritual conference in Kerala, India. "Come on and enjoy the fountain-head of all joys in life, enjoy the overbright chambers of your own inner personality. All suffering will cease, all agony will go, and all peacelessness and misery of life will simply disappear."

Taking his message west, Maharishi continued to elaborate on his definition of enlightenment. "Fulfillment of human consciousness lies in the attainment of divine consciousness," he wrote in his 1963 book, *The Science of Being and the Art of Living*. "Every perception, the sound of every word, the touch of every little particle and the smell of whatever may be, brings a tidal wave from the ocean of eternal bliss. Every right thought, word or action is a rising of the tide of this bliss."

Perhaps I didn't grasp the subtle nature of the bliss that is experienced "whatever may be," even when tragic events and violent acts occur. It might not be emotional joy that Maharishi and many other spiritual teachers seem to be describing, but rather the bliss that arises from an awareness that accepts that the flow of negative and positive is the natural expression of creation. Enlightenment may be the attainment of a powerful consciousness that replaces resistance and revulsion with contentment and understanding.

Whatever Maharishi meant by enlightenment, some of his disgruntled followers claim that he was lying when he made his prediction that within five to eight years, TM can bring meditators to the kind of awakened consciousness that he had described. Perhaps he made his prediction just to motivate people, so that they would not be discouraged by the more likely prospect that it would take decades, not years, to reach enlightenment. Some critics charge that Maharishi deliberately deceived people to popularize his teaching or himself or only to make money. I am not one of them. I believe that Maharishi was sincere, just mistaken.

Maharishi underestimated how long it would take, and what it would take, to bring people to enlightenment. This misjudgment might have partly been due to his definition of an enlightenment that permanently frees us from all forms of suffering, which may take forever. But I never felt misled by Maharishi or resentful at my own failure to attain the state that he described. His teachings inspired me, his vision sustained me, and his meditation expanded me. Maharishi wasn't infallible, just human. Well-intentioned, but sometimes wrong. If Moses wasn't perfect and couldn't predict the future, why should any of us have expected Maharishi to always be right and even clairvoyant?

For many spiritual seekers, the belief in human perfection often ends in disillusionment when they discover that they have been following fallible gurus or, much worse, following scandalized preachers like Jimmy Swaggart, who confessed to adultery while preaching fidelity, or criminal Catholic priests such as Oliver O'Grady, who admitted sexually abusing the same children he was pastoring. The imperfections of each spiritual leader varies, and our revulsion is in proportion to the severity of their flaws. Whatever the flaw, a belief in spiritual perfection can lead to intense spiritual frustration.

A realistic recognition of the faults and limitations of our spiritual idols may be so disheartening that we renounce the journey toward an awakened awareness. After so many years of linking higher levels of consciousness to flawless behavior, disillusioned seekers who have failed to attain such states themselves may eventually give up on the search for any kind of enlightenment. We become a casualty of spiritual naïveté, a victim of our own faith.

When our attachment to infallibility falls away, those of us who might have been neglecting families and careers to chase an immaculate enlightenment may suddenly find ourselves confronting a stark environment that is emotionally challenging and financially threatening. Spiritual perfection was supposed to yield perfect results, including perfect health, perfect happiness, and even perfect wealth, so we may be unprepared to deal with the realities of an imperfect world. Deprived of our belief in the inflated promises of seductive spiritual texts and their alluring promoters, many of us find ourselves struggling with the same mundane challenges that others face, whether they are spiritual aspirants or stalwart secularists. We feel forced to accept the fact that human beings are fated to a lifetime of labor in order to survive, that it is an ongoing challenge to stay healthy in a body destined for death, and that our drive to find constant emotional security in a world of uncertainty is futile. The cynical pragmatist might celebrate the fall of the spiritual seeker, but the cynic's delight is premature.

Those who persevere in their search for enlightenment regain their spiritual bearings, emerging with a more realistic yet still optimistic view of what is possible. They embrace a reasonable spirituality that balances the fulfillment of perfect inner silence with the emotional disruptions of an imperfect world. Instead of fixating on the attainment of an unattainable state of consciousness, where imaginary mystics not only behave perfectly but supposedly see everything in the world as similarly perfect, spiritual realists learn how to live side by side with flawless inner silence and the flaws of the external world.

On the path to enlightenment, spiritual realists often encounter those who insist that nature has no flaws, seeing the benign and the cancerous alike and proclaiming, "It's all good!" as if the slogan was the battle cry of the true spiritual soldier. Modest spiritual realists leave room for the implausible: it may be all good—but not to me. They do not seek or even want to achieve a state of consciousness that perceives tumors destroying brains and breasts as the expression of nature's perfection, a fact that should uplift us rather than repel us. Spiritual realists rejoice over health and decry disease and make no excuses for their bias. Spiritual realists are comfortable with their own humanity. Their inner silence enables them to make peace with inhumanity, without feeling compelled to excuse it.

People suffer not only because they do bad things to each other, but also because bad things happen to them that have nothing to do with human behavior. The world around us can only follow its own dual nature, which is to create negativity alongside the positive, error alongside wisdom, imperfection alongside perfection. We human beings must also follow our own nature, which is to try and act humanely. This means that we do not react to the negative as if it were positive. Insisting that the pains inflicted by nature do not blemish nature's perfection is inhumane and heartless.

"I do not trust the man who never weeps," said Swami Vivekananda, who in 1893 became one of the earliest Vedic masters to popularize Indian philosophy in the United States. This is a basic tenet of spiritual realism.

Spiritual realists do not attain happiness because they are happy with all circumstances, be it the birth of a child or the untimely death of one. In their peaceful inner stillness, they can still weep, and, more often than not, they should weep.

If we keep clinging to spiritual fantasies, our recurring anxieties and disappointments will eventually grind us down. The duality of positive and negative events, and the positive and negative emotions that they trigger, cannot be eliminated by your enlightenment or mine. But we can experience a spiritual reality where the unity of perfect silence can bring us peace while we deal with the dueling contrasts and contradictions of daily life.

We may become agitated when we begin to consider that just maybe, all of our problems will not be solved simply by our reaching a higher level of consciousness. We may become increasingly unnerved as we slowly begin to realize that not only might the difficult conditions of the present continue to challenge us, but the memory of anything that has severely undermined us in the past can also be troubling. Our private hurts leave public scars that are not so easily hidden by an expanded consciousness.

Despite the promise of supreme enlightenment, even the Vedic masters acknowledged that the lasting influences of our pre-enlightened lives continue to have consequences despite our awakening. The gurus refer to this as *lesha avidya,* Sanskrit for "the remains of ignorance." It is like the faint stain that is left after a slice of butter is removed from a plate. As long as we inhabit a human body, the stresses inflicted on our physiology—both mental and physical—still linger and will continue to influence us. They can weaken our bodies, cloud our understanding, and harm our personalities, and enlightenment is not enough to reverse the damage. Lesha avidya, the stains from our previous unenlightened lives, will keep us from acting with perfect wisdom. Mistakes will be made.

Even in our enlightenment, virtue and selfishness will continue to coexist. Our wisdom will still compete with our ignorance. Aggressive coworkers and unintentional blunders might revive previous fears of failure, isolation, and helplessness. Current circumstances may also cause us to react negatively. When we are confronted by real threats—an unwanted divorce, a lost limb, natural disasters, accidents, injuries, crime—the butterflies in our stomachs may burst forth so quickly that they feel more like physical instincts than reasoned reactions. Recoiling is often a natural response to a turbulent world. The only relaxing refuge is inner silence, which calms the turbulence so that we may overcome destructive impulses and act on our positive ones.

Sometimes, life's turmoil seems too much to contain, and we may keep stumbling out of silence and eventually wander so far away from the path back into it that we forget that it is even there. Without the awareness of the soothing stillness within us, daily life may start to feel like the grinding tedium of just getting by. Yet even a flash of hope is enough to show us the way back. And as we turn inward and once again head into silence, we realize that the achievement of inner peace is still in sight. We are reminded that life is not only about getting by, but about living with a stabilizing awareness that gets us beyond self-doubt, depression, and pessimism.

The return to inner silence may not completely eliminate the influence of our previous traumas. But like the stain of lesha avidya, they fade as the presence of our current fulfillment expands. The sting of having been fired from a job or the heartache over being rejected by a lover diminishes when we place our attention on the quiet stillness within. Because our bodies and personalities are imperfect, we will likely encounter future hurts that shake us out of silence. We will then have to return to silence once again to heal them.

Letting go of our obsession with spiritual perfection liberates us. It frees us from the distraction of a constant search for an enlightenment that knows no pain. We can then see that there is no place left to go other than into the painless presence of inner silence. Therein lies the spiritual perfection that can bring us the peace that we truly dream about—one that is realistic and immediate.

Spiritual realism shows us that although the dream of absolute perfection is charming and at times motivating and worth imagining, the reality of the silent healing stillness of this moment offers us the serenity we seek, here and now. When the dream is over, awakening follows. Our perfect inner silence offers us enduring peace as we pass the time in an imperfect world.

Chapter 6

OUR IMPULSE TO LOVE

If we return to inner silence quickly enough, it can seem as though it never left us, even when we are momentarily distracted by external challenges.

A 35mm still photo moving through a movie projector at twenty-five frames per second gives the illusion of seamless motion. Similarly, the repetition of the illuminating silence within, which is only momentarily interrupted by the dark gaps of negative circumstances, can be experienced as constant serenity. Each break in our awareness of inner silence, triggered by external circumstances, is quickly followed by yet another instance of inner calm. The faster our return to the silence within, the more we experience this quiet inner stillness as a constant reassuring presence, comforting us during the inevitable ups and downs of daily life.

The alternating awareness that switches between the pull of outside upheavals and the rapid return to inner silence may not be the state of unbroken contentment that many spiritual seekers dream about, but it's close. "You lose the Now, and you return to it, again and again. Eventually, presence becomes your predominant state," wrote the German spiritual teacher Eckhart Tolle, who champions the inner stillness present in every moment. This repeated movement between outer sensation and inner stillness keeps us centered when life's difficulties threaten to overwhelm us.

When I was growing up in New York City, there were frequent encounters with gangsta wannabes trolling the streets, looking to knock some innocent kid onto the pavement or break a baseball bat over someone's leg, for no other reason than the perverse joy of randomly expressed rage. I can still feel a palpable tingling in my body whenever I walk through troubled urban areas or hostile foreign neighborhoods where similar dangers lurk. It's as if those early years of daily fears helped me to create an energetic field that still follows me around, ready to become activated to warn me of impending danger.

When the danger does arrive, despite the usual adrenaline jolt, my return to inner stillness keeps me centered, eventually calming me down, clearing my mind, and sometimes leaving me wondering why I put myself at such risk. Yet I don't forget that every day battlefield medics, war correspondents, rescue workers, missionary doctors, police officers, and tens of thousands of heroic peacemakers are placing themselves in far more dangerous situations to help the helpless. As for my own less perilous wanderings, I no longer rely on a contrived vision of a powerful enlightened consciousness that would make it possible for me to ignore surrounding dangers, as if the energetic field that feels like an early warning system could evolve into a ring of spiritual love that would shield me from serious attack. My only real protection has been the silent inner stillness that keeps me present, out of panic, and capable of figuring out a proper mix of advance and retreat.

Inner stillness centers us and makes us calm, but it does not always generate joy. Depending on the circumstances, we may be worried, relaxed, sad, discouraged, happy, or inspired—but our inner quiet does help us make peace with these shifting sensations. At times, certain spiritual teachers have hinted that their own enlightenment is a state of permanent joy, by describing the experience of the inner stillness as blissful. But, as Krishnamurti explained, "bliss is not pleasure." The silent space within the mind is simply filled with nothing but silence. Not even our joyful emotions can be found there. But neither can our sorrowful ones. Contact with this empty mindspace is not sensuously gratifying in the way that a sumptuous meal or an evening of lovemaking is pleasurable. But it is utterly peaceful, which for many people is the meaning of bliss.

Our connection with inner silence may not be flashy. Yet it does help us create the conditions for more lasting emotional and sensual enjoyment. We feel freer, less inhibited, more confident. "I call it stillness," Tolle explained, "but it is a jewel with many facets. That stillness is also joy, and it is love." The inevitable outgrowth of the repeated experience of inner silence is expanding loving kindness. The stillness within makes us calmer, gentler, more sensitive to our primal urge to love and be loved.

Experiencing inner silence is a subtle, transcendent joy. It is a joy that comes from an underlying feeling of peace. Silence activates a spiritual love more abiding than ordinary emotion. It is a love that is not based only on sentiment, the shifting moods that leave us open to giving one day and susceptible to closing down the next. You may not always be able to hold on to the inner silence, but the longer you do and the more quickly you return to it, the more capable you are of sustaining your inner peace—and your commitment to loving others, regardless of the mood of the moment. You may not always be exhilarated by the thrilling emotional kick of being in love, but being in silence will prompt you to keep on quietly loving. As the German philosopher Friedrich Nietzsche observed, "Not the intensity but the duration of high feelings makes high men."

The respected Roman emperor and military leader Marcus Aurelius understood the process whereby we may encounter distressing outside circumstances and then, when the opportunity arises, promptly return to the equanimity within. As a solider, Aurelius knew firsthand the power that external events have to instill fear in the most courageous of men. The battlefield is no abode of uninterrupted bliss, whether one is enlightened or not. Although enlightened men might not seek battle, others may still choose to battle them. And sometimes ordinary life can seem like a battle as well. Aurelius celebrated the ability of the wisest among men to swiftly let go of their anxieties, knowing that war is the most anxious time of all. "When thou hast been compelled by circumstances to be disturbed in a manner," he wrote, "quickly return to thyself and do not continue out of tune longer than the compulsion lasts; for thou wilt have more mastery over the harmony by continually recurring to it."

The recurring return to the silent self enlivens an inner harmony that can be experienced even in the midst of turmoil. When uncertainty and disappointments inevitably distract you, remain mindful of that which can calm you. Inner silence is a gift that is readily available. All that is required is the continued practice of turning inward whenever possible, in every circumstance. "The man who in his work finds silence, and who sees that silence is work," the Bhagavad Gita teaches, "this man in truth sees the Light, and in all his works finds peace." Inner silence is always present and readily accessible, whether we are walking or talking, working or relaxing, writing or reading.

Inner silence is readily accessible, yet the outside world is alluring and it is easy to get drawn into its drama, causing us to forget to connect with the quiet stillness within. All kinds of thoughts and emotions, good and bad, can overshadow our awareness of it. Even our own simple forgetfulness keeps us from experiencing inner silence. But trying to concentrate on inner silence, struggling to block out distracting thoughts and repress uncomfortable emotions, merely contracts us and prevents us from relaxing into quiet awareness.

Do not concentrate on holding onto inner silence. You will only wind up thinking of little else but your effort to avoid slipping out of silence. It is stressful, frustrating, and ineffective. When we relax our awareness, easily putting our attention on the surrounding stillness, the mind naturally opens up to the silence within. Even when we are meditating, using a mantra or the inhalations and exhalations of our own breath, if we try to hasten the journey into silence it becomes more elusive because the mind can't quiet down if it is too busy working on quieting down.

In his acclaimed spiritual novel *Siddhartha*, the Nobel Prize–winning author Hermann Hesse has the title character explain the problem with thinking our way into silence. "When someone is seeking," Hesse wrote, "it happens quite easily that he only sees the thing that he is seeking; that he is unable to find anything, unable to absorb anything, because he is only thinking of the thing he is seeking, because he has a goal, because he is obsessed with his goal."

Relentless thinking about not thinking drowns out our ability to absorb the quiet that lies in between each thought. Let your thoughts and emotions come and go. Easily place your awareness on the inner silence that underlies all thought and emotion. Stay relaxed about your distractions. Just favor the stillness as the shifting feelings and stream of thinking move in and out of your awareness. Let them run their course as you become conscious of the ongoing silence. Gently return to inner silence whenever you remember that you have forgotten your connection to it.

Our commitment to the value of inner silence must not give way to the pretense of experiencing it. Imagining that we are already in a state of consciousness where our awareness of inner silence is never-ending at all times in every circumstance is an impediment to authentic spiritual expansion. Conjuring up imaginary states of consciousness prevents the mind from fully resting in stillness. We are so busy striving to sustain the idea of stillness that we cannot really settle into the present quiet within.

We cannot force ourselves into our empty mindspace. How can you get there? Many people choose to set aside a certain period of time to meditate, when they close their eyes and simply listen—to their breath, to their mantra, to the sound of their inner prayers or outward chants. They sit quietly, attentive to the empty mindspace within where only silence abides. They gradually become awakened to the silent gaps in between their thoughts, letting their minds effortlessly sink deeper into the silence. When they do get distracted by physical sensations, a series of intense thoughts, or captivating emotions, they gently return to their listening or their chanting or their breathing or whatever vehicle they have chosen to bring them back to silence.

I have found it beneficial to learn a meditation technique from an experienced teacher, in person, firsthand. It is difficult to learn how to dive into inner silence from books since they naturally keep the conscious mind preoccupied with words, concepts, judgments, and speculations. An experienced teacher can help to quiet the mind, answering questions, sharing the stillness, offering techniques that can bring a student into that inner place where thought and analysis become fainter and the underlying silence appears.

If the method you choose to experience stillness is effective, the regular practice of turning inward will gradually enable you to remain centered in silence even when your eyes are open. This centeredness will nurture a self-esteem that is extraordinarily reliable because it no longer depends on the fickleness of changing external events. You will still experience joy and sorrow, depending upon life circumstances, but your spiritual tranquility will eventually override most emotional upheavals. Your self-worth will be nourished by the continuous return to silence. Your connection to silence will give you the confidence to withstand the rough times and more easily generate good ones, knowing that neither one can permanently separate you from the simple peaceful experience of your own silent self.

Confident in the ability to experience inner silence, you acquire the capacity for a courageous love that unfolds naturally. This love is natural because it is not the product of an abstract ideal or rigid rules of behavior. Our simple spontaneous gratitude for having finally found inner peace prompts us to humbly want to share its benefits with others. It is a courageous love since it prevails amid all kinds of challenges. It triumphs over our previous impulses to hold back when confronted by rejection, ingratitude, or spite. Since this love is deeper than emotion, independent of mood, we are eager to serve others whenever the opportunity arises, unencumbered by judgment, intimidation, resentment, or defensiveness. We are more caught up in the pleasure of loving others than of merely being loved by others.

Established in our own quiet sense of well-being, we spontaneously strengthen the ability to serve others, even when they do not serve us in return. This altruism is not forced upon us by a guilty conscience or an intellectual concept of virtue or even a commitment to spiritual values. It is not a thing to be manufactured, but rather the natural outgrowth of a life rooted in inner silence that nourishes our own inherent loving kindness.

When you are connected to the quiet within, you feel so good that you cannot help but share your good feelings with other people. You are so grateful for finally experiencing inner calm that your natural inclination is to show your gratitude by helping others find joy.

The intention to be kind and merciful to others is as primal as the instinct to survive, as natural as any fear arising from external threats. Wasn't your basic childhood desire simply to be happy and to joyfully play with others? Before all the weirdness of childish insults and hidden backbiting, we were all innocent, eager to smile and enjoy. There was nothing complicated about our desires: they were pure, innocent. There was not yet any of the complex defensiveness that would be later thrust upon us; none of the psychological machinations that would absorb us for years as we increasingly fixated on a life complicated by a confusing mix of friendship and vindictiveness.

Before we became callous and cynical and adopted an emotional stinginess that posed as hardnosed adult maturity or wary reserve, our fulsome impulse to love was youthfully unashamed. We felt no need to hide our exuberance. We were not ashamed to show our eagerness to be liked. We were charmingly immature; we innocently assumed that our good intentions would always be reciprocated. It was a loving, Christlike innocence, one that is difficult to recover. "If you do not turn about and become as children are," Jesus said, "you shall not enter the Kingdom of Heaven." By turning toward the uncomplicated awareness of our own inner silence, we can recapture our childlike, Christlike readiness to love others—and let ourselves be loved by others. You will find yourself growing into a spiritualized maturity that is more innocent and carefree. You will no longer be dominated by a battered spirit that is preoccupied with the cycles of emotional profit and loss, bedeviled by the constant demands of an ego that fears neglect and disrespect.

Liberated by our unbounded capacity to love, we can look back at our days of stultifying inhibition and selfish reserve as a bygone era, relieved that we are no longer bogged down by social anxieties and inept attempts to overcome them. We will indeed become born again, reborn through the newfound freedom that arises from our liberating connection to inner silence. This spiritual rebirth might make your troubled past seem shameful, as it has for me. Yet as Bob Dylan put it: "Ah, but I was so much older then, I'm younger than that now." And, of course, the antidote to regret is love.

Spiritual realism may be youthful, but it is not naive. It will not make us perfect on the outside, only aware of the perfect silence on the inside. We may recoil if a parent insults us or may shout down a lover who betrays us. We may fear angry young toughs who punch pregnant women in the streets and suicidal terrorists who fly planes into office buildings. Yet we will know that nearly everything that threatens us will eventually subside. And that when our silent calm returns, our compassion will automatically rise again. Then our spiritual love for our adversaries will be able to thrive, despite our imperfect personalities. Spiritual realism means realizing that while we may still have to fight our enemies, we do not have to hate them.

This altruistic love is the aspiration of spiritual seekers everywhere. When the Israeli political journalist Yossi Klein Halevi embarked on a spiritual quest through his war-torn homeland, he came upon Sister Johanna, a devout Catholic nun who had been cloistered in a convent inside Israel for more than twenty years. "What has been your hardest spiritual struggle?" Halevi asked her. "Overcoming sentimental love," Sister Johanna responded. "The difficulty is to love truly, without discrimination. To love like Him. Totally and unequivocally, beyond the likes and dislikes of the personality." Is this not your aim as well?

The return to stillness brings us closer to this goal. Buoyed by inner silence, we can better rise above the likes and dislikes of our personalities. When we are attuned to the gratifying stillness within, even when we are emotionally hurt or threatened, we are less likely to engage in petty retaliation or to flee into cowardly isolation.

When inner silence dominates our awareness, although others may reject or threaten us, we can instead choose to forgive them or even help them, rather than impulsively condemn, strike, run, or capitulate.

When we do have to protect ourselves, physically or emotionally, once the threats subside our prompt return to the calming quiet within gives us an opportunity to quickly open our hearts again and again. "Once we become conscious, even dimly, of the Atman, the Reality within us, the world takes on a very different aspect," wrote Swami Prabhavanda and Christopher Isherwood in their introduction to the teachings of the great Indian sage Adi Shankara. "Every experience offers us the chance of making a constructive reaction to it—a reaction which helps to break some chain of our bondage to Maya and bring us that much nearer to spiritual freedom."

Our spiritual calm, replenished by our connection to the reality of our silent being, the Atman within, helps to tame our emotions, keeping us flexible, leaving us poised to assist others whenever the chance arises. By speedily regaining our composure through the experience of stillness, we become better equipped to drop our defenses once the danger has passed and able to express our love more fully, without reservation.

This realistic spirituality means that although we recognize that there may still be moments of fear and even anger in an enlightened state, there are no perpetual anxieties or lasting grudges. While we are vigilant to real threats, the unbounded love that inner silence releases leaves us ready to help our adversaries whenever it is safe to do so.

Spiritual realism is not about a high-minded but fanciful ideal where the world around us is made peaceful simply because we have a passion for peace. Positive energy is not always reciprocated with positive energy. The love arising out of inner silence is brave enough to reject the negative and resist the cruel. It is also tough enough to keep us compassionate amid the negativity and the cruelty.

A realistic spirituality integrates our basic human need to resist harmful forces with our ardent spiritual desire to forgive those who wish us harm. It is free from the sentimentalized love touted by exaggerating yet well intentioned spiritual pundits and so rarely achieved by their followers. We do not expect enlightenment to always make us feel good. It takes all serious things seriously, including past hurts and present dangers, the tragedy of defeat, and the tragedy of having to be victorious. Spiritual realism promotes a love that is youthful but not infantile. Although we may have to regretfully attack our enemies, we are eager to heal their wounds once the battle is won. Spiritual realists are wise enough to resist and kind enough to forgive.

As we courageously drop our illusions and boldly emerge from a mystical pretentiousness that promises a worldly utopia dwelling in the recesses of liberated minds, spiritual realism unveils a truth that perfect harmony is only found in the perfect silence that exists in an imperfect world. It is a truth, perhaps not *the* truth, but it is a spiritually realistic one that offers a practical, attainable, and beautiful opportunity for fulfillment in real life.

Chapter 7

EASING ANXIETIES THAT
COME AND GO

There is an old Indian aphorism: avoid the danger that has not yet come. Meditating does expand our consciousness, which helps to bring us into greater harmony with our surroundings by freeing us from persistent anxieties. Yet it does not keep all dangers at bay. Being forced to choose between anger and acquiescence, cowardice and freedom, is a common predicament, regardless of our state of consciousness. Inner peace can keep us from being overwhelmed by bad situations, but it will not totally insulate us from them.

Look at the world around you. If a friend betrays you, your lover cheats on you, a business associate deceives you, or a family member undermines you, what choice will you make? Resist or acquiesce? Lead or appease? Can spirituality truly dissolve all outside aggression and free us from making tough choices in bad situations? Is it really possible to retreat into a spiritual haven that can shield us from all negative surroundings?

Unfortunately, it appears that no one has yet found Shangri-La. If they have, it has not been located on a map that any of us have seen. Some have speculated that the mystical paradise is in Tibet. If so, it is no paradise any longer. Chinese troops invaded the country in 1949 to put down an uprising by Tibetans opposed to their rule. The Chinese seized the capital of Lhasa, slaughtered monks, destroyed thousands of Buddhist monasteries, and forced the Dalai Lama to seek refuge in India. Two years earlier, during a political power struggle among the Tibetans themselves, the monks of the Reting Gompa monastery led a rebellion against their political rulers. Troops from Lhasa were dispatched; they destroyed the ancient monastery, and the surviving monks fled to safety. The violence spread. "Enraged by the happenings at Reting," wrote Lama Anagarika Govinda, a German-born Tibetan Buddhist who was trekking through Tibet at the time, "a section of the monks of Sera rose against the government, and only after a bombardment by artillery was peace restored."

Do you think that such Tibetan violence was confined only to recent history? More than a thousand years ago, King Ralpachan, a devout Buddhist who is considered one of the great religious monarchs of Tibet, was assassinated by a follower of an indigenous Tibetan religion called Yungdrung Bn that predates Buddhism. The Tibetan Yungdrung Bn Institute claims that the faith is the authentic religion of Tibet, having originated eighteen thousand years ago in what its practitioners believe was the enlightened community of Shambhala, which is Sanskrit for "place of peace."

As for the Chinese occupation of Tibet, it has certainly been a violent one. Although Tenzin Gyatso, the exiled fourteenth Dalai Lama of Tibet, has emphasized nonviolence throughout a long and often brutal occupation, thousands of Tibetan guerrillas were trained by the CIA to take up arms against the Chinese. One of their leaders recalls telling the Dalai Lama, "Stop waiting for the world to save us. Stop hoping the Chinese will change. Whether the cat is white or black, it is going to eat the mouse. To get our freedom we must fight, maybe die. That is our only chance."

The CIA-backed guerrillas were eventually disbanded in the 1970s at the urging of the Dalai Lama, yet recently, activists within the Tibetan Youth Congress have become increasingly disenchanted with the apparent futility of nonviolent resistance. One young Tibetan activist told a reporter, "I want to ask the Dalai Lama: 'If you could achieve Tibetan independence in a day by killing a hundred Chinese, would you do it?' If he says no, he cannot be the leader of the Tibetan people. He values his philosophies more. Monks are good people but perhaps too good for the raw politics consuming us." Another young Tibetan concurred. "It's not that I believe in violence," he said, "but even a street dog, if he's cornered, will bite you."

Such is the troubled state of the venerated Tibetan Plateau. Tibet has not been a place of peace, or, at best, perhaps it hosted such a spot around eighteen thousand years ago. Neither is it a modern-day Shambhala. But to be fair, do you know of any other community of spiritual seekers that is so evolved that it is peopled only with those who always treat each other kindly? Is it to be found inside a remote Hindu ashram in the Himalayas, a Buddhist monastery on a mountaintop in Burma, a Sufi center in Old Jerusalem, a neighborhood church, a temple, a mosque, or a synagogue? At the very least, are there not armed security guards or police patrols ensuring that the inhabitants of all these places are not victimized by thieves, assailants, or even murderers?

Many of us might assume that an exotic corner of India frequented by various yogis and numerous spiritual seekers might likely be free of the everyday potential for violence. I wish. When I was traveling with one of my teachers, Chalanda Ma, we visited an ashram in the tiny village of Bet Lar, located in the secluded foothills of the Himalayas. It was a long and arduous trip, twelve hours by bus from Delhi and another five hours off-road in an unsteady truck bouncing over rocks, streams, and steep drops. At one point, a truckload of armed Indian soldiers suddenly appeared. They were there to provide us with safe passage through the dense, isolated jungle. Bandits were known to swoop down on unsuspecting travelers, and apparently neither the higher consciousness of my spiritual teacher nor the collective consciousness of her loyal disciples was sufficient to protect us from attack.

If there is no such community on earth where a heightened spirituality has freed its adherents of all conflict and periodic violence, if higher states of consciousness have not yet created a single village that is completely invincible to serious danger, then are we destined to keep finding ourselves in difficult circumstances despite our expanded spiritual awareness? Probably. The only truly peaceful refuge lies within.

What about those legendary souls who are said to have achieved a rarefied state of supreme enlightenment? If there are no communities that are untouched by negativity, aren't there at least a few great individuals whose consciousness has given them mastery over the consequences of negative behavior? We are all familiar with the eternal conundrum: why do bad things happen to good people? Some spiritual seekers hasten to add: bad things do not happen to enlightened people. But is this really the case?

There are a few examples that can shed some light on the correlation between high consciousness and lowly outcomes. There was once a revered saint who lived in a cave near Rishikesh, a Himalayan village long considered to be the abode of many of India's greatest sages. His name was Tat Wale Baba. He was said to be over eighty-five years old, yet to have the remarkable appearance of a middle-aged man. He was actually rumored to have stopped aging at thirty-five.

Tat Wale Baba lived in a jungle cave with a giant cobra for a pet, as evidence of his contagious serenity. On December 2, 1974, he was murdered by a gunman who led a nearby ashram.

"The man was crazy with jealousy," one of Tat Wale Baba's disciples, Swami Shankardasji, told a biographer writing about the murdered spiritual leader. "He tried to set himself up as a great saint and wanted people to go to his ashram. But few went to see him. He noticed people from all over the world coming here to visit my guru. He thought that if he would kill my guru then people would go to see him instead." Can you do the mental acrobatics that could translate this tragedy into a blessed benefit that serves a higher spiritual purpose? Is this the way to reconcile cosmic consciousness with horrific happenings?

Perhaps the assault on Tat Wale Baba was some sort of cosmic fluke, like the one that happened to Charlie Lutes, the first person in the continental United States to learn Transcendental Meditation (TM). He had personally been taught by Maharishi himself. I came to know Charlie during a series of interviews I conducted with him in 1978. He was a devout meditator, well-versed in esoteric knowledge. As far back as 1959, he was organizing the U.S. branch of the Spiritual Regeneration Movement to teach TM to the rest of America. For years, Charlie's regular Friday night lectures in Santa Monica were a popular event for hundreds of Los Angeles spiritualists.

Surprisingly, Charlie was a straight-talking conservative businessman with a military-school upbringing. Nevertheless, he was always available for counseling the many meditators who sought him out during more than four decades of spiritual service. Charlie was blunt but gentle, confident yet humble. He never charged a fee for his consultations or courted a following in any way. "He maintained a twenty-four/seven hotline for anyone who wanted to reach him, and the phone rang off the hook," recalled Vincent Daczynski, one of Charlie's numerous admirers. "He was a clairvoyant, a healer, and a lecturer. He was also accomplished in many yogic siddhi powers."

I never heard Charlie make the claim that he was adept at the siddhis, which are supernatural abilities delineated by the Indian sage Rishi Patanjali nearly fifteen hundred years ago. These yogic powers include such feats as being able to acquire enormous physical strength, understand the language of animals, become invisible, levitate, and predict the exact time of one's own death. Whatever the scope of Charlie's mystical abilities, many people honored his extraordinary generosity and long-standing commitment to spiritual development.

One evening, during one of his weekly talks, someone from the audience suddenly attacked Charlie with a knife. Charlie survived the assault, yet it was stunning that anyone would try to harm a man so dedicated to selfless service. Then again, this paradox is not new. One of history's most vigorous advocates of nonviolence, Mahatma Gandhi, was assassinated by a Hindu extremist opposed to reconciliation between his coreligionists in a newly independent India and the Muslims of the recently formed Pakistan.

Despite his commitment to selfless service, was there a serious deficiency in Charlie's spiritual awareness that made him vulnerable to attack? Regardless of his standing as a man of great spiritual development, was Tat Wale Baba's tragic fate actually the result of his inability to burn off his bad karma? And even though Gandhi was devoted to elevating politics by infusing it with a deep spirituality, was his possible failure to reach enlightenment really the reason for his murder?

To bring us to more recent events, were there no people of virtue or dedicated spiritual seekers among the more than three thousand people who died in the World Trade Center on 9/11? Had any one of them been truly enlightened, would he or she have been able to block the suicidal pilots and thereby help everyone else evade the awful circumstances that befell them? It may be comforting to think so, empowering us with the feeling that we can completely control our earthly destiny by raising our state of spiritual consciousness. But is it realistic?

We cannot deny the infinite potential for tragic outcomes in the relative world. Good people encounter bad situations, including the almost enlightened and those purported to be fully enlightened. Spiritual progress does not alter the laws of nature, which often bring saviors and murderers into cataclysmic confrontation.

If spiritual advancement does not completely eradicate the surrounding negativity, then how can we find contentment when we are shadowed by potential violence, such as the newly emerging threats from suicidal terrorism? It takes practice. And often a bit of courage.

In order to sense inner quiet, we must be willing to stop our habitual effort to immediately rid ourselves of worries. Patience can be uncomfortable. Despite our return to silence, we frequently have to wait for the physical discomfort triggered by fear to run its course. Often, our thoughts move faster than adrenaline. The mind can settle down more quickly than the body since the heart rate and the breath rate usually need more time to recover. Even when we relax into silence, the butterflies and the tightened muscles take a while to go away.

Rather than resisting, we can instead accept the temporary unease as we gradually return to silence. Without struggling to instantly repel the negativity, we can keep focusing effortlessly on our return to the source of calm, turning our attention to the soothing stillness within us, as we patiently wait for the physical discomfort to dissipate.

Instead of bumbling around in the dark, cursing the blackness of negativity, we can head toward the light that will eventually be rekindled inside us. Gradually, the soothing glow of our inner silence will once again illuminate our true nature, which is to survive—emotionally, physically, and spiritually—and to forgive, love, and radiate peace.

Inner silence is worth the wait. The presence of the stabilizing stillness within is the source of spiritual strength. The powerful love released through silence goes beyond the world's virtues and vices. It outlives our subsequent positive and negative reactions to them. We still have our judgments and continue to honestly label the good and the bad, but the confidence and the inspiration that naturally emerge from our contact with the silent presence within give us the strength to love even in the face of terror. As Nietzsche said, "Whatever is done from love always occurs beyond good and evil."

This impulse to love is who you really are, the true self that defines you. It is not based only on the surface qualities of your personality, which may have been traumatized by abuse, neglect, or rejection. Inner silence reveals that your essence is loving kindness. This lofty view of the human capacity for love is not merely the belief system of pampered suburban pundits who live charmed lives. Even those who have had to endure the most horrendous suffering have embraced this optimistic view of the human condition.

Victor Frankl, a noted Austrian psychiatrist, spent three years in the Nazi concentration camps at Theresienstadt and Auschwitz. In those hideous factories of death, Frankl lost his wife and his mother. His brother was killed, and his father died of starvation. When describing his ordeal, he reinforced the notion that a loving impulse is at the center of the human character.

"The more one forgets himself by giving himself to a cause to serve or another person to love—the more human he is and the more he actualizes himself," Frankl wrote. He believed that self-actualization is linked to the transcendence of selfishness and self-pity. Reinhold Niebuhr, the famed Christian scholar, agreed with his Jewish counterpart: "The highest form of self-realization is the consequence of self-giving." The more you love, the more enlightened you become.

The regular return to inner silence brings you into repeated contact with your basic human impulse to love fully, creating a virtuous circle: silence leads to increasing love, which in turn is nourished by your return to silence. The continuous cycling of silence followed by love, followed by silence once again, takes us into an authentically human state of self-realization.

Frankl's enormous capacity to love even while surviving the unspeakable horrors of the Holocaust may seem too extraordinary for the rest of us to ever achieve. Yet his experience as a concentration camp survivor and his nearly sixty years as a professional psychiatrist treating a range of despairing patients who suffered from a variety of ailments did not alter his belief that the true essence of all ordinary human beings consists of a basic hunger for selfless service.

Obviously, Frankl was well aware that many people on the planet are not in touch with the refined longings of their authentic natures; they are driven instead by barbaric cravings that are satisfied only by their own ghastly cruelties. But for the rest of us, the infinite love within us can easily be released by our immersion in spiritual silence, cleansing us of egoism and anger and enabling us to uncover our amazing capacity for compassion.

Immaculée Ilibagiza, another holocaust survivor—the tragedy in Rwanda where two million helpless people were slaughtered in just three weeks—demonstrated man's extraordinary ability to forgive. She attributed it to coming back to an inner experience that she described as a return to the inner light of God. "Seeing my home in ruins and visiting the lonely forgotten graves of my loved ones had choked the life out of my forgiving spirit," she recalled. Then she turned inward. "A sudden rush of air flooded my lungs. I heaved a heavy sigh of relief," she wrote. "I was at peace again. Yes, I was sad—deeply sad—but my sadness felt good. I let it embrace me and found that it was clean, with no tinge of bitterness or hatred." The inner source that calms us does not keep us from the sorrow that comes from grief. As Vivekananda said, do not trust a person who never weeps.

We can weep for the world's tormentors, for they are often victims of their own weakness, susceptible to the vice that is constantly in play alongside virtue in this world of duality. "There was no doubt that they had to be punished for their crimes against humanity," Ilibagiza wrote, thinking about her own tormentors. Yet the need for justice need not overshadow our impulse to show mercy. "The people who'd hurt my family had hurt themselves even more, and they deserved my pity," Ilibagiza explained.

The experience of the inner silence that we return to does not always last, so the powerful love that defines our true natures is not always active. Many things can push us out of silence, preventing us from expressing the pure loving compassion that our nature wants to manifest. We then become so preoccupied with analyzing, justifying, calculating, manipulating, and striving that we are incapable of simply loving honestly, openly, and not defensively. When we are lost in thought or waylaid by emotion, unrestrained love can only appear sporadically, depending on our volatile feelings, shifting judgments, and emotional needs. If we believe that we are justified in holding a grudge, forgiveness seems foolish. If we are depressed, receiving love becomes more urgent than giving it.

In the absence of an awareness of inner silence, our hearts may contract. We become bound by the threats we face, the challenges we anticipate, the obligations we feel. This contraction can generate a downward spiral, further narrowing our awareness, diminishing our ability to hold the very inner silence that can expand us and that would give us a greater capacity to love. The way out of this vicious cycle comes from our determination to return to silence again and again, however much we might believe that inner stillness has become irrelevant.

When I was in Burma, the awareness of inner silence did begin to feel irrelevant. During my journey through the remote Burmese countryside, I became gripped by fright while climbing up onto the roof of a high temple. It seemed as if inner silence was not relevant to my panicked effort to keep from falling.

My spiritual guide, Gayuna Cealo, a Buddhist monk from Japan, was leading a group of us on a pilgrimage to Burma's holy sites. At one point, he convinced me to follow him up to the top of an ancient Buddhist shrine and sit precariously on its narrow edge. My overwhelming fear haunted my experience of silence. Why am I putting myself through such misery? I wondered as I made my way upward. I did feel as if my spiritual convictions were being tested. Would I succumb to irrational fear or stay faithful to my belief that spiritual stillness could empower me to go beyond fear?

During my early teens, I lived on the eleventh floor of a Bronx apartment building. In my more mischievous moods, I often leaned halfway out of my bedroom window to toss eggs and drop water balloons on the unsuspecting elderly ladies chatting below. When I decided to earn a little extra cash to spend on pizza and movies with the neighborhood kids, I carelessly reached out of high-rise apartments to wash windows for fifty cents apiece. After I left New York for the desert flatlands of Phoenix, I inexplicably developed an irrational fear of heights. I remember being surprised to discover that barely looking over the rim of the Grand Canyon was enough to give me the willies, even though the likelihood of my falling was far less than my chances of plunging to death had been while leaning out of towering apartment buildings.

My determination to conquer my fear of heights in Burma was reinforced by a decision to open myself up completely to Cealo's teaching. In a similar vein, I had once tried going up in a hot-air balloon over Northern California. I figured that floating in a wicker basket over a thousand feet in the air would be so terrifying that a special state of mind would surely kick in and I would be able to calmly enjoy the ride like almost everyone else. It didn't happen.

I wound up being terrified for more than an hour in that drifting wicker basket, without a moment of letup. Although some people might think the fear was well-founded, my irrationality became evident when I realized that my fright ratcheted up when we started to climb toward a thousand feet and that it decreased when we lowered to a few hundred—as if I'd be any less dead by falling from either height. This time, in Burma, with my spiritual teacher to guide me, I hoped that I might actually experience a special state of spiritual calm, enabling me to overcome my fear of heights. I was so wedded to Cealo's guidance that I even shaved my head, took vows, and became a Buddhist monk.

There is a tradition in Burma in which men can become monks for only a few months or even a couple of weeks. Many Burmese men consider it a right of passage, a religious obligation to fulfill at some point during their lives. I was granted the special privilege of being one of the few Westerners who would be allowed to become a monk. It was to be temporary, I was told, although the head of the monastery later tried to persuade me to leave my wife and kids to join his group permanently. I didn't know whether to be flattered or offended.

As an aspiring monk, I first had to have my head and beard ceremoniously shaved on the humid, sweltering monastery grounds. I then participated in a lengthy ritual conducted with Pali scriptural chants amid local Burmese gawkers. I donned traditional orange robes and black rubber sandals and set out carrying a symbolic begging bowl on a journey to dispense rice and candy to the country's poor orphanages. We also made pilgrimages to the numerous Buddhist shrines that seemed to be everywhere, from the teeming capital of Yangon to the remote mountaintop of Kyaiktiyo. That's the place where my fears began to percolate.

Legend has it that in Kyaiktiyo, a strand of the Buddha's hair is housed in a pagoda built high atop a giant boulder covered with gold leaf. The hair is said to keep the huge golden rock precariously and mysteriously balanced on the edge of a steep hill overlooking a deep chasm below. Maneuvering around the narrow walkway that encircled the holy rock sent my pulse into high gear. The transcendental calm that I longed for had not yet arrived.

Luckily, most of the trip was on flat land so there seemed to be no hurry in my mastering extraordinary heights. Other than the queasiness of inching around Kyaiktiyo's leaning boulder, nothing else in Burma gave me the slightest trepidation. I knew that the country was governed by a ruthless military junta that used slave labor, forcing even children and pregnant women to work long hours under horrible conditions, employing gang rape as an official weapon to terrify and subdue the population, and committing numerous other atrocities to satisfy their demented ambitions. But despite the repression, nothing scary happened and my rare encounters with Burmese soldiers were quite friendly. I was a privileged outsider, a tourist protected by my U.S. passport. Nothing alarming took place until we reached Bagan, a desolate ancient site revered as the city of a thousand Buddhist temples.

The heights of Kyaiktiyo were a piece of cake compared to what awaited me on one of those thousand shrines in Bagan. One evening, we climbed the ancient crumbling steps of a very high temple, stopping on a flat spot about a third of the way up. The plan was to meditate while the sun set. So there I sat, meditating but mostly struggling to stay calm while the sun went down and my heart rate went up. Everyone else meditated serenely, occasionally opening their eyes to take in the vast view and gradually inch closer to the edge. Meanwhile, I discreetly shimmied my way toward the rear of the temple terrace, where I pressed my back against a large stone wall as if I were glued to it and it might somehow keep me from falling. I glanced up now and then, tentatively peeking at the grand expanse all around me. I noticed that there was not even a handrail to keep me from plummeting over the side.

The next afternoon during lunch, my fellow travelers enthusiastically recounted their delight with the previous evening's twilight meditation. So much so, that Cealo agreed to take us back up on a return visit to the temple terrace. I tried to conceal my displeasure, sensing that he might be one of those spiritual teachers who enjoyed taking a tough love approach to the development of higher states of consciousness. If he picked up on my fear, he might try to stop me from cowering in the corner.

My phony nonchalance during dinner was pitifully transparent. Cealo quickly noticed that I was the only one not smiling. I cringed when he asked me why. I felt forced to confess my fear of heights, and he let out a high-pitched laugh after hearing it. When Cealo's cackling finally died down, his mischievous smile seemed to promise that he would make sure that I climbed back up the temple and stayed out of its corners.

That evening, the group cheerfully hurried back up the wide steps leading to the temple platform. I was about to take my familiar spot next to the rear wall when I heard Cealo shouting in the distance. A few people pointed to a small tunnel that led from the platform to a higher landing. I bent down to look inside. It was a dark, narrow passageway with stone steps that seemed ready to crumble after centuries of use. I then saw Cealo in his striking orange robe waiting for me at the other end, calling out my name. He waved and smiled at me, hurrying me to come on up.

Dutifully, perhaps stupidly, I entered the dank, shadowy staircase. I slowly rose one step at a time, lifting the heavy robes above my ankles to avoid tripping, as I struggled to climb in my flimsy rubber sandals. Instead of wearing a comfortable pair of jeans and sneakers, I clumsily hiked up the narrow ancient stairs practically barefoot and wearing what felt like a disheveled dress. Cealo was gone and all I could see was a bright circle of daylight at the exit high above me. It seemed as if the only thing worse than falling down that steep staircase would be climbing out above it.

Somehow, I was still convinced that spiritual consciousness could overcome irrational fear. I soon realized just how isolated this area of Burma was and how much the place had deteriorated from centuries of disrepair, with no park rangers or any of the other protections that I had become accustomed to when traveling through America's national parks. I started to wonder whether my fear of climbing all the way up to the temple roof was really that irrational. Perhaps inner stillness was irrelevant. Its presence was beginning to fade, leaving me alone with my fear. Still, I was determined to rid myself of as much fright as possible. It was an impulse arising out my deep-seated desire for complete spiritual freedom.

Fyodor Dostoyevsky, the Russian novelist who often tackled spiritual predicaments, seems to have accurately described my intention. "There is only one occasion, one only, when man may purposely, consciously choose for himself even the harmful and the stupid, even the stupidest thing," Dostoyevsky explained, "just so that he will have the right to wish the stupidest thing, and not be bound by the duty to have only intelligent wishes." I, too, yearned for the freedom to be stupid, to be able to not only rid myself of unreasonable fears, but to also free myself from reasonable ones. That seemed like total liberation to me. And so up I went, perhaps foolishly, even irrationally, but quite devoutly.

When I finally emerged from the dark covered staircase, the scene was more staggeringly frightening than I had imagined. The landing was shaped like one of those Mayan pyramids with a small zigzagging roof at the top. I stood there with nothing but miles of empty space all around me. The temple towered over the other smaller ones below, and there were no buildings to break the view, no structures to block the horizon and ease the feeling of being so high up. The soft wind blew around us unobstructed, and the eerie quiet added to the sensation of standing at the edge of the world.

I thought about crouching down on the small platform and gripping the floor as if this might keep me from flying off the roof. Before I could, I noticed Cealo smiling. He shook his finger and beckoned me to follow like a stern father demanding that his obstinate son obey him. He suddenly stepped onto the narrow brick ledge that ran round the jagged perimeter of the temple and practically began jogging around the temple's edge.

Balancing perilously close to the side, Cealo moved fast. He was not quite running, but almost. Stunned by his insistence that I follow him, I meekly obeyed. I stepped absentmindedly onto the edge and hurried to catch up with him. My mind emptied, but not because I transcended thought to arrive at pure inner silence. There was so little thought because the only things I could experience were total unrelenting fear and a strange hypnotic force that pushed me to follow him. I walked straight along the jagged edges, hoping to keep my robe from getting caught under my feet and trying not to slip out of my flip-flops. I turned sharply each time the narrow ledge switched directions. I fixated on Cealo who was speeding along as if he were in one of those Chinese martial arts movies where the fighters leap up into the air and furiously kick and punch while miraculously hovering above the ground.

Finally, my harrowing trek around the narrow precipice was interrupted when the brick-lined temple perimeter came to an abrupt end. I stood transfixed, facing a high stone wall that slanted upward to the left, with a very slim ledge on the right. It was much too narrow to even consider walking on. That's what I figured, anyway. My body eased somewhat as I prepared to settle in to whatever temporary solace I might find in not yet having to resume my crazed jaunt along the edge. The reprieve didn't last long. In a matter of moments, Cealo walked straight onto the tiny ledge and sat down. There was barely enough room for his rear end, yet there he sat, crossing his legs, his knees not quite sticking over the edge, but almost. He looked at me, smiled, and gave me that authoritative finger wagging to signal that I was to join him immediately. Beyond reason, I obeyed.

I practically tiptoed across the slender shelf, keeping my eyes on Cealo as I crept closer to him, my peripheral vision taking in the incredible drop just to my right. After I got next to him, Cealo motioned for me to sit. I slowly squatted, placing myself on the ledge I cautiously maneuvered to cross my legs and pressed my hands downward as if I could actually anchor them into the sliver of stone beneath me. I kept my gaze transfixed on Cealo's eyes. There were no more smiles. He just stared back at me reassuringly.

As I sat there, a warm wind slowly drifted past us. Long swaths of slightly rolling hills stretched out below until they merged with the blue sky far off in the distance, as if the empty lands converged on the edge of some vast and distant ocean. I looked into Cealo's eyes as if they were capable of holding me safely in place. Cealo rarely spoke

English. This time, he did. Leaning into me, he said with a soft resonant voice, "I, too, was once afraid, like you." He nodded as if to make sure that I knew he really did understand what I was going through. He then lifted his arm and held his hand out into the air in front of us. He pointed slightly downward toward the ground far below, then pulled his hand back, this time pointing down at the ledge we were sitting on. "There is no difference between that and this," he said. I looked up at the emptiness in front of us, then back down at the flat stone holding us.

I pondered for a moment. There is no difference between this and that? Then a flash of insight seized me. An amazing calm descended, wrapping my entire being. I felt that I had awakened and finally perceived that the same energy was sustaining both my body and the empty space in front of me. It was a feeling of astonishing unity, connecting the solid stone upon which I sat with the open atmosphere around me. They were both formed by the same energy. It merely manifested itself in different forms. It was like sitting on a sandy beach with the waves rolling in front of me and first becoming aware that both beach and ocean were supported by the common ground of earth. Of course, had I not been able to swim, I would have had to watch the tide rather than step into it. Likewise, not being able to fly, I continued sitting on the ledge and did not fling myself over it and into the air.

Rather than being frightened by the immense emptiness before me, I realized that the ether was actually an extension of my own being. Body, ground, and atmosphere were all linked by a common spiritual connection. And although the surrounding expanse was connected to me, it would not pull me down into it against my will. As long as I was prudent, I would not slip. Nothing was there to push me. I would not fall. If I did go down, I would have to jump. And I had no intention of jumping.

I sat there on the tiny ledge for quite a while, calmly gazing out in all directions. I felt amazed that I could peer out to the distant horizon and survey the immense expanse of ground without being shaken out of the deep, comforting stillness that was so powerfully present within me. Cealo and I sat quietly beside each other, held up by a small slice of ancient stone. In peace, we looked into the distance and shared the breathtaking silence. I glanced down at my crossed legs and protruding knees, then back up at the floating horizon in front of me. There was no difference between this and that.

I'm not sure how much time went by, but after a while Cealo stood up and walked across the slender ledge to the other side. He stepped back onto the narrow brick-lined path and continued his speedy journey around the temple's perimeter. I, too, stood up and followed. This time, I walked briskly behind him with absolute confidence and an eerie calm that still surprises me.

We were on the very top of the temple. We quickly worked our way down to the next level, which was still quite high. It gave us another vantage point from which to absorb the magnificent view. We stopped for a moment to enjoy it. I continued to be amazed by how naturally comfortable I was, standing there at such a great height. My bright orange robe was draped around me like a superhero's cape, and the soft wind seemed to whip up an even greater stillness within me. Inner silence was relevant. It was centering, reassuring, empowering. Suddenly, I noticed an old Burmese woman on the ground below, peering up at me with an otherworldly stillness.

It is a tradition in Burma for people to bow when coming into contact with Buddhist monks. They place their heads on the ground with their hands outstretched to express their respect. My eyes met the woman's silent smile and I felt as if my chest instantly opened, releasing a pure rush of love that flowed down upon her. We both lingered for a while, looking at each other without reserve or embarrassment. Then, with great reverence, she slowly bowed down before me. It was a surreal moment as I stood there on the temple landing, high above the ground, effortlessly connecting with a stranger, both of us radiating love.

When the elderly woman lifted herself up, I placed my palms together the way people do when praying. I gently moved them up and down to gratefully acknowledge the honor she had so generously bestowed on me. As I did, I was struck by the realization that had I not overcome my fear of heights, I never would have been able to experience that loving moment. Either I would have cowered in the corner instead of stopping on that high platform, or I would have stood there faking calmness while my thoughts and emotions could focus on nothing but my overpowering fright. The fear would have so constricted my heart that I could not have offered that dignified, reverential woman the effusive love that so effortlessly vibrated out of the peaceful silence within me.

Maharishi often repeated the Indian teaching, "Avoid the danger that has not yet come." He explained that we can steer clear of danger more often once we attain a higher state of consciousness that will give us the wisdom to act in accordance with the supportive laws of nature. Yet sometimes there is no avoiding danger so instead we have to rely on our spiritual courage. Everyone must make his or her own judgment regarding which fears deserve to be respected by showing sensible restraint—and which ones require a spiritually courageous push to pass on through them. For me, at that special moment in time in that specific place, with someone at my side in whom I decided to place my trust, my decision to rely on the presence of silence and the spiritual guidance of that particular teacher felt right.

The terrifying climb that brought me to that moment of loving stillness was not easy; perhaps it was more perilous than any reasonable person should make. However, sometimes, as the *Tao Te Ching* says, "The path into the light seems dark." Yet when you finally arrive at the silent divine stillness within, then, as the mystical Sufi Muslim Sidi Muhammad al-Jamal explained, "you will not see the darkness, and you will not see the Light, because there is no darkness and there is no Light, only God."

Whether you are high or low, in danger or far from it, a survivor or a potential victim, when you experience silence as the light of God or as the simple, quiet presence of your essential self, there is no ecstasy, but there is also no fear. No surging emotion exists within that vast silent emptiness, only the simplicity of an intense quiet feeling of inner peace.

Chapter 8

THE VALUE OF CHANGING

BELIEFS

Thought is power. Chalanda Ma, one of my spiritual teachers, observed that the most powerful thoughts we can have are the ones that follow "I am." If we think, "I am unattractive," how will this influence our behavior? Or "I am sexy." Then what? We know that there are lots of other possibilities: "I am successful" will give us confidence. "I am unlucky" will undermine our ambition. "I am appreciated" feels good. "I am neglected" might trigger resentment. "I am incompetent" may haunt everything we do. "I am loved." The best of them all.

When you awaken to the quiet presence of your own inner being, you grasp who you really are, and the thoughts that follow "I am" become more positive. A thought that adequately expresses our contact with inner silence is "I am That," the experience of the Self as That quiet stillness within. When we integrate our experience of

"I am That" into our everyday activities, the thoughts that best express our internal reality become "I am loving," and "I am at peace," and we subsequently become more peaceful and more loving.

Without the experience of inner silence to help transform our thinking, it may seem that there is little we can do to change the kind of thoughts we have. Our thoughts arise spontaneously. Often, all we can do is choose which thoughts to act on and which ones to ignore, guided by some general principles that help us decide what is ethical, what is useful, and what is pleasurable.

Thoughts raise or shake our self-confidence. If you believe that certain flashy states, such as visions of light when meditating or praying, are signs of spiritual advancement, then experiencing them will reassure you. But if you don't have them, you might unnecessarily begin to question the validity of the path you are on, or worse—you may mistakenly doubt your own spiritual potential.

Dogma, the thoughts we hold to be true, governs our search for spiritual fulfillment. Our spiritual beliefs determine what actions to take, which ones to avoid, what practices to emphasize, and which experiences to ignore.

If you believe that inner silence is the key to enlightenment, and that it can be attained only when the mind is still and virtually empty of thought, then you are more likely to take the time to engage in a specific spiritual practice, such as meditating regularly so that you can transcend your thinking and arrive at the silent mindspace within. If you are convinced that spiritual progress is best achieved by serving others, then you are more likely to spend most of your time engaged in charitable works, volunteering to help feed the hungry, care for the elderly, or mentor disadvantaged children. Of course, you can do both.

Our beliefs shape the perspective we have on life. If you have a fundamentalist interpretation of karma that insists that we are ultimately the cause of whatever happens to us, then you might blame yourself for everything, including losing your job when it is outsourced to China or even getting cancer. You are also likely to take credit for the good things, whether it be an unexpected rise in the real estate market that doubles the worth of your house or giving birth to a healthy child.

Spiritual realists have a more practical view of karma. This view does recognize that immutable laws of nature link cause and effect. In accordance with the laws of gravity, if you throw a heavy rock at a fragile plate glass window, you will cause it to shatter. According to the laws of physiology that determine the frailties of the human body, if you break someone's leg, you will cause that person pain. Yet this acknowledgment of cause and effect is balanced by a realistic understanding that many things happen that have nothing to do with our own actions. A distant star in another galaxy explodes regardless of how we behave. All of us will eventually die, no matter what we do. Both of these things have nothing to do with our karma.

We are not helpless, but our power is limited. We can't take all the credit for what happens to us, but neither should we take all the blame.

Our beliefs are not only shaped by our thoughts. Our overall state of mind also influences our opinions about life. Low self-esteem may tempt us into a despairing belief in a harsh karmic system that sees suffering as the justified consequence of our past failures, further intensifying self-doubt. A faith in your essential goodness can free you from defeatism and guilt, generating thoughts that are positive and enthusiastic.

Napoleon Hill, the motivational speaker and the author of *Think and Grow Rich*, a groundbreaking best-seller on self-development published more than seventy years ago, wrote about the connection between thought and attitude that influences our capacity for personal growth. "A person who maintains a positive attitude will find every possible *Yes* in that circumstance and make it part of his life," he explained. "A person who maintains a negative mental attitude will lean toward the *No* side, miss much that is good, live with much that is painful and damaging."

Many of us do appreciate the power of positive thinking. Still, we can't force positive thoughts into our minds, even when our ideas do not accurately reflect the reality of our situation. Excessive praise from a parent might encourage a negative attachment to the notion "I am usually right," creating a smug attitude that our opinions are superior to those of other people. Constant criticism from a lover may eventually give rise to the thought "I am unworthy," causing us to feel that our insecurity is justified. It may seem too hard to break these cycles of negative thought.

Our own lifestyles also color our thinking. If we are tired, stressed out, and working under a tight deadline with barely enough time to finish a project, our bad mood might activate a series of distressing thoughts: this is unfair, this is unreasonable, this is impossible. When we are rested and well prepared, the same pressure may lead to another way of thinking: this is expected, this is an opportunity, this will lead to success.

How can we generate more positive thoughts? Relaxing into stillness calms the emotions, reduces negativity, and allows us to experience the quiet serenity of the present moment. This serenity spontaneously generates positive thoughts: I am at peace, I am loving, I am hopeful. The positive thinking that emerges from our quiet sense of inner well-being creates a cheerful attitude, which in turn generates more optimistic thinking.

Repetition deepens the impact of that which is being repeated. The more we put our attention on negative thoughts, the more powerful they become, and the more they influence us. Frequently returning to the spiritual stillness within calms us, enabling us to experience more positive thoughts more often.

The thoughts that we choose to engage over and over again have a greater influence on us than those that we tend to ignore. If we repeatedly dwell on the notion "I am spiritually confused," instead of choosing to consistently embrace the idea "I am exploring my spirituality," a belief in our own confusion will naturally begin to dominate our thinking. Convinced that we are hopelessly mixed up, we may feel increasingly lost and eventually give up on ever finding a clear path toward spiritual fulfillment.

If we turn away from the idea "I am floundering spiritually" and instead favor a more positive thought, such as "I am learning about spirituality," the resulting optimism gives us the resolve to keep on experimenting and expanding.

Just as the repetition of a thought increases its power, a repeated reference to our spiritual beliefs increases their ability to influence us. This ability of repetition to increase the impact of something can be seen in the way we get to know someone. When I first meet people, there may be only a few things that I notice—what she likes to talk about, whether he seems uncomfortable or easygoing. But all I have to do is continue to spend time with someone and the repeated attention allows me to get to know that person even better. I pick up on more subtle qualities, such as how her family may have influenced her opinions and whether someone is shy in groups or is much less so when he is talking one-on-one with another person.

By repeatedly seeking out a person's company, we establish an intimacy, allowing us to perceive finer aspects of that person's personality. Our impression of people becomes stronger the more we hang out together. It changes automatically. A powerful intimacy flows naturally from the familiarity bred by repetition. There is no effort except the one that comes from our determination to be with someone more often.

Similarly, when we mull over a particular set of thoughts several times a week, they become more familiar, more intimate, and the impact they have on us increases. This constant thinking about a subject can form a pattern, a system of beliefs. When we adopt a specific belief system about spirituality, our continuous thinking about it strengthens its impact in our daily lives. This deepening commitment to our beliefs about spirituality alters our attitudes and shapes our lifestyles.

We may not be able to control the thoughts that pop into our minds, but a small shift in the ones we choose to emphasize over and over again is enough to make everyday life more rewarding. When we stop characterizing spiritual uncertainty as confusion, we might recognize that our complicated mix of beliefs is often a natural outcome of the transition from one level of understanding to another.

Spiritual realists avoid becoming too attached to belief systems. They are realistic because they recognize that however devoted we are to a particular spiritual path, over time, our thoughts will change. If this new thinking does not clash with our previous approach to spirituality, then we will continue on the path we are taking. If our new thinking convinces us that there is a more effective road to spiritual development, then why not allow our belief system to change accordingly?

When commenting on the New Age generation of seekers, my father once said, "What's wrong with you people is that once you've learned all you can from a spiritual teacher, your gratitude keeps you from moving on to someone else." I have seen this happen during my nearly forty years of involvement with various spiritual paths. And his advice also applies to belief systems. Once they no longer serve us, it is time to move on.

Beliefs are like clothes. When we first try them on, they look attractive. They fit perfectly. So we buy them and wear them often. They help us to feel good about ourselves. Gradually, they wear out and are no longer in sync with changing circumstances. As they continue to lose their shape and resilience with each passing year, we begin to notice that they no longer fit us anymore. As times change, our old beliefs may likewise lose their fit. They may seem out of fashion, no longer attuned to our current circumstances. Our convictions might not look as appealing as they once did, nor are they as useful. Like a worn-out coat that is torn and frayed, outdated belief systems may no longer comfort us, leaving us vulnerable to the world outside.

When a system of beliefs no longer serves us, we can discard it just as we would exchange an old set of clothes for new ones. There is no shame in changing our beliefs, nothing disloyal about embracing a fresh set of thoughts that can comfortably take us into new territories of spiritual experience. As the spiritual poet Ralph Waldo Emerson noted, "A foolish consistency is the hobgoblin of little minds." Why continue on a spiritual path that is no longer taking us where we want to go?

We may resist taking a more effective spiritual path out of a misplaced devotion to a particular belief system or guru. Our devotion is to spiritual growth, not to any one person or set of beliefs.

A former girlfriend once left Maharishi for another guru. After a year she wanted to return, deeply upset by her belief that she had betrayed Maharishi, her true spiritual master. Jerry Jarvis, a longtime confidant of Maharishi, advised her to just start practicing Transcendental Meditation (TM) again and not to worry. "The path is the master," he explained. Gurus and dogmas are there to help us realize our spiritual goals. The best teachers do not demand our devotion, nor do they need it. They are there to aid our spiritual development. There is no coercion, emotionally or psychologically. We are always free to choose whether to continue accepting their help.

Our resistance to spiritual change is often delusional, a pretense that hanging on to people or paths that are increasingly outmoded will somehow make them relevant over time. "Don't be trapped by dogma, which is living with the results of other people's thinking," advised Steve Jobs, who went on a pilgrimage to India before returning home to launch the personal computer revolution by starting Apple Computer. "Don't let the noise of others' opinions drown out your own inner voice."

Although our spiritual beliefs may change, the desire to expand our consciousness does not. It is better to remain loyal to our own inner voice than to become attached to a set of beliefs that now seems too rigid and increasingly obsolete and that prevents us from making further progress.

When people remain stuck in a spiritual belief system that fails to move them forward, blame the believers, not their beliefs. A belief system cannot be forced upon anyone. Some people may be susceptible to brainwashing, but that is because the mind is weak and the character is willing. Most believers have a more realistic choice. You do not have to allow beliefs that now seem stagnant to override your own natural impulse, which is to increase your understanding of yourself and move toward greater happiness.

We know that belief systems are fallible, so why not be open to changing them? We can't be so sure that our current judgments are correct that we can predict with certainty the future consequences of our decisions. Our intellects are incapable of grasping the totality of creation, which is subject to unpredictable change. If we are growing spiritually and intellectually, our thoughts about reality are always evolving. So it makes sense to remain open to revising our beliefs as the world changes around us. Although spiritual realism accepts the mystical aspects of life that appear irrational, it does not require irrationality. Spiritual realists rely on the obvious logic that says if one method isn't working, use another one.

Spiritual practices take us beyond the limitations of logic. They open us up to the metaphysical silence that underlies all thought. Yet the path into transcendent stillness can still be a reasonable one. A spiritual path need not demand a stubborn devotion to ideas that are no longer consistent with our own experience of daily life.

"The meaning of life differs from man to man, from day to day and from hour to hour," the psychiatrist Victor Frankl reminds us. "What matters, therefore, is not the meaning of life in general but rather the specific meaning of a person's life at a given moment." This observation is the essence of humility. It acknowledges that all we can do is articulate our own understanding of the present, realizing that we come to know ourselves and the world around us a piece at a time, without ever fully comprehending the infinite complexity of the universe. Frankl's words pertain to my own view of spiritual realism. My perceptions may serve some, and be wholly or partially discarded by others, but they will never grasp the totality of life's mystery.

The unquestioning devotion to a guru, a teacher, or a technique throughout our entire lives hinders the flexibility of mind needed to accept an ongoing change in beliefs. This receptivity to evolving convictions does not mean that we are too flighty or lack real commitment. On the contrary, it reflects an understanding of the personal growth that can accompany every new life experience.

Although spiritual realists are sensitive to the reality of changing circumstances, they are not spiritually fickle. They do not constantly change their core spiritual convictions. Yet spiritual realists are ready to change their thinking about the nature of spiritual enlightenment. They are humble, realizing that not every idea is true for us at all times in every circumstance. Spiritual realists share a flexible belief system that is not unnecessarily rigid. It gives them the confidence to act decisively, while also being secure enough to switch directions whenever it makes sense to adjust.

An illogical attachment to an outworn system of beliefs can be spiritually damaging. But the inability to make any sense of this world can be worse. Most of us believe that even in the most dire situations, people act in accordance with basic rules of human behavior. If a woman is screaming for help and you rescue her from a burning building, she will be grateful. If you offer money to a man begging on the street, he will accept it. For these people to do otherwise makes no sense. That is one belief system that we all share. But what if there is no belief system that can account for the unfathomable cruelty of people? What if the world seems totally and utterly beyond belief?

During the Holocaust, the behavior of Nazi concentration camp guards frequently defied reason. The German Nazis not only systematically murdered six million Jews, they worked them to death as slave laborers, performed gruesome medical experiments that involved horrible surgeries without anesthesia on fully conscious victims, and frequently degraded camp inmates with such incomprehensible viciousness that the Holocaust survivor and author

Primo Levi wrote that their ferocious torturing resulted in the complete "demolition of a man."

Levi describes how inmates were starved into a state of such utter delirium that he saw people "bestially urinate while they run to save time, because within five minutes begins the distribution of bread." Why employ such sadistic methods on helpless prisoners who are marked for certain death? What reasonable purpose could they possibly serve? The belief system that gave rise to such madness was so inhumanly bizarre that it seems more accurate to say that the concentration camp overlords believed in nothing at all, driven by a monstrous fury that defied any semblance of reason.

Elie Wiesel, another Holocaust survivor and a Nobel Peace Prize winner, described a concentration camp incident in which a young boy was sentenced to hang alongside two adults. The entire camp was forced to watch as the three condemned inmates mounted the gallows and a noose was placed around each of their necks. The chairs were tipped over, killing the two adults. "But the third rope was still moving, being so light, the child was still alive," Wiesel remembered. "For more than half an hour he stayed there, struggling between life and death, dying in slow agony under our eyes. And we had to look him full in the face. He was still alive when I passed in front of him. His tongue was still red, his eyes were not yet glazed." The guards would not cut him down, nor would they even show enough mercy to fire a bullet into him to at least end his suffering. They probably would have shown more kindness to a wounded dog, putting it to sleep to stop the pain. What kind of thoughts go through someone's head when they allow a child to dangle for half an hour, struggling for breath as the noose slowly tightens bit by bit?

Nothing can explain the unimaginable acts perpetrated by those running the concentration camps, many of them Nazi officers who were well educated and highly cultured. It's as if an entire group of people just went insane. What other explanation could there be?

When we no longer have a belief system to help us make sense of the world, the result is often so frightening that we frequently cling to any collection of thoughts, no matter how outdated they might be or implausible they may seem. We need something to believe in, and until there is an adequate replacement, many of us will just stick with what we've got. It's like people who realize they are in a bad relationship that is destined to fail, but they refuse to end it until they've met someone else. Having someone is better than having no one. And when it comes to belief systems, something may seem better than nothing. So we cling to the same tiresome programmed answers that, deep down, no longer make any sense to us; we deny that our spiritual beliefs are trying to explain away the unexplainable. Still, we hold onto them anyway, desperately insisting that such absurdity is merely the illusion of maya, that inexplicable suffering is due to karma, that despite our sorrow over the pain of others, everything in life is all good.

For many of us, it is true that the only thing that may be more debilitating than having a mistaken belief system is having none at all. Victor Frankl emphasized the importance of believing in something so that we can find meaning in our lives. "It is not the physical pain that hurts the most," he wrote when describing the arbitrary cruelties that he was subjected to during his years as a Nazi concentration camp inmate, "it is the mental agony caused by the injustice, the unreasonableness of it all." It can be disorienting to live in a world in which our belief system can no longer reasonably explain events that previously seemed so easy to understand. To lift ourselves out of such an intellectual morass, we often feel compelled to choose something to believe in, almost anything that gives us hope. Yet as long as we remain open to changing our beliefs as our thinking evolves, then fresh thoughts will propel us forward, guiding us toward self-realization.

When we remain open to new ideas, our long-standing spiritual beliefs can be changed without causing us any significant discomfort. Rather than feeling foolish at having believed in something that now seems so obviously unrealistic, our shift into a new under-standing will often give us an unexpected opportunity for spiritual advancement, creating fresh opportunities to express our intention to increase knowledge and reach enlightenment.

A jolt to my own belief system occurred on a visit to Israel. One of my persistent beliefs was that any Nazi who served in a concen-tration camp was a sadistic creature whose evil was beyond the reach of compassion and forgiveness. This view is fairly common-place, but because I am Jewish, the horrors of the Holocaust felt personal. The fate of the inmates was heartbreaking, and my compassion was reserved for the overwhelming pity that I felt for each of them. There was no room in my heart for the perpetrators. I could sympathize only with the tortured. I hardly gave the Nazi tormentors any thought, other than the disturbing realization that people like them actually exist on this planet.

One day I was about to enter the Yad Vashem Holocaust memo-rial in Jerusalem with Chalanda Ma, who was leading a group of us on a pilgrimage to spiritual sites throughout Israel. It seemed like an odd place for spiritual seekers to visit; we expected to do things like meditate by the river Jordan and feel the holy energy in the Bethlehem church that was built over the spot where Jesus was born. Few of us anticipated spending time viewing exhibits that depicted the savagery of the Holocaust.

As we were about to enter the memorial, Chalanda Ma asked us to gather around so that she could speak to us before going in. "Don't think you are separate from this," she said. Since almost everyone in the group was Christian, except Chalanda Ma, who was Hindu, I figured that she was urging the non-Jews to avoid thinking that the Holocaust was a Jewish catastrophe that had little to do with them. I, of course, was very familiar with the tragedy, the memory of the six million deaths casting a shadow over the lives of nearly every Jew since then. I had already visited the Holocaust Museum in Wash-ington, D.C., and the Dachau concentration camp near Munich. I had grown up with constant reminders of the anti-Semitic madness.

When we went inside, I began to move quickly through the exhibits. I felt no need to linger. I had seen it all before. I was more interested in seeing the reactions of the others in our group, wondering how optimistic spiritual people would process the horrifyingly displays. There were scenes of emaciated inmates, their ribs sticking through their flesh. There were photographs of the railroad tracks leading into the concentration camps, the long lines of cattle cars packed with men, women, and children who were slowly disembarking, about to be systematically separated into two groups. The elderly and the sick would be told to join one group that would be led to their immediate death in the gas chambers. The others would practically be worked to death before being stripped and forced into a large shower room where poison Zyklon B gas, instead of water, would be released from the showerheads, killing them all.

As I was about to leave the building, Chalanda Ma gestured for me to stop. She pointed to a large picture hanging on the wall and told me to look at it. I reluctantly agreed, thinking that it was unnecessary because I had seen photos like that many times. It showed a huge pile of dead bodies stacked up in the shape of a pyramid, the lifeless heads and limbs sticking out in just one of many ghastly examples of the Nazi genocidal determination to eradicate Jews from the planet with machinelike efficiency. I knew all too well how close they had come to succeeding; they had slaughtered nearly a third of the entire global Jewish population at the time. What was the point in my looking at yet another photograph of concentration camp corpses?

Suddenly, as I stared at the pile of dead Jews, I noticed a young German soldier standing nearby. Although my eyes were repeatedly drawn back to the Jewish victims, which was my usual habit, this time I found my gaze returning to the soldier with increasing frequency, as if compelled to do so by a powerful force. Eventually, I let my attention settle only on the young German. He was clean-cut in his crisp uniform and handsome, with typical Aryan features: the Nazi model of German youth. A disciplined solder with a rifle in his hand, he dutifully stood guard near the stack of Jewish bodies as if someone might try to steal them before they could be shoveled into the massive ovens that incinerated hundreds of bodies per day.

The more I looked at the lone German soldier, the more I became aware of just how young he was. His stance looked tentative, his face innocent, with an expression that seemed obedient but downcast, as if he were stunned at being drafted to serve in hell rather than in the army. I imagined myself at his age, involved in a war that I didn't choose, led by a madman whose henchmen were not patriots but sadists and whose underlings ordered me to participate in his crimes and pushed me to obey or be imprisoned or worse.

I felt sympathy for the young soldier's plight. I realized that rather than being a callous monster, he might have been someone just like me, who in his early twenties had not yet been forced to choose between honor and death. He may have been too inexperienced and immature to decide when to make a stand and when to join the crowd to avoid being hounded and hunted.

My compassion had finally gone beyond the Jewish victims of the Holocaust, extending to that young generation of soldiers who might have been unconsciously complicit but not deliberately evil. Perhaps the reason why I had never pondered this reality was because the Holocaust seemed to be at least one example where there were obviously clear distinctions between the good guys and the bad guys. All Nazis deserved unqualified condemnation. Simple. Maybe the thought that the situation was more nuanced, that it is not always so easy to identify the truly wicked, was too disturbing. "Beware those who are quick to censor," wrote the Beat poet Charles Bukowski. "They are afraid of what they do not know." If even one Nazi concentration camp guard was entitled to my sympathy, wouldn't that challenge my belief system, which had always used every enabler of the Holocaust as the baseline for my judgments about who is clearly unworthy of any forgiveness?

This shift in my thinking about the Holocaust was unexpected, even shocking. It changed the way I thought about perpetrators and their victims. Certainly, an incredible number of Germans were enthusiastic anti-Semites who embraced the Nazi effort to rid the world of all its Jews. Hitler made no secret of his poisonous ideology. It was saluted by millions of average Germans who willingly participated in massive Nazi rallies that celebrated a relentless hatred of Jews. They freely expressed support for Hitler in local shops, in neighborhood schools, and even inside the safety of their own living rooms. If they had felt compelled to publicly embrace Nazism, there was no need to proudly display their support in private. Yet I was now able to make more subtle distinctions, using my expanded awareness to connect with someone who may have truly felt forced to mouth the anti-Semitic slogans, hail the calls for genocide, and even pull a trigger to bring it about, yet who still may have had sincere innocence in his heart.

I remembered Chalanda Ma's instruction, "Do not think you are separate from this." She may have wanted the gentiles to avoid feeling separate from a tragedy that befell mostly Jews. But my spiritual mission was to move beyond my exclusive connection to the Jewish victims. I was no longer able to hold onto my belief that I was absolutely and eternally separate from any German who stood by and watched the atrocities in the Nazi concentration camps. My newfound awareness dramatically altered my belief system, allowing me for the first time to relate to those Germans who might have been victimized in their own way by a terrifying dictatorship that made rebellion seem futile, especially those who were just a tad older than teenagers at the time. I already had a deep respect for the German resistance movement, those brave souls who tried to assassinate Hitler and the others who risked their lives to weaken his regime and even hide Jews. But to contemplate a concentration camp guard, who was at the center of the genocidal depravity, and absorb the possible truth of his innocence was unprecedented.

My consciousness had shifted, new thoughts emerged, and my belief system changed. It had not happened through the usual methods of reading or studying, which, of course, offer new facts and fresh ideas to stimulate our thinking. This unexpected shift was achieved through inner silence. Not a word was spoken. Not one new piece of historical information was considered. All I did was gaze at a single revolting photograph with a spiritual teacher at my side to quietly urge me on, as I felt my own inner silence freeing me of rigid outworn notions and allowing me to spontaneously absorb new ones.

Whenever we keep ourselves open to a range of new experiences, there is an opportunity to revise our thinking and adjust our belief systems. The experience of inner silence, in and outside of meditation, takes us to that calming space within, which can give us the freedom and confidence we need to let go of attachments to beliefs that are no longer relevant.

Chapter 9

FINDING THE CALM OF
UNCERTAINTY

No belief system can explain everything. There is a deep mystery in life our minds cannot fathom. Our solace remains in the inner silence that transcends the narrow limitations of our reason. Yet spiritual realists also go beyond transcendental silence to boldly engage the contradictions of daily life. Many hope that when they are sufficiently enlightened, all of life's difficult contradictions will disappear. Harmony will prevail because of our realization that duality is an illusion. Yet does this kind of consciousness help us deal with the reality of life's problems or just make it easier to ignore them?

Should we long for a state of mind that either minimizes or ignores the clash of positive and negative events that seems to dominate everyday life? We know the saying "Ignorance is bliss." So is ignorance the basis of enlightenment's bliss? Does spiritual nonattachment mean that we no longer pass judgment on what is good or bad, that we are indifferent to both because our expanded consciousness no longer makes such unenlightened distinctions? The rhetoric may be appealing. But is it virtuous? And is it realistic?

Staying in the present moment does bring us into the quietness that allows us to find inner peace, whether we are enjoying the good times or living in a world of trouble. Inner silence calms us, but not because our lives are always calm. The world we are making peace with can be disturbing, and often is. Spiritual realists perceive the quiet stillness within, while simultaneously keeping their eyes open to the positive and negative events that we all encounter every day.

Spirituality is frequently viewed as being separate from the mundane happenings of worldly life, allowing us to rise above its daily conflicts. Some seekers do not read newspapers, avoiding the news as if its appallingly negative reports might infect their positive outlook and slow their progress toward enlightenment. But can we ignore our way to self-realization? Does spiritual awakening actually require us to put part of our minds to sleep?

In the Dhammapada, the Buddha teaches that peace comes to those who accept that they are always facing death. Acceptance is not easy, since we celebrate life and mourn death. We also long for goodness and dread its opposite. Yet we know the world is filled with negativity and death. How can we accept and eventually make peace with life's contradictions between harmony and conflict if we keep on blocking them out? If there were no conflicts, there would be no need for peace.

Using spirituality to bypass the reality of negativity brings a fragile contentment, one that depends on our looking only at that portion of the world that we want to see. Can spiritual understanding really explain away all of life's harsher realities?

When we integrate inner silence into all aspects of everyday life, we may not be able to explain away all suffering, but we can find a way to accept it. Peace comes to those who know that suffering always exists, not to those who pretend it doesn't.

The groundbreaking therapist Carl Jung noted, "If, in physics, one seeks to explain the nature of light, nobody expects that as a result there will be no light." Enlightenment gives us an understanding of the nature of negativity, but can we expect that as a result there will be no negativity? As the Christian theologian and novelist C. S. Lewis explained, it is only "the senseless writhings of a man" who "still thinks there is some device (if only he could find it) which will make pain not to be pain." If we don't engage the painful energies as well as the positive ones, how can we make peace with both of them?

Yitzhak Rabin, a former Israeli prime minister and Nobel Peace Prize winner, defended his controversial decision to negotiate with Yasser Arafat, the chairman of the Palestinian Liberation Organization and a longtime bitter foe who had orchestrated numerous terrorist attacks against Israel. "You make peace with your enemies, not with your friends," Rabin explained. When we engage our enemies, we can talk with them, listen to them, and hopefully make peace with them. The same goes for the negativity that is so clearly at odds with the spiritual goals we seek. We can feel the world's negative energy and use our inner silence to help us make peace with it.

Like Rabin, a veteran soldier of Israel's many wars who was not afraid to look directly into his adversary's eyes, we can develop a consciousness that is tough enough to look at the negativity in life without weakening our ability to overcome it. In order for us to make peace with our enemy, we must first know the enemy. Our spiritual adversary is the negativity that causes needless suffering. When we insist that there are no enemies, that all things are equally good, then how can we come to terms with negativity when we do eventually encounter it? Peace doesn't come by pretending there already is peace. Spiritual peace comes from recognizing that real problems in the outside world can threaten our equanimity, and that inner silence is the weapon we use to conquer them.

The silent self is our perpetual defender. It allows us to boldly open ourselves not only to the positive energies but also to the negative realities. The quiet stillness within protects our inner peace, strengthening us so that we can confidently face everything in life. We can read both scripture and newspapers, learn about sacred sites as well as war-torn ones, attune ourselves to the enlightened along with the cries of the anguished. And we can still return to the spiritual calm of inner silence.

We may be open to all of life, but we can't know everything in life. Yet when we listen carefully enough, the cries on this planet can be heard just above the peaceful silence we experience within. If we won't listen to them, then we hardly know anything. We won't know how to love those who need it the most. What else is worth knowing?

"The whole world groans and is in labor together," St. Matthew said. Everyone yearns to be reborn into a world where suffering ends and only goodness reigns. Even though our heightened consciousness diminishes our own personal pain, the groans of many others continue. If we refuse to hear them, if we will not look at them or read about them, then what kind of spiritual peace have we really found? A spiritual peace rooted in fantasy rather than in reality? A cowardly one? A selfish one?

The realities of this world can be harsh, which is why we hunger for a state of consciousness that will enable us to perceive harshness as a mirage masking the higher truth that all of life is actually unfolding in sweet harmony. But the reality of the outer world is both sweet and bitter. Only inner silence offers the peace that is beyond taste. Still, our spiritual serenity cannot eliminate all of the bitterness on this planet. Animals will still eat each other, people will still kill each other, everyone will still die. But our expanded consciousness can change how we react to the bitterness.

"You cannot control what happens to you in life," Rabbi Harold Kushner wrote, "but you can always control what you will feel and do about what happens to you." This ability to change how we feel and what we do arises from our repeated return to the serene presence of inner silence.

"It's not what happens to you in life that makes a difference. It is how you react to each circumstance you encounter that determines the results!" the popular televangelist Robert Schuller wrote, sharing the rabbi's view. Traditional religion offers traditional methods to change our responses to negative circumstances. Spiritual realists share this goal, although they follow a different path. They accept the fact that even the enlightened cannot prevent all negative events from happening in the world. But enlightened people try to react to them more positively by expanding their consciousness so that they can repeatedly experience the peaceful silence within.

Much of our response to life's difficulties depends on how much self-confidence we have. "The ultimate human value is the will to self-dignity, self-esteem," Schuller told me when I interviewed him. For Schuller, self-esteem comes from a relationship with Jesus Christ. For spiritual seekers who don't follow traditional religions, self-esteem flows from self-realization, which is the awareness of our silent self. This experience can indeed feel like the quiet presence of God within. Many do describe this state of mind as a Christlike consciousness. Whatever we choose to call it, we feel as if we've discovered a positive truth about ourselves that is the very source of our self-esteem.

Emboldened by the self-esteem that emerges from self-realization, we are able to deal effectively with the problems in our own lives and those faced by friends and family. Of course, there are other problems, often more difficult ones, such as political and environmental ones, that are occurring on this planet. In order to deal effectively with those as well, we must be willing to face them. Our compassionate reactions can make a difference even if we are not directly involved in solving these problems.

Spiritual realists do not have to become political activists. Yet a small segment of spiritually enlightened people can influence world events. "Political change occurs when a percent or two of the public changes opinions or changes sides. That's all it takes," explained Professor James Stimson at the University of North Carolina.

The way we think about issues can help others, especially in a democracy where leaders are responsive to the views of its citizens. "The superpower of the world is public opinion," noted Peter Weiss, a Middle East peace activist and the president of the International Association of Lawyers Against Nuclear Arms.

Professor Diane Heith of St. John's University studied the activities of five consecutive U.S. presidents: Richard Nixon, Gerald Ford, Jimmy Carter, Ronald Reagan, and George H. W. Bush. "All five administrations employed polls during their most active legislative period," she reported. "These presidents sought public input for the agenda, and to some degree for the options available as answers."

How are political opinions formed? Primarily through casual conversations around the office water cooler, over dinner, in the everyday exchanges of ordinary life when people are expressing their viewpoints and values. Pollsters seek out opinions from diverse segments of the population. They do not exclude spiritual seekers.

When we are familiar with the issues, our opinions can naturally arise out of our inspiring experience of inner silence. We can then express our positive responses to world problems, which may one day be picked up by pollsters. If we ignore negative events in the world, how can we form any opinions about them and make a positive contribution to efforts to address them?

Professor Scott Althaus of Northwestern University reported that "People who are ill-informed tend to give 'don't know' and 'no opinion' responses more frequently than well-informed respondents." Those who don't know don't matter. Their values have little impact on political decision makers. If we want to improve life on this planet, then shouldn't we apply our spirituality to help formulate specific views about events on this planet?

Any one of us could find ourselves on the other end of a telephone pollster's survey. Caring words, emerging from inner silence, carry a positive energy that can provoke acts of compassion. We can use our spirituality to make political conversation more compassionate.

In 2000, a national Kaiser Family Foundation telephone survey of American public opinion asked whether respondents favored or opposed reducing the amount of money that certain African countries owed to the United States "so they can use the money to deal with the problem of AIDS." An overwhelming 65 percent majority supported debt relief. The following year, the U.S. Congress authorized $435 million for international debt relief. Most of the countries qualifying for American relief that year were also located in Africa. In democracies, compassionate thoughts have power. Elected officials listen to their constituents.

Our thoughts can even influence what's reported in the daily newspaper. "Today, survey results are quite intentionally treated by reporters and editors as news," explained Susan Herbst, a professor at Northwestern University. "Polls may be used by a paper to set the public agenda or highlight an issue or problem the editors believe to be critical." Don't like what's being reported in the news? Form an opinion, talk about it, and it may eventually filter into the ears of pollsters, who in turn pass along the results to editors deciding what to print. Then our repeated peaceful experience of inner silence can increase the power of the compassionate thoughts they produce and help to raise the consciousness on this volatile planet.

News reports can assist us when we apply our expanded awareness to help reduce global negativity. There are tragedies and crimes that we may not know about, so how can we even begin to form opinions about them? We can, however, choose to look at them and read about them by watching the news and reading the newspaper. Some people believe that engaging in such activities is beneath us, that following the news is irrelevant to spiritual development. Or that it may even get us caught up in the negative energy of politics, crime, and competition. But isn't all of reality worth grasping? Is our consciousness so fragile that it can't withstand the whole truth of human existence? Spiritual realism integrates both the tranquility of inner silence and the volatility of outside circumstances, including the political ones.

What are the volatile circumstances that spiritual realists choose to deal with? Often, the most troubling ones do not occur in our own lives. They take place elsewhere, affecting other people in faraway places. They involve appalling events that are hard for us to imagine.

If we read about such events or watch or listen to the news, we won't have to try to imagine them. On May 12, 2005, the *Chicago Sun-Times* reported that "A man with a sword cut off the hands of a government social worker in central India for trying to stop child marriages." Although child marriages have been banned in India, the tradition still continues in some rural areas where girls as young as nine years old are married off. That such an atrocity can still take place in the modern world seems incomprehensible, but such things are happening every single day. Should spiritual seekers avoid reading about them? Should they try to hide from this reality in order to protect their state of consciousness from the shock?

What is the value of an enlightened consciousness that must rely on happy ideals and shut out life's harsh realities in order to survive? We can instead harness the steadiness of inner silence to bring our unwavering compassion into this troubled world.

Once we open our hearts to whatever negativity exists on this planet, it becomes increasingly important to tap the peaceful stillness within so that we may express greater compassion.

On May 29, 2006, the *New York Times* described how thousands of people fleeing from the savagery in war-torn Somalia were forced to seek safety in nearby Yemen. Ruthless smugglers were paid to take them across the sea, packing eighty to a hundred people into small fishing boats that risked being confiscated by sailors trying to block their arrival in Yemen. The small vessels were barely capable of navigating the water. When it got too rough, many of the helpless men, women, and children drowned. "But it is when the Yemeni Coast Guard appears and the boat owner risks losing his craft that things get even worse," the *Times* reported. "The crew is likely to force all the passengers into the sea at gunpoint. If anyone hesitates, the crew will sometimes tie the hands of the passengers and throw them out, or simply shoot them." It is hard for most of us to imagine anyone committing such vile acts. Yet it happened, not centuries or even a generation ago, but as recently as 2006. Does our spiritual progress demand that we remain ignorant of such things? Or can our spirituality be harnessed to help prevent such things?

When we want to use the fruits of our expanded consciousness to help reduce the world's negativity, we must be willing to put our attention on any aspect of it, without restraint. We do not need to dwell on negativity or seek it out continuously, but we can take a balanced view that does not try to hide from any of it. Merely by our staying alert and unafraid, the numerous cruelties of this world will unfortunately reveal themselves on their own. Their existence is one aspect, a tragic one, of life on this planet. Yet ironically, our willingness to take an unblinkered look at the wrenching presence of tragedy strengthens our ability to hold onto the sublime peace of inner silence. We are less likely to be yanked out of silence by the shock of life's negativity since we are already familiar with the shocking. We become more resilient so that even when we are pushed off center, we are more able to quickly return to stillness because we are used to moving from the inspirational to the tragic and back again. This resilience helps us to stay open and eager to express our loving kindness, instead of shutting down and getting stuck in our disgust and our fears.

Spiritual realism is about enlightenment with power, a state of consciousness that is powerful enough to deal with the horrible cruelties taking place everywhere on this planet, many of which are not even confined to our fellow human beings. Animals are routinely tortured for profit. Not for food, but for profit. In China, the fur industry is big business. It exports more than eleven million skins a year, bringing in nearly two million dollars, and it is the biggest fur producer in the world. On April 16, 2006, the Swiss

Animal Protection agency issued a report detailing how Chinese furriers make sure that their furs stay clean and free of damage by using an excruciating form of killing that keeps the furs from getting stained with blood. The details are ghastly, but should we turn away because our awareness of inner silence is too weak to keep us centered in its peaceful presence? Is inner peace available only when all things are peaceful?

When we defiantly stand before brutality, refusing to turn our love away from its awful product, our gentle love becomes even more determined to express itself. Anchoring ourselves in silence, armed with our compassionate intent, our commitment to loving kindness expands. Our love matures. Our spirituality becomes wide-eyed, grown up, able to soothe because we can see what needs soothing.

Spiritual realists do not experience harmony only when everything is already harmonious. They are not afraid to look at acts of hideous disharmony. They face them so that they might better use their transcendent calm to prevent them. At those Chinese slaughtering sites, the foxes, minks, raccoons, rabbits, dogs, and cats are "stunned with repeated blows to the head or swung against the ground," the Swiss animal rights group reported. "Skinning begins with a knife at the rear of the belly whilst the animal is hung upside-down by its hind legs from a hook. A significant number of animals remain fully conscious during this process. Supremely helpless, they struggle and try to fight back to the very end. Even after their skin has been stripped off, breathing, heart beat, directional body and eyelid movements were evident for five to ten minutes." I watched the skinning process on a video put together by the Swiss animal rights organization. Viewing it was even more harrowing than reading about it. Yet learning about it creates a channel that connects the quest for inner peace with the need to pacify others.

The extent to which people can engage in such unspeakable cruelty is unfathomable. But life's negativity doesn't come only from deliberate human actions. Terrible accidents happen. Although they are the result of tragedies that occur naturally every day, they produce the same anguish as anything inflicted by man.

Do our spiritual convictions demand that we ignore life's inexplicable assault on the innocent?

On November 4, 2004, an Irish news service ran a story about a thirty-six-year-old construction worker who returned home and parked his truck in a pile of leaves. After stepping down, he heard his ten-year-old daughter call out. "Daddy, I can't breathe," the news service reported. The little girl had been playing with her friend, hiding inside the pile of leaves that her father had just driven over. She died shortly after being taken to a local hospital. No state of enlightenment worthy of its name will yield anything but a deep heart-wrenching sadness over such a tragic event. But our spiritual realism will make us resilient, keeping us centered in the presence of comforting stillness while we feel profound sympathy and sorrow.

Spiritual realism helps us to process mankind's madness and life's shocking accidents. It does not allow us to hide life's heartbreaking tragedies under a cheerful spiritual veneer that proclaims all is good in the face of all that clearly is not. It is our enlightened realism that gives us the compassionate strength to look at pain while we remain centered in our ability to heal.

It is tempting to keep looking away from the world's negativity. The unpredictable cruelties are too depressing. So the veneer of spirituality gives us a way to keep turning away, without having to show our own weakness. "When confronted with the unknown," my son Jesse wrote, "one is either happily resolved to not understand or unhappily feeling the passion to understand." Authentic spirituality is about having the passion to expand our consciousness and our understanding, as we grasp the reality of life in all its awesome majesty, and encompass all aspects, the uplifting and the crushing.

Our senses will naturally react with horror to life's cruelties. "Skin is what allows humans to feel. We can touch and we can be touched," my daughter, Mia, wrote. "When the skin has been peeled away the face of God appears." Spiritual realism removes the veneer of a spirituality of denial, exposing us to the full spectrum of God's creation and allowing us to feel our own humanity when we sympathize with suffering, as well as experience the awesome expanse of divine stillness. Our spirituality helps us to peel away emotional pain and discover the underlying divine compassion that can help to heal us. Uncovering the silence within is how we make peace with the world. Not because we condone its cruelties or close our eyes to its brutalities. We see the world as it is, and our spiritual realism shows us how to use our inner silence to cope with all of its aspects. Keenly aware of what is inspiring and fully aware of what is horrifying, we spread our love across both realities to increase joy and minimize pain.

Spiritual realism helps us to develop a consciousness that is expansive enough to include both the virtue that we honor and the viciousness that we despise. It allows us to confront life's inevitable sorrows without sacrificing our inner peace. Even death is not a threat to the peaceful presence of silence.

After my father turned eighty, he suddenly became severely weakened by post-polio syndrome, a debilitating condition that emerges decades after polio victims are originally struck by the disease. Within months, my father became unable to lift himself off the bed to go to the bathroom. He was confined to a hospital room with little hope of ever recovering his strength. I stayed at his bedside for days, never turning away from his sad plight and giving him the caring companionship that was the only comfort left to him.

At one point, my father looked into my eyes and told me that he was ready, that it was time to move on. I knew how serious he was. He was a man who could have long ago chosen to spend the rest of his life in a hospital ward for disabled patients. Instead, he made the hard journey back into the world, wheeling his wheelchair into the office where he worked for thirty years, struggling to live within a meager budget, helping to raise two children while his wife cared for them full time, and providing for all of them as the only breadwinner in the family. He had learned to enjoy his life despite its difficulties. So when my father told me it was time to move on, I knew that he was right. He wasn't giving up, just gracefully giving in.

I asked my father whether he was afraid of death. "Not really," he said, "although there is always some fear of the unknown." A few days later, he began gasping for air. I held him tightly, whispering in his ear that it was okay, and that I loved him. He took his last breath while I held him in my arms. Though my heart was shocked and trembling, my inner silence calmed me, keeping me present and allowing me to feel how much I already missed him. I would enjoy missing him, knowing that he was worth missing. He had been my satguru, my original and highest teacher. His soul still lingers inside of me, and my inner silence can take me to him whenever I choose. Silence can expand your heart, even when life breaks your heart.

The Buddha said, "Peace comes to those who accept that they are always facing death." Tragedy and cruelty will always be with us. Do not turn away, just go within, toward the silence that never dies or wavers, into the peaceful stillness that can never be taken from us.

Chapter 10

THE NATURAL CYCLES OF EXPANSION AND CONTRACTION

Our emotional responses to the harshness of the world are powerful. They influence our health, belief systems, and behavior. An expanded consciousness does not push these emotions away. It changes the way we experience them. Instead of allowing our unpleasant emotions to dominate us, the awareness of inner silence lets us use them as tools.

Worry is one of our most uncomfortable emotions and one of the most persistent. If we are not aware of the stabilizing quiet within, all that we are conscious of is the anticipation of future problems. There is no peaceful stillness inside to anchor us. We are tossed by our nervous thoughts, overwhelmed by our preoccupation with the difficulties to come, and filled with doubts about our ability to cope with them.

Our level of fear naturally varies with the severity of the expected crisis and the likelihood of it ever happening. If we suspect that there is a slim chance that we might not have enough money to pay off a credit card, we may be worried, but not nearly as much as if we expect that a test for cancer will show up positive. When we are stabilized by inner silence, we can step back from our worries and consider which ones are reasonable, which are helpful, and which are exaggerated and useless. Then, with a clear, calm view, we can shape a positive response to our concerns.

When can worry be helpful? When it makes us more effective. Worry, of course, is usually associated with excessive pessimism and obsessive thinking. But worry, moderated by inner silence, can be transformed into a balanced concern. In this sense, worry can be useful. If we anticipate financial problems and are in a position to reduce spending or work a little harder to earn more money, then a reasonable worry about the future can have a positive effect. The emotional energy of immediate concern prompts us into taking quick action.

Does spiritual fulfillment mean that we are free of all worries, at all times in all places, regardless of the circumstances? If worry is useless, if our concerns have no basis in reality, or if they are no help to us in avoiding future problems, then yes, the calm of inner peace will reduce, even eliminate, such worries. If our concern is rational, and it does serve a purpose, then what kind of spirituality would eliminate such a practical emotion? Would it be spiritual freedom or spiritual denial?

Can we reduce the discomfort that comes with worry? Yes. The return to the silence within can calm us, giving us greater perspective on the nature of our concerns. Since we are able to experience something other than anxiety, its impact diminishes. If we are eating only onions, and we don't like onions, the meal seems inedible. If the dish includes rice and beans, zucchini and curry, plus onions, the food becomes much more palatable. We still may not like onions, but they don't ruin the whole meal. We can just enjoy what we like and more easily tolerate what we don't. The same goes for worry. The appealing presence of inner stillness reduces the bitterness of our anxieties, making our concern about the future just one aspect of our overall emotional experience and often not even the dominant one.

How can we tell whether our worries are excessive? It depends on the circumstances. If a stomachache starts out as a minor discomfort, inexplicably grows worse without letup, and suddenly the pain becomes excruciating, then a hurried drive to find immediate treatment is useful. When we are clear, we can tell the difference between caution and "catastrophizing." If there are alternative possibilities for recovery, then a reasonable amount of concern for the future may help us to focus our minds more intently, so that we can clarify the present situation and choose the best options. The return to soothing inner silence may not eliminate all of our concerns over a potentially terminal illness, nor should it. But it will keep us from panicking so that we can assess our future problems and options more clearly and calmly.

Inner silence does not block us from tapping the energetic power of legitimate concern that fuels our search for a solution to real problems. To remain complacent in the face of a preventable failure is not spiritual contentment; it is spiritual foolishness.

Sometimes our worries are not linked to external circumstances. They arise out of our own self-doubt. We may anticipate the worst without even knowing what is possible, so we can't plan realistically because we don't know what to plan for. This type of anxiety has no value. It doesn't energize our search for solutions. It serves no purpose. We are just reacting to the world's future uncertainties, rather than to life's immediate realities. We harbor doubts about the future, but mostly we have doubts about ourselves. Worse than pessimism, this is defeatism. Yet the certainty of inner stillness can reassure us, giving us the confidence to assume the best and discard the rest. This goes deeper than optimism; it is spiritual realism.

Spiritual realism favors discernment over denial. The presence of a soothing inner silence helps us to calmly determine which concerns about our personalities will help us change and which ones will merely keep us from changing. Is it wise to rely on an imagined state of consciousness where we will be completely free of all concerns, complacent about our habits, whether they serve us or undermine us? Or is it more practical to experience a state of awareness that helps us to formulate positive approaches that will develop and strengthen the personality traits that we feel are most useful? We are all growing, learning from our mistakes, mindful of our weaknesses, and inspired by our talents. The stabilizing presence within gives us the peace we need to accept ourselves with calmness and the confidence to see ourselves clearly. This acceptance represents a spiritual realism that is mature and liberating; it is not a spiritual complacency that whispers, "I am perfect in all ways."

The expanded awareness that opens us up to the peaceful stillness within is the source of constructive solutions to real problems. Our connection to silence provides a lifeline of inner calm that can rescue us from the downward pull of unnecessary anxieties. When there are solutions to problems, we find them and take them. When there aren't, we can accept them—and use the presence of inner silence to help us make peace with them.

"God grant me the Serenity to accept the things I cannot change, the Courage to change those things I can, and the Wisdom to know the difference," Reinhold Niebuhr wrote. The quiet stillness of the present can keep us from getting entangled in anxieties that make change difficult.

The freedom from unnecessary worry allows us to take a step back from our problems. This wider view gives us a clearer picture of our situation. We can see whether our continued concern is likely to lead to a positive change in our behavior and whether this change can actually have a positive impact on future events. If not, we will soon realize that our worries are pointless. If there is nothing we can do to alter the outcome, then continuing to struggle is a waste of time. This clarity enables us to move through our negative emotions more quickly.

Sometimes, we are so gripped by our own anxieties that we can't tell which concerns are reasonable and which ones are exaggerated. Our worries may become so powerful that they jolt us out of silence, sending us headlong into fear over future failures, depressing us with the feeling that there is no way out. But if we are committed to the return of silence, then silence will return. At some point, the powerful emotions will subside. We will be released from our worries, even if only for a few minutes. In the space between our dreadful thoughts and feelings of helplessness, silence will make it easier for us to let go of excessive worrying. These calming silent moments can help us use our discrimination to determine the best course of action. The continual movement from worry to silence, to worry, and then back to silence develops spiritual resilience and eases us away from pointless panic.

We need not be discouraged that our worries about the future can sometimes pull us out of the silent present. The movement between the silence that centers us and the worries that overwhelm us is natural. The emotional discomfort that accompanies problems, even when they have solutions, is often distracting, so it may take a while for us to remember to return to silence. Rather than doubting our level of spiritual development because we still have worries, it is more useful to quickly move back into the silence that frees us from our attachment to them.

At times, the shift away from peaceful stillness might seem unavoidable. If you are worried that you will be attacked, and there is indeed a possibility that you will be, your justified concerns will cause you to either flee or figure out a way to defend yourself. Worrying about a possible assault can push silence to the periphery of your awareness. The adrenaline fueled by your survival instinct can take over your body, your mind, and your emotions so completely that virtually nothing else fills your awareness other than the intention to protect yourself. You may need to harness all of your human resources to survive. And when the threats against your survival have passed, the stillness of the moment will eventually reemerge.

Our survival instinct is powerful and is almost impossible to resist. It can overshadow all other motivations and drives. Only in rare cases is our intense will to survive overcome by an awareness of profound inner stillness.

In 1963, Thích Quảng Đức, a Buddhist monk, protested government repression in South Vietnam by setting himself on fire. He sat upright in a meditation pose with his legs crossed. "I could hear the sobbing of the Vietnamese who were now gathering," a *New York Times* eyewitness reported at the time. "As he burned he never moved a muscle, never uttered a sound, his outward composure in sharp contrast to the wailing people around him."

Thích Quảng Đức had prepared himself for self-immolation by meditating for weeks, putting himself into an extraordinary state of mind that enabled him to overcome his survival instinct with amazing calm. His remarkable acceptance of deadly pain kept him motionless as his flesh and bones fell to the ground and the heat turned them into blackened ash.

Most of us are unwilling to sacrifice ourselves in fiery protest and to calmly experience the harrowing pain that goes with it. The threat of a violent death would cause us such dread that the presence of inner silence would be almost impossible to experience. We would be too busy defending our lives to remain open to stillness. Luckily, few of us face the kind of violence that can keep us away from silence. Yet we do have other worries, and they may still feel quite ominous to us.

We may not be facing death daily, yet our instinct to protect our emotional lives can drag us into such anxiety that nothing seems to exist but worry. Our insecurities can push silence out of our conscious awareness. But as long as we allow silence to reenter our lives, we will again experience the peaceful stillness of the present that can diminish these insecurities. What matters most is not the movement away from silence, but our swift return to it.

"Man runs back and forth, in and out of the divine Presence, and the Presence itself seems to be running back and forth, in and out of the human soul," wrote Rabbi Arthur Green in his commentary on the sacred texts of the Hasidic masters. The Jewish mystics had a Hebrew term for this movement in and out of the spiritual presence, calling it *razo wa-shov*, literally "a running back and forth." The rabbi noted that, "In learning to live with the rhythm of our inner tides there may be a path that brings some peace." It is not a path that leads us into a pond of perpetual emotional pleasure that arises from an uninterrupted awareness of the silent presence within. Rather, it is a path to "the peace of the waters of Ocean, ever churning, smashing, rising and falling," Green explained, where seekers find "their peace in the regular breathing of tides, seeing themselves and their beauty in both ebb and in flow."

The Kabbalists realized that although our churning feelings of failure and worry give way to triumph and joy, only to fall again into unease and concern in a cycle of highs and lows, when we accept the rise and fall of our emotions as a normal occurrence, we are better able to make peace with these natural rhythms of life. This accept-ance gives us the ease we need to relax and settle back into the inner peaceful waters below, where we can discover the spiritual content-ment that we seek.

When we are gripped by worries that push us out of silence, we can be patient, knowing that silence is always waiting for us to return. This will take the edge off our concerns and allow us to be more content as we move through the spiritual phases of awakening to silence, then falling into worries that make us oblivious to silence, and then gradually reawakening to the presence of silence.

Are enlightened men and women confident and content because they know that everything that happens is good, that the cycles of life persist despite our will, so there's no point in trying to change anything? If so, then what is the point of doing anything? Does being in the moment mean not caring about the future, because the stars or karma or nature's grand design has already determined what will happen to us? If so, then why bother to plan ahead for anything?

Enlightenment is empowering, not preposterous. It makes us stronger, not dumber. Inner silence brings us into the now, but the future still matters. Otherwise, why not sit back and be in the world but never act in it? Because, whereas trees barely move so that they can grow, human beings must constantly move in order to grow. Even a spiritual recluse living in a remote cave knows that at least one thing in this world is worth doing: loving others. Love radiates. It is an energy that moves.

Desires that are denied do not disappear, they merely remain unmet. Facing our worries and our desires is more useful than hiding from them. Enlightenment doesn't leave us emotionally docile. We remain fully alert to everything: the calm of the moment, the troubling events in our past, our inspired visions of the future. We favor emotional awareness over dullness, resilience over emotional cowardice.

Spiritual fantasies promise continual emotional calm instead of helping us to develop the ability to calmly experience troubling emotions. Spiritual realism takes unpleasant emotions seriously enough to pause and consider them, instead of rejecting them without cause. It recognizes that some of our worries, and at times even our anger, can help us to create a more positive future.

Spiritual realists understand that not only is the attempt to eliminate all unpleasant emotions futile, it can be harmful. It would remove a powerful emotional tool that can actually serve us. It would be like a cook losing the ability to feel pain when he picks up a hot frying pan. Instead of jerking his fingers away, he would be able to firmly grip the handle because of his lack of sensation, but his hand would eventually burn down to the bone. He would not feel pain, but he might wind up crippled as a result. The same goes for emotional hurt. What good are perpetually pleasant emotions if they fail to protect us from disaster?

Enlightenment allows us to use all of our everyday human emotions with more balance and calm, without ignoring those that are temporarily unpleasant. Even if we wanted to eliminate our unpleasant emotions, the pursuit of uninterrupted pleasure often ends in ceaseless frustration. Not because our consciousness is not high enough, but because our spiritual expectations are not realistic enough.

A realistic spirituality, one in which we are aware of both inner silence and life's difficulties and uncertainties, liberates us from the illusion that our unpleasant emotions are a reflection of a lower state of consciousness. The embrace of spiritual realism bolsters our self-esteem, giving us confidence to react more honestly, more authentically, and more positively to feelings that may be uncomfortable, but at least they are real. Rather than repressing or rejecting difficult emotions, we are centered by our spiritual experience of inner silence.

An awareness of inner silence gives us the calmness we need to decipher which worries help us to move forward, and which ones keep us stuck in fear. Once I had to make this distinction when I was traveling through the tense West Bank territories in the Middle East. It was the quiet presence within that kept me centered enough to make peace with those who frightened me. I was visiting with angry Palestinians who had been locked in a century-old war against their neighbors in Israel, and all that I had to reassure myself was an intuition that came from inner silence.

I went to the West Bank to meet with Ibrahim Issa, the director of the Hope Flowers School in Bethlehem. Although the school's ideology opposes Israeli policies and adopts the official Palestinian curriculum, in which maps that exclude Israel imply its eventual dismantling, Palestinian Muslim and Christian students are taught nonviolent approaches to political problems at Hope Flowers.

Bethlehem, the birthplace of Jesus, is only 25 percent Christian. A Muslim stronghold, the city has seen intense fighting between Arabs and Jews. I was wary as I made the trip to meet with Ibrahim.

Just two years earlier, a month-long siege between Palestinian gun-men and Israeli soldiers at the Church of the Nativity, which was built over the spot where Jesus is believed to have been born, resulted in a shootout that left bullet scars on its sacred walls. For many terrorists, Bethlehem was home.

An Israeli blockade had been set up around Bethlehem to prevent suicide bombers from slipping across the border into Israel. Security was so tight that I had to take an Israeli taxi to the outskirts of Bethlehem since the driver would not enter the city. I could then pick up a Palestinian taxi on the other side to continue the drive to the Hope Flowers School. My inner silence faded as my anxiety increased.

I got out of the car at the Tantur checkpoint and walked around a series of concrete barriers. Then I went through a small makeshift corridor where an Israeli soldier skeptically checked my passport. I was the only Westerner among a dozen or so Palestinians waiting to walk into Bethlehem. The Palestinians looked at me blankly, half of them curious, the other half suspicious. After I went through the checkpoint, I entered the city. I had visited Bethlehem four years earlier, and at the time, Palestinians and Israelis were in the midst of a promising peace process. The city had been bustling with tourists and local vendors hawking souvenirs to throngs of people, many of them visitors from Europe and the United States. During that visit, I was completely at ease, almost giddy at the prospect of a budding Arab-Israeli peace. This time, Bethlehem looked like a ghost town. The streets were empty; nearly every souvenir shop was closed. The fighting between Palestinians and Israelis had chased away the tourists, and almost all commerce had ground to a halt. I began to wonder whether the fighting should have chased me away, too.

I had barely walked a few yards into the city when I heard shouts from a Palestinian who was heading toward me. He called out to me in Arabic. I had no idea who he was and why he was hurrying toward me. I was already on edge. Prior to my visit, when I was riding in a taxi in Israel, the driver had cautioned me to be on guard when spending time with Arabs. "Sleep with one eye open," he advised. "Someone will rise up in every generation to kill you."

I continued walking through Bethlehem while the unknown Palestinian kept shouting at me. Rather than being bolstered by inner silence, I relied on the confidence of Eliyahu McLean, the Jewish peace activist who had set up the meeting with Ibrahim at the school. "Peaceworkers are protected," Eliyahu had assured me.

The unknown Palestinian got closer to me as I walked deeper into the city. He eventually realized that I was a Westerner and switched to Arabic-accented broken English to ask whether I needed a taxi. I did, so I got in, nervously and a bit exhilarated. We rode toward the school, and as usual, I started asking questions. He told me about his background. "My name Khalid Abu Osama," he offered in halting English. "I'm Bedouin." He had been born in a stable, one of ten children. He got married when he was just fifteen years old. He pressed me to let him take me on a tour of the city when my meeting was over. "I'm not a tourist," I explained. "I've already seen the city." Realizing how difficult it must be for Palestinians to earn a living when there were so few tourists to keep them busy, I finally agreed to let him take me around after my meeting. Peaceworkers are protected. Are they really?

When my discussion with the school's director was over, Khalid was waiting for me outside. I got into his car and we drove through narrow dusty roads. "You like chicken?" he asked suddenly. Khalid insisted on taking me to his house for lunch before beginning our tour. I told him that instead I would like to buy him lunch. But Khalid would not budge; his traditional Arab hospitality did not weaken. His wife would cook lunch for us, he insisted. But first, we would have to buy some chicken.

We turned into a cramped back street with ramshackle storefronts, then wound through the unpaved roads, and eventually stopped in front of a tiny shop. I had assumed that we would be going to a Safeway or another typical supermarket where we would pick up a frozen chicken and head over to his house. A few elderly men were seated at the entrance to the store. They were wearing traditional checkered black-and-white Arab headscarves, smoking hookah pipes, sipping tea, and playing backgammon in the heat. They eyed me curiously as I walked into the store. I smiled at them. Their faces did not change. The atmosphere seemed thick with rising tension. Should I be afraid? I couldn't tell whether my growing fear was helping me to survive or merely keeping me from expanding more deeply into silence.

After entering the shop, most of the others inside greeted me in Arabic. Khalid talked loudly, gesturing excitedly. I soon realized where I was when I noticed rows of cages lined from floor to ceiling just to my left. They were packed with live chickens.

A young Palestinian in a worn white tank top came out from the counter behind the shop and approached the cages. He reached inside one and grabbed two fluttering chickens by their feet. He walked back behind the counter and picked up a gleaming knife with a long sharp blade. Khalid walked closer to the counter, signaling me to follow, and I did. The tough-looking young Palestinian held a squirming chicken in one hand, his blade in the other. He flipped the struggling chicken upside down with the breast and the outstretched neck facing the ceiling. He lifted up the knife, suddenly leaned toward me, and looked me straight in the eyes. "You American?" He asked. I nodded yes. "America shit!" he shouted. Then he slit the chicken's throat, and the blood shot toward me in a streaming arc, barely missing me as I jerked away.

The Palestinian butcher swiftly slaughtered the other chicken, disemboweling both birds in a few short minutes. He sliced off their heads and feet. He placed the dead chickens in a vat filled with hot water that made it easy for him to remove their feathers. He wrapped them in paper and handed them to Khalid. Then he stepped out from the counter and walked intently until he was just a few feet in front of me. "Where you from?" he asked. "Los Angeles," I answered. "Hollywood, the movies!" I said smiling. I figured that by ignoring the tension, I could somehow change the energy in the room. If I didn't react with fear, perhaps my pretense of confidence and goodwill might lighten things up. Distracted by worry, I returned to the inner silence that would steady me. And then we left.

I got back into Khalid's taxi and when we reached his house, he brought me into a large living room and told me to wait. He took the chickens into the kitchen for his wife to start cooking. I knew better than to ask him anything about her. I assumed he was a Muslim traditionalist. His wife had not come out to greet me. She would not even show her face to a strange man. To ask Khalid any direct questions about his wife would be a sign of disrespect. Unless he made it obvious that it was all right for us to talk about her, it was best for me not to show any interest whatsoever.

I waited in the large room alone, uneasily wondering when Khalid would return. I sat on the couch fidgeting, staring at the multi-colored Persian rug spread across the floor. I looked up to see whether there was any artwork decorating the room, something authentically Middle Eastern. To my right, I noticed two posters taped to the wall. One was a picture of Sheikh Ahmed Ismail Yassin, the founder of Hamas, the radical Islamic terrorist group that was responsible for the majority of suicide bombings that had struck Israel during the previous ten years. The founding charter of Hamas declared, "Israel will exist and will continue to exist until Islam will obliterate it."

Yassin had been assassinated by Israeli security forces just three months earlier, following a double-suicide bombing by Hamas. Next to the large poster of Yassin was another one heroically depicting a very young Palestinian with explosives that looked like sticks of dynamite placed in a converted tool belt wrapped around his waist. I was beginning to think that perhaps the nervousness I felt was indeed a reasonable fear, a useful one that could protect me.

I had found my way into the home of a Hamas supporter or, even worse, a Hamas member. Two years earlier, Daniel Pearl, a *Wall*

Street Journal reporter, had been beheaded in Pakistan by al-Qaeda terrorists. Osama bin Laden's al-Qaeda openly praised Hamas. The al-Qaeda killers had made a videotape of Pearl's gruesome murder, holding up his bloodstained severed head as a victory trophy and titling their film *The Slaughter of the Spy-Journalist, the Jew*. Pearl was not a spy. He was a peaceful Jewish writer from California. Like me.

I returned to inner silence. I also returned to my general, if somewhat careless, optimism. I waited patiently for my host to return. When Khalid finally showed up, he walked over and stood next to me. "Sheikh Yassin," he said proudly, pointing to one of the posters. "A martyr," he said with equal pride, looking at the picture of the young suicide bomber next to it. I leaned over to him, smiling mischievously, hoping to lighten my anxiety and perhaps his. "Are you sure it would be okay with the Sheikh for me to be here?" I asked. Khalid seemed surprised. "Why not?" he asked, somewhat confused. "He started Hamas," I answered, pointing at myself to gently remind him that I was a typical target for Palestinian terrorists. I had told Khalid I was Jewish on the ride over. "No problem, my friend!" Khalid assured, lifting up his hands to pull the posters off the wall. "I will take them down." I shook my head no. "This is your home," I insisted. I would respect his choice, although it was a horrible one.

I gazed at the posters for a few more moments. "You can see why I might be a bit nervous," I said half-jokingly. "The guy at the chicken place told me, 'America is shit,'" I explained, running a finger simulating a knife cutting across my throat, as if I might soon wind up like one of those chickens. "And now here there are pictures of Sheikh Yassin." Khalid let out a loud laugh. When he entered the butcher shop, Khalid explained, he introduced me as his friend from America. But everyone thought I was Palestinian. After I told them that I was from Los Angeles, the man with the knife didn't believe me. According to Khalid, the man meant to say, "America? Bullshit!" Not "America shit," or, as I had taken it, "America is shit."

"You look like an Arab," Khalid declared. "I first saw you, I talked Arabic. I called you uncle, what we call to someone. You look like Arab. Like my father!" he laughed. "Remember that my wife looked at you? She was angry for never telling her that I had family in America." I had noticed Khalid's wife peeking out from the kitchen, dressed in a black covering that hid almost her entire face, except for her eyes. The story seemed reasonable. Khalid then left the room. I returned to silence.

Khalid soon came back with an old photograph. "Look," he said, holding the picture in front of me. "My father. You look like my father!" The old-fashioned picture showed his mother and father on a couch seated next to each other. His father was sitting upright, stiff and proud in his Arab headdress, looking like he was straight out of a scene from *Lawrence of Arabia*. His complexion was much lighter than those of many Arabs, and his short salt-and-pepper beard looked just like mine, as did his angular features. I did look like him.

This was not the first time someone had thought I was an Arab. Years earlier, when I was visiting old Jerusalem, a kid sold me an Arab robe and a white keffiyeh, the traditional Bedouin scarf that drapes around the sides of your face with a woven black rope circling your head. "You look like a Palestinian!" the boy insisted after I had put on the Arab clothes. I was flattered, as if the resemblance was physical proof that the heart connects despite divisions of politics and culture. Standing in Khalid's house where I had again been mistaken for a Palestinian, I felt my worries slowly begin to subside. The explanation seemed reasonable. For now.

Khalid and I enjoyed a lunch of fresh chicken, stuffed grape leaves, rice, and strong Arabic coffee. I met his two boys, one of whom was a little older than my daughter. Khalid suggested that we arrange for them to get married. American girls choose their own husbands, I explained. He was modern, too, Khalid told me. Not like when he got married. Nowadays, if the boy sees a girl that he likes, he can visit her family and if the family approves, then they can get married. So at least the groom gets to suggest which girl he likes and is allowed to look at her once before the wedding. I told Khalid, almost apologetically, that maybe, as modern as this was, the arrangement still might not be okay with my seventeen-year-old daughter. In the West, parents don't arrange marriages for their children, although I often wondered whether it might be a good idea for them to arrange divorces. Both the husband's and the wife's parents could tell them, "You're not getting along; it's time for you kids to separate." Less grief, smaller lawyer fees.

After lunch, we set off, Khalid's oldest son included, for our sightseeing trip through Bethlehem. We went to the Church of the Nativity, where Jesus had been born. Khalid showed me the hideaways in the church where Palestinian terrorists had held out during the month-long siege when they fought off Israeli soldiers. I asked Khalid whether I could visit the nearby Mosque of Omar. "Yes," he said cheerfully, without hesitation. "It's okay for me?" I asked again. "Of course!" he answered. I went inside and stood quietly in the back while others faced Mecca, the birthplace of Muhammad, to offer up their Muslim prayers. In that holy Muslim place, the silence within me began to expand.

A little more than three miles from Bethlehem is the Herodium, an ancient hilltop fortress built by King Herod. We parked nearby, hiked a little way across the desert, and entered an underground tunnel inside the palace. We walked up a steep incline, and Khalid soon got tired. We stopped to rest. While waiting, I told Khalid to pay attention to his breathing, to use his breath to help him walk. "Breathe in when you take a step," I offered. "Breathe out after taking another." I knew that the kundalini energy that runs up the spine would help to move him along. In explaining the power of focused breathing, I slowly turned my palms upward as if I were praying in the Muslim style. "Breathe," I said softly, looking up. "Allah," I said, gesturing to Khalid and his son, indicating that they could practically draw God's breath down from the heavens and into their bodies through opened palms.

I stood in silence. Khalid and his son also stood still and silent. A Jewish supporter of Israel beside a Palestinian supporter of Hamas, with the Arab's teenage son next to him, all standing in prayerful silence inside the palace of an ancient Hebrew king, a few miles from the birthplace of Jesus Christ where the former Christian city now had a Muslim majority. The three of us were sharing a moment of deep silence, linked by our common inner stillness, a quiet brotherhood that transcended ethnicity, nationality, race, and religion. My worries had been pointless. This time, just beyond fear, a common humanity waited.

Had I chosen fear over friendship, I might never have let myself been taken to the Palestinian butcher shop and into an Arab Bedouin's home. It was silence that centered me when the knife's blade cut and the suicide bomber's face looked down at me from Khalid's wall. The inner stillness had not completely taken away all my fears, but it allowed me to calmly judge what was excessive, what was useful, and what I should ignore.

Spiritual realism doesn't try to push conflicting emotions away. It can even help us use our unpleasant emotions as tools, making us reasonably cautious, but also giving us a silent reassuring boldness when there is a good reason to go beyond our fright.

There is a spirituality defined by levels of consciousness where awakened people have no fears or need for caution. Where a supreme state of consciousness gives them perpetual confidence and emotional pleasure regardless of the external circumstances, however troubling they might be. The death of a child? He or she will one day reincarnate. Beheadings by al-Qaeda terrorists? Bad karma. London wiped out by suicidal nuclear bombers waging jihad? Part of the eternal cycle of birth and destruction. When you are in the now, it's all good. Perhaps there are those who never have to return to silence because nothing ever takes them out of silence, even for a single brief moment, no matter what the danger, whatever the emotion. Is that you? If not, does this mean that you are a spiritual failure or, at best, a spiritual underachiever? Once we throw away such self-recrimination and replace it with an awareness of the silent stillness of the moment, we achieve the spiritual success that we cherish, right here and now.

We do not have to be dispirited because we experience everyday life's emotional ups and downs. There is no shame in accepting a spirituality that mixes inner tranquility with emotional volatility. This liberating acceptance lets us return to silence more quickly since we are not distracted by useless self-doubt. When we return to the silent stillness within, our attachment to volatile emotions lessens. Reunited with the inner calm that we need to respond positively to our negative feelings, we are once again free to act kindly and feel more loving.

The process of flowing in and out of stillness is not to be resisted or criticized but rather accepted and respected. Spiritual realism honors this natural flow as a sacred human experience. Disparaging the movement in and out of silence as a lesser state of consciousness can actually take us out of the silent now. If we are obsessed with a belief in a distant utopia, we may overlook the blessings of the present. Imagining a state of hyperconsciousness might give us inspiring visions of the future by energizing, uplifting, and motivating us to seek out new ways to evolve and to remain dedicated to the ones that are already working. But the vision of a utopian hyperconsciousness devoid of all suffering, both physical and emotional, can serve us only if our attachment to it does not slow our return to the transcendent reality of the silent peace within us.

Chapter 11

THE MYSTIC'S FREEDOM

How might imagining states of hyperconsciousness inspire us? As long as we don't allow our spiritual imaginations to keep us from accessing the inner silence that's available to us now, our visions of the future can open us up to life's enduring mysteries. Staying open to these mysteries can be liberating since they allow us to accept that the infinite complexity of life is beyond our comprehension.

To many people, especially those unfamiliar with descriptions of higher states of consciousness, a belief in various spiritual talents is in actuality a belief in the supernatural. For others, what is considered supernatural may be inspiring.

Even spiritual realists acknowledge that many seemingly impossible things are often quite possible. "There are those who look at things the way they are, and ask why," Senator Robert Kennedy once said. "I dream of things that never were, and ask why not?" This sentiment can be applied not only to political progress, but to spiritual development as well. "You can often measure a person by the size of his dream," wrote the televangelist Reverend Robert Schuller. "Champions aren't made in gyms," explained boxing champion Muhammad Ali. "Champions are made from something they have deep inside them—a desire, a dream, a vision."

Dreaming about a state of hyperconsciousness, replete with extraordinary psychic abilities, may inspire us to keep moving further along on our spiritual paths. Not to dream extraordinary dreams might even be considered unnatural.

"The Hebrew word 'I imagine' is *Adamah*," wrote the eighteenth-century Jewish mystic Rabbi Nachman. "For this reason man was called Adam. He is formed of *adama*, the dust, the physical, but he can ascend above the material world through the use of his imagination" [italics added]. The Book of Genesis says that God made Adam from *adama*, the Hebrew word for "dust," to miraculously create a spiritual being. Perhaps we can also use our physical bodies to attain a miraculous level of spiritual consciousness. Such imaginings can be useful, as long as we do not overlook the realistic spirituality of the silent presence within, which can be experienced in everyday life, right here and now.

What kinds of extraordinary spiritual experiences might we imagine that go beyond the quiet peace that naturally emerges from inner silence? More than fifteen hundred years ago, Rishi Patanjali described a state of consciousness that enables us to develop a highly focused awareness called *samyama*. By practicing samyama, Patanjali wrote in his yoga sutras, "the yogi can fly through the air."

Paramahansa Yogananda, the Indian guru who in 1920 began to popularize meditation in the United States, explained how the enlightened mind can create matter out of thin air. The manifestation appears as real as any other physical object. Yogananda wrote about his visit to Drongiri Mountain in the Himalayas, where he met Mahavatar Babaji. A companion told Yogananda that the legendary saint had manifested "a spectacle of unparalleled grandeur," an ornate gold palace surrounded by exquisite gardens and decorated with diamonds, emeralds, and sapphires.

Yogananda also wrote about a discussion with a friend who had visited the advanced yogi Bhaduri Mahasaya. The friend reported that he had personally witnessed Mahasaya rise into the air, and he explained that the yogi used certain meditation techniques that lightened his body so that he could "levitate or hop about like a leaping frog."

In a book published in 1932, the French explorer Alexandra David-Neel reported that she had seen a Tibetan monk moving quickly across the mountains with one arm swinging a stick as if it were there to help balance him—except that his feet barely touched the ground. His body was more like an elastic ball bouncing in the air with each step. She was told that by doing a Tibetan spiritual practice called *lung-gom*, the monk was able to make his body lighter than air.

The initial stages of lung-gom involve "jumping cross-legged" on the ground without using the hands, much like the leaping frog described by Yogananda's friend. The next stage requires sitting cross-legged at the bottom of a pit, then rising out and over a curved pole that is equal to twice the height of the lung-gom practitioner. After years of practice, one becomes a *lung-gom-pa*, one who has mastered lung-gom. It is then that the ability to completely levitate is achieved.

David-Neel once saw a lung-gom-pa with chains dangling from his body. "They wear those chains to make themselves heavy," her Tibetan companion explained. "Their bodies have become so light that they are always in danger of floating in the air."

I once regularly practiced a technique based on Patanjali's yoga sutras, taught by Maharishi. I was able to hop into the air with my legs crossed in a full lotus, without using my hands, in a manner similar to the one described by the Tibetans. I also hopped about like a leaping frog, as explained by Yogananda's friend. I felt as if my body had indeed lightened. I doubt that I could have achieved the same result by mere physical effort. As David-Neel explained, "the object of this exercise is not acrobatic jumping." The practice "does not aim at training the disciple by strengthening his muscles."

I did not master the yoga sutras enough so that I could actually levitate off the ground and float in the air. Nor had I ever seen anyone who had. Yet I remained eager to meet someone who had managed to succeed in doing this. When I was granted an audience with Tenzin Gyatso, the fourteenth Dalai Lama, I asked him whether he knew of any Tibetan lamas who could levitate using lung-gom. Yes, he told me, he knew someone. "Come to Dharmasala," he invited, and he would introduce me. The Dalai Lama hastened to add that such feats are not the aim of spiritual development. Enlightenment, not the development of supernatural abilities, is the goal.

As eager as I was to see someone really levitate, I wasn't able to make the long journey to Dharmasala, where the Dalai Lama and other Tibetan refugees lived after seeking sanctuary in India. I wonder what would have happened if I had.

I am still open to the spiritual feats of magical wonder that might reveal themselves sometime in the future. Yet my focus is on the practical spirituality of the silent now, which can be experienced in our everyday activities. "If you really want to judge the character of a man, look not at his great performances," Swami Vivekananda advised. "Watch a man do his most common actions; those are indeed the things which will tell you the real character of the great man."

Reading about supernatural feats may motivate us to continue searching for states of higher consciousness. Recognizing that such abilities usually reside only in our imaginations ensures that they will not become a yardstick for spiritual development.

Inner silence, which is the foundation of everyday spirituality, does not require mastery of any ability that we do not already have within us. As the Dalai Lama explained, the goal is enlightenment.

Of course, certain human experiences happen daily that cannot be explained logically. Even Western science has documented events that seem almost as miraculous as those described in India and Tibet. They are not grand feats such as humans flying and the psychic manifestation of golden palaces, but they do seem to defy scientific analysis and common sense.

Modern medicine has demonstrated the incredible power of thought. There are numerous scientific studies proving that the conditions of sick patients can dramatically improve when they are given pills that the recipients are convinced can help to cure them—even though the tablets are placebos, little more than small doses of sugar that contain no active medical ingredients whatsoever.

The ability of thought to directly impact physical events without any direct action has been documented by numerous reputable researchers. The results of an experiment conducted at the University of Michigan, in which participants were treated for pain using placebos, showed that placebos can initiate significant changes in brain chemistry. Tests revealed that those treated with the placebo showed a greater release of opioids, a chemical that the brain produces to reduce pain. "This deals another serious blow to the idea that the placebo effect is a purely psychological, not physical, phenomenon," wrote one of the researchers, Jon-Kar Zubieta, M.D., Ph.D., a professor of psychiatry and radiology at the university's medical school and a research scientist at its Molecular and Behavioral Neurosciences Institute.

Patients can show startling improvements even when they are not convinced that the placebos will work because they haven't been told that they will. Instead, it is the physicians who believe the tablets are effective and are unaware that they are merely placebos. "There is ample evidence to indicate that the nature, character, personality, behavior, and style of doctors can influence a good deal of human response not only to inert but also to active medication," reports Daniel Moerman, a professor of anthropology at the

University of Michigan. "It is as if the physician's demeanor activates medication, inert or otherwise.

Even the experience of pain can somehow miraculously be influenced by our interpretation of the meaning of that pain. One study compared a group of wounded soldiers with another consisting of civilian patients. After receiving a certain surgical procedure, 90 percent of the civilians complained about severe pain and requested a narcotic. Yet only 25 percent of the soldiers who underwent similar surgeries after being wounded on the battlefield reported the same level of pain as the civilians. "For the soldiers, a wound meant a highly welcome escape from imminent danger of death," Doctors Jerome and Julia Frank explained, "while the civilians had no such comfort." What we think about something can have a direct impact on how we experience that thing.

A positive attitude can yield a positive result, even when there are no outside circumstances directly influencing the outcome. The same goes for negativity, which can produce negative results. In one study, a group was told that leaves similar to poison ivy were harmful. Then the leaves were brushed up against one of each person's arms. Another group was told that similar leaves that were known to cause skin rashes were actually harmless. Each of their arms was then touched with the harmful leaves. "All thirteen subjects displayed a skin reaction to the harmless leaves," reported Professor Irving Kirsch of the University of Connecticut, "but only two reacted to the irritant leaves." How you think can often determine what you get.

Western science has also studied astrology, which is often a centerpiece of certain spiritual beliefs. Professor Daniel Moerman of the University of Michigan wrote about a study of Chinese Americans who died from lymphatic cancer. Those whose birth years were considered by Chinese astrologists to make them "susceptible to diseases involving lumps, nodules, or tumors" lived to about sixty years of age. But Chinese Americans who had the same disease but less ominous birth years lived nearly four years longer.

The same study also revealed that Chinese Americans suffering from lung diseases who had birth years that astrologists claimed made them more susceptible to lung ailments died five years earlier than those with similar problems yet less dangerous birth years. The link between longevity and Chinese astrology was scientifically proved to be particularly prominent in the Chinese community. The same study measured Caucasian Americans who had similar diseases as the Chinese Americans, yet there were no such discrepancies in life span. "It is clear from this case that these significant differences in longevity among Chinese-Americans," Moerman concluded, "[are] not due to having Chinese genes, but to having Chinese ideas." Belief in an idea, whether astrological or otherwise, can sometimes turn the supernatural into the natural.

Western science has not yet figured out how differences in belief can cause certain bodily changes that would normally seem to be beyond the mind's ability to influence one way or the other. Perhaps when science does, researchers will also learn how certain thought processes can lighten the body enough so that it can eventually lift off the ground and float in the air. Our belief in an implausible future where inexplicable supernatural feats are the attributes of a godly hyperconsciousness relies mostly on faith, but it may also contain a dash of reason. "Trust in the Lord with all your heart," said the Old Testament proverb. "Do not rely on your own understanding." What we don't understand today may be perfectly reasonable tomorrow.

Sometimes, unexplained spiritual experiences can become a bit clearer over time. Years ago, I received a cryptic message from a close aide to Chalanda Ma. He called me up and said, "Ma says you should teach with grace." I asked for some clarification since I was a publisher and had not taught in decades. "That's all Ma told me," he explained. He had been asked to pass along her message, word for word, without elaboration, so he had nothing else to offer. No further explanation, no context, nothing to add whatsoever. At the time, I did not understand what she was talking about. Teach with grace? It didn't make any sense to me.

Within a few years, I was teaching writing at the University of Southern California. It hadn't been planned. I had not seriously considered teaching when I received Chalanda Ma's message. A coincidence? Maybe.

Miraculous healings, amazing supernatural feats, uncanny happenings are all difficult, if not impossible, to explain using our ordinary understanding. They are examples of the larger mystery of creation that is beyond the ability of human beings to comprehend. Why is the world the way it is? We cannot fathom why. "How" questions can often be answered. But certain "why" questions must remain unanswered. Seeking the "why" of creation is like asking for an explanation from a cosmic intelligence much greater than ourselves and more capable of grasping the ungraspable. "Who are you to argue with God?" St. Paul explained. "Shall the work of art say to the artist: Why did you make me the way you did?"

One of history's most enduring "why" questions has been, "Why is there suffering in the world?" The ancient Persian poem the "Rubaiyat of Omar Khayyam" expresses the sentiment that many of us share: we would have done things differently had we been consulted when this universe was created. "Could thou and I with Fate conspire, to grasp this sorry Things entire, Would not we shatter it to bits—and then re-mould it nearer to the Heart's desire." The heart's desire of nearly every man and woman has always been to banish all suffering from this world. Yet its continued presence is a mystery that will always be with us.

If only the criminal and the cruel were punished, we might be able to find a bit of solace by attributing their sad plight to some overriding need for fairness. Their punishment would simply be a function of the karmic laws of reciprocity, the inevitable consequence of the balancing hand of justice. But this mechanistic view of creation breaks down when the most innocent among us appear to be victims of an arbitrary fate. Birth defects and crippling diseases strike newborns at random. Loving fathers are suddenly felled by unexpected heart attacks. Doting young mothers develop malignant tumors. Entire families are crushed by natural disasters. Are life's tragedies the only way for us to appreciate life's triumphs? Is the presence of these opposing forces really necessary? Does the absence of total harmony make sense? Or is the clash of opposites merely another essential part of life's enduring mysteries?

The world needs brutality so that mercy, its opposite, can exist. But is the presence of mercy worth brutality's pain? Unless there is sin, there can be no virtue. As the poet T. S. Eliot wrote, "Virtues are forced upon us by our impudent crimes." Those who are always sober because they do not like drinking alcohol have little reason to be praised. Yet alcoholics who love getting drunk but manage to stay sober deserve to be congratulated. Temptation allows for virtue, its opposite. Yet are the temptations that lead to self-destructive behavior really worth the virtues that help us overcome them?

We can see that the same creative force that brought all things into existence seems indifferent to life's contradictions. There are energies that contradict one another, hateful ones and loving ones, opposing forces that clash and are sometimes harmonized. Creation continues its cycle of opposites, and its creator does not appear to care about the human consequences.

Inner silence is likewise indifferent. It transcends the duality of good and evil. Silence itself is neither positive or negative, although our experience of it is a pleasurable one. Silence merely exists. Like the God of the Old Testament, whose Hebrew name is simply YHWH, I Am That I AM, silence Is What It Is. Silence has no quality other than its own eternal existence. Our awareness of inner silence may be comforting, pleasing, and peaceful, yet silence itself is none of these things.

When we identify with inner silence, we become more able to drop the need to figure out the reason for the outer world's clash of opposing energies. "In the beginning was the Tao. All things issue from it," wrote Lao Tzu, the ancient Chinese sage. "The Tao doesn't take sides. It gives birth to good and evil. The Tao is ungraspable." In the Tao of silence, we transcend active positive and negative forces that arise from perfect stillness. In silent stillness, no answers are to be found because there are no questions. Silence is beyond questioning, beyond thought, beyond analysis, beyond our understanding. In silence, we are able to simply be. To be at peace.

When we are at peace with the unexplainable, there is no longer any need to ask why life is the way it is. We cannot truly discover the ultimate meaning of life, so what else is there left for us to do, other than to love fully, unafraid, and without reservation? We do know that all of us are soothed by love. Couples are falling in love at this very moment. Parents are loving their children, friends are loving one another. We know that love is unfolding somewhere every second of every day, as it has from the dawn of time up until this very moment. Why does love exist? We do not know. Some things, like love and peaceful silence, need not be explained because we are not looking for an explanation. We are just grateful that they exist. "If you look at things with the eye of ordinary reason," wrote Farid ud-Din Attar, the twelfth-century Sufi mystic, "you will never understand how necessary it is to love."

The silence that transcends logic opens our hearts so that we may peacefully embrace life's mysteries. Experiencing the quiet presence within reminds us that at least we do not have to understand why love exists in order to receive the benefits of loving. Love itself has its own mysterious power, which helps us to overcome all things, and for that, we are thankful.

Chapter 12

USING OUR COLLECTIVE
CONSCIOUSNESS

Is love of country too narrow-minded for spiritual seekers? Is patriotism an outdated notion that encourages nationalistic divisiveness rather than global harmony? Doesn't love begin with our loving those closest to us—our mothers, fathers, siblings, and grandparents. As we grow, our affection extends to friends, colleagues, even neighbors. But an abstract love of country? Isn't loyalty to government and geography the root cause of most wars?

Our sentiments may be tied to the culture into which we were born, rather than to a piece of land or a particular nation. The customs of our cultural heritage are familiar—its foods, fashions, music—so they might have a special resonance even for those of us who are focused on spiritual development. Yet others might feel confined by their cultural heritage, finding it too conservative, too rigid to allow for a free and open exploration of nontraditional spiritual paths.

Yet isn't the pace of self-realization influenced by the spiritual and material expectations we have developed as a result of living in a safe, affluent culture? If we are well fed and our spiritual rights are well protected, then aren't we better able to pursue enlightenment in our daily lives?

Those born into poverty and living under a system of massive government corruption, where the everyday search for a decent meal is a tedious, perilous path, may look upon our spiritual practices as a narcissistic indulgence. Yet they, too, might just as easily take up the search for spiritual awakening if survival were not a daily preoccupation.

For us to experience inner silence, all we have to do is go inward, knowing that our country's economic policies help to make it possible for us to eat well and our political system helps us to sleep safely in our beds. Although we know that heartbreaking poverty and urban violence exist in affluent democracies, they do not compare to the plight of more than one billion people living elsewhere who barely survive on less than one dollar a day and the millions of others who live in fear of political and spiritual repression.

Can our spirituality grow regardless of where we live? Perhaps, but it would be a more difficult task. Economic, political, and spiritual security make a difference. They make things easier. We do not have to meditate with one eye open, constantly looking behind us to make sure we are safe and are able to sit peacefully in a comfortable room. Is this because we have good karma? Maybe. But then perhaps our good karma is that we were simply lucky enough to have born in the right place at the right time. Even our most successful business leaders recognize that their success is not merely the product of their own efforts. Perhaps the same goes for our spiritual success.

"There's a myth that achieving wealth is a function of personal intelligence and energy," noted William Gates Sr., the father of Bill Gates, the richest man in the world. "Let's take the example of the intelligent, hard-working, ambitious human being who tries very hard to accumulate net worth, except let's just move him from Chicago, Illinois, to somewhere in Ghana. So how much of an estate is this intelligent, hard-working person going to create? Very, very little. Wealthy? No way. What is the difference? The difference is being an American. We live in a place which is orderly. It's a place where people can own property and protect it. It's a place that has a court system that works. It's a place that has basically a government that works, so that you have the opportunity to think and to plan and to build and to create."

Those of us who are living in free countries protected by stable governments have the opportunity to think, meditate, and engage in spiritual practices that help to awaken us to the presence of inner silence. Our spiritual progress is a consequence of our own devotion, but it is also aided by our good fortune in being able to live in a political culture that respects our right to pursue whatever spiritual path we choose.

Many of us may believe that we can progress spiritually regardless of where we live, whether it be in another country or within another culture. Yet can't our individual approaches to spirituality be hindered by a culture's traditions or by certain forms of government? Isn't it spiritual presumptuousness, perhaps even spiritual arrogance, to assume that politics and patriotism are beneath us because we are committed to a higher path that values universal spirituality?

"To improve the world, improve the nation," Maharishi has written, "to improve the nation, improve the community, to improve the community, improve the individual." Sometimes, if we are lucky, our nation also helps to improve us.

Our commitment to universal values does not preclude us from acknowledging the unique values of our individual communities. The interaction between spirituality and culture is profound. Patriotism is a concept that honors the distinct collective consciousness that generates a community's cultural values. The collective national consciousness can make it easier, or harder, for us to expand spiritually.

Nationalism defines cultural differences in language, temperament, and perspective. "Every age has its scripture," the Koran says. Why can't the same scripture be applied in every age in every culture? Is there really such a big spiritual difference between one age and another? The Bhagavad Gita says that in order "to save those who are good, destroy evil, and establish righteousness," Krishna returns "in every age, again and again." Why can't Krishna speak to us in the same way throughout all ages? Or do we need different messages and different messengers for each different age and each different culture?

We all know that we are living in an age of technology, of unprecedented global communication. We are developing our spirituality in a unique era. The Internet enables us to convey spiritual ideas freely to one another, almost instantly. Sometimes we do not even know the gender, the race, or the nationality of the blogger we are reading. It is pure mind-to-mind communication, almost mystical in its intimacy and immediacy. In a society that is open and free, diverse spiritual teachings can be disseminated almost instantly over the Web to millions of aspirants. The Internet lets us bypass the usual prejudices that might ordinarily cause us to misjudge the merits of someone else's ideas. If an insightful comment is posted on a blog or a website, we may carefully consider it even though it might have been written by a twelve-year-old from Dublin or an eighty-one-year-old from Des Moines. We frequently don't know much about the writer and have nothing to go by other than the clarity of the posting.

In closed societies, such as North Korea, the use of the Web is virtually nonexistent, and the exchange of spiritual ideas that are not specifically endorsed by the regime is not only nearly impossible, it is illegal. The era of technology has been thwarted, along with the unprecedented array of spiritual teachings that today's new media disseminate.

Never before has there been such intimate instant communication among so many people in different places with a variety of backgrounds. Yet is technology really the defining feature of our age? Are cell phones and PCs and BlackBerries and iPods really the most useful tools propelling us on our spiritual path? Or is it a country's political values that determine whether we can freely make use of the new media, rather than the technologies themselves, that have the greatest impact on our spirituality?

We can see how technology has led to increasing globalization, which has blurred the lines between nations and cultures. Computer software is written in India, CD-ROMs are produced in Malaysia, computers are assembled in Mexico, their components are manufactured in Singapore, and the finished products are sold in America, Germany, Japan, and elsewhere. Business executives move capital and personnel across numerous national boundaries with the ease that was once reserved for transactions within a single country. The result is a global corporate culture revolving around the universal mission of every businessperson regardless of nationality—to make a profit. Yet there is also a spiritual globalization taking place: teachers and seekers around the world are connecting to create a vast universal network of knowledge.

The impact of technology and the globalization that it helps to create, either economically or spiritually, is wholly dependent on the political practices of each country. Yes, certain human values that are common to us all have little to do with politics. For instance, when I was publishing in China, sitting in an American-style TGIF restaurant in Beijing discussing ad sales with a Chinese client, the experience was almost exactly the same as the ones I had when having similar conversations in New York City. Even the small talk was relatively the same: the weather, kids, food, music, sports. Yet how would my spiritual life differ if I was living in Beijing instead of New York? Would the political climate in China allow me to develop my spirituality just as easily?

China is a communist country, officially atheist, although no one is forced to become an atheist. Of course, how would any regime do that? Yet the government is careful not to allow any spiritual group to coalesce into a force that might become an alternative center of power capable of challenging its exclusive authority. Even something as innocuous as attending a Passover seder in Shanghai is restricted to foreigners. When I asked whether I could bring a Chinese guest to the Jewish holiday meal, the synagogue representative explained that the celebration was not open to locals because the authorities wanted to ensure that there would not be any attempt to convert them to Judaism. As if being a Jew in today's world is so appealing that millions of Chinese would be eager to sign on. Still, the authorities wanted to block any possibility of an emerging religious movement that could eventually grow into a political threat, much the way that the Catholic Church in Poland was able to help mobilize opponents of the communist regime prior to its fall in 1989.

"Communist Party members do not believe in any religion," China's President Jiang Jemin reiterated in 2001. "Religion should never be allowed to be used to oppose the party leadership or the socialist system." For many spiritual seekers, this might seem just fine since they have little interest in becoming political activists. Yet the regime's assessment of the political ramifications of a particular spiritual practice could very well keep us from learning it.

The fourteenth Dalai Lama's political calls for greater Tibetan autonomy within China are considered a threat to Chinese national unity by Communist Party leaders. Chinese authorities have banned the Dalai Lama's teachings in Tibet. Even the possession of any pictures or photographs of him is illegal.

If we are not Tibetan Buddhists living in Tibet but instead practice yoga in Shanghai, then perhaps the banning of the Dalai Lama's teachings does not matter much. Perhaps we can still proceed on our own spiritual path without government interference, as long as the Chinese regime does not consider it a threat to its rule. But what if we had been born into Muslim families in Egypt and decided to become Hindus?

I once rode bareback through Cairo's suburban desert sands on an Arabian horse. I was accompanied by a young teenage Egyptian rider who kept screaming "I won't let you fall, my friend!" as I tightly gripped the horse's mane, and we galloped toward the pyramids. When I managed to arrive without being tossed off the animal, I was free to enter the pyramids and use my Vedic mantras to meditate inside. Yet if I had been an Egyptian citizen and born a Muslim, I am not so sure that I could have done the same thing without being subjected to the wrath of the religious police.

In Egypt, a Muslim who adopts another spiritual path is guilty of the crime of apostasy. Nasr Hamid Abu Zayd, an Islamic scholar living in Cairo, did not even renounce his Muslim faith, yet he was found guilty of doing so nevertheless. Zayd had made the fateful error of asserting that the Koran had two natures, human and divine. He said that the Koran's divine nature was evident because Muhammad's revelation came from Allah. Yet the Koran's human aspect was also obvious since it was expressed in Arabic, a language created by human beings.

Zayd's analysis of the dual nature of the Koran challenges certain Islamic fundamentalist beliefs that the scripture is literally the word of God. According to these fundamentalists, to suggest that the Koran was created or even interpreted by any human being, including the Prophet Muhammad, instead of being directly revealed to Muhammad by God, word for word, is to reject Islam itself. After finding Zayd guilty of apostasy, an Egyptian Family Court declared that his marriage to a Muslim professor at Cairo University must be annulled, ruling that Islamic law forbids the marriage of an apostate to a Muslim. To protect his marriage and to save himself from death threats, Zayd and his wife went into exile in Europe.

Some people might wonder whether Egypt's spiritual intolerance is an exception. We know that not all Muslim countries are alike.

There was even a time when Iran, the symbol of contemporary Islamic extremism, was considered to be one of the most socially liberal countries in the Muslim world. But what if we were Muslims living in Iran today and we decided to practice Christian contemplative prayer, a form of meditation espoused by the Catholic monk Thomas Merton? We would be considered apostates by Iran's religious authorities for having moved away from traditional Islam in order to adopt another form of spirituality. And unlike in Egypt, the punishment for apostasy in today's Iran is much more severe than merely being forced to divorce your spouse.

Many of today's young people in Iran do not subscribe to the government's extremist Muslim ideology. They prefer Western fashions and rock music. Many teenage girls and boys secretly get together to party in defiance of the fiercely conservative restrictions instituted by Iran's militant Muslim mullahs. They are rebelling against authority, as lots of us did when we were kids—except these kids have to dodge Iran's roving moral police. In July 2001, officers from the Office to Enjoin Good and Inhibit Evil came knocking on a door in a wealthy section of Teheran and arrested several dozen youngsters between the ages of eighteen and twenty-five for "insulting Islamic sanctities in a depraved party." The nature of the depravity? In Iran, dancing with the opposite sex is forbidden. The young party-goers were given sentences that ranged from thirty to ninety-nine lashes.

If we had been born in Iran, our rejection of tradition might have less to do with secret partying and more with pursuing a spiritual path that differed from the one offered by Iran's ultra-conservative Islamic authorities. We might choose to practice a meditation technique taught by a Hindu guru or a Catholic monk or follow some other spiritual practice at variance with those of mainstream Islam. If so, the risks would be enormous.

In Iran, apostasy is a capital crime. A decade ago, Hussein Soodmand, a Muslim who converted to Christianity and became a minister, was tried and executed by Iranian authorities for the crime of insulting, abandoning, and encouraging others to reject Islam.

If rejecting Islam is so risky, why not embrace it and just follow a Muslim path that is more compatible with our spiritual goals? Not all Muslims have to abandon Islam in order to follow a mystical path that deepens the experience of inner silence. Many Sufis practice a form of Islam that believes that traditional Islamic teachings do not always reflect the true spiritual message of the Prophet Muhammad. Surely, there are alternate ways of interpreting and practicing Islam that do not run the risk of our being charged with apostasy. Yet the opportunity to publicly redefine an Islam that we believe is more accurate and in harmony with our own core values depends on where we are living.

In 2000, Dr. Abul Husnain Muhammad Younus attended a meeting of the South Asia Peace Movement in Islamabad, Pakistan. Younus issued a statement criticizing Pakistan's terrorist attacks against India during their fight over who had the right to rule the disputed border region of Kashmir. After this statement, a Pakistani intelligence officer threatened Younus for taking this position, warning that he would "crush the heads of those who think and talk like that."

The day after the South Asia Peace Movement gathering, Younus, a medical doctor, gave a lecture on physiology at the Capital Homeopathic College, also in Islamabad. He was asked a question about the ritual shaving of pubic and armpit hair by religiously conservative Muslim men. Younus was falsely accused of having answered that the practice was not always followed by Muslims, noting that Muhammad himself did not become a Muslim until age forty. And since Arabs did not engage in the cleansing ritual prior to the arrival of Islam, Muhammad would not have shaved these body parts before receiving his revelations from Allah.

Three days after allegedly giving this response, Younus, himself a Muslim, was arrested and formally charged with blasphemy under Section 295-C of the Pakistan Penal Code. According to the court, his statements defiled the image of the Prophet Muhammad. Younus was sentenced to death. Although no one has actually been executed in Pakistan for blasphemy, many of those sentenced, such as Younus, spend years in solitary confinement under brutal conditions. "I remained constantly under threat of murder by Islamic fundamentalist inmates in jail for murder and gang rape, and by some religiously minded prison wardens," Younus recalled. After serving two years in "a dark and dirty death cell," he was eventually acquitted and released. Still fearing for his life, Dr. Younus fled to Europe.

We might say that these instances of repression have nothing to do with us. We're lucky, those people are not. We're okay, they're not. We don't live in Egypt, Iran, or Pakistan. Let them fix their own spiritual mess.

Yet what if others decide that it is our culture that needs fixing? What if they are convinced that our religious tolerance and spiritual liberalism are actually just licentious permissiveness and degrading decadence? "We want you to know that we'll try to be merciful to you, once we do overtake the West," Osama bin Laden promised. "Abandon your greed, your promiscuousness, your licentious women, your lifestyles, your free enterprise, and your secular government, and commit your lives to Islam," he warned. "Because if you haven't done so by the time we overtake you, according to our holy laws, it is you who must be executed first."

Are bin Laden's followers just a small band of terrorists who might inflict more violence but whose views are too extreme for most people to take seriously? A public opinion poll released four years after 9/11 showed that 26 percent of the public in Morocco actually support bin Laden, as do 35 percent in Indonesia, 51 percent in Pakistan, and a whopping 60 percent in Jordan. Perhaps this makes our own political values more relevant to the pursuit of higher states of consciousness. In a world dominated by bin Laden's theocratic politics, our spiritual pursuits would be severely threatened. Books like this one would be banned, and publicly practicing meditation would be a crime. Yet in a culture free of bin Laden's theocratic thuggery, we can pursue our spiritual path into inner silence publicly or privately, at any time, in any place, without being harassed or arrested by the moral police.

I have had many opportunities to experience inner silence any time, anywhere, in a variety of places. When traveling in the United States and elsewhere, I have found churches to be one of my favorite places to meditate. Even in the middle of a bustling city, whether it be morning or evening, in northern Italy or southern Spain, I could always find a quiet place inside a church where I could sit comfortably and freely meditate in silence. I have never once been asked about my religion by any priest or minister or asked whether the meditation I was practicing used the mantras of India or the prayers of the Vatican. Whether I was praying, meditating, or reading the Bible, the Vedas, the Koran, or the scriptures of any other religion, it did not matter to any of the priests or ministers. All they expected from me was that I respect the church's quiet space.

This acceptance of spiritual diversity also exists in a small part of the Middle East—in Israel, a land revered by the three major religions of Judaism, Christianity, and Islam. The Baha'i faith also has its holiest site located in Israel's port city of Haifa, a city that has been a model of peaceful Arab-Israeli coexistence. When I traveled through Israel, the culture's respect for spiritual freedom allowed me to easily practice techniques that deepened my experience of inner silence without the threat of being jailed by the country's religious enforcers.

There are so many young Israelis visiting Hindu sites in India that in Rishikesh, the renowned home of the country's most honored gurus, located on the banks of the holy Ganges River, there are numerous signs written in Hebrew. "The Hebrew on all the restaurant menus is incongruous enough," one travel writer reported, "but nowhere nearly as weird as my glimpse through the thick Indian jungle of a Hassidic rabbi in full regalia conducting a service before a ritually nodding congregation." The numerous Jews throughout Israel and the West who practice Buddhist meditations have earned them the name JewBus. We may be able to experience inner silence anywhere, at any time, but it is easier to do so in democratic cultures that honor spiritual diversity.

When traveling through Israel, I once went to the Jordan River. I was with a friend of mine, Suzanne Lawlor, who had been raised Christian but practiced a Hindu form of mantra meditation. As we waded into the river, Suzanne told me to let my entire body sink down into the water and to completely submerge myself. When I emerged a few moments later, Suzanne surprised me by sprinkling some drops on my head to baptize me in the River Jordan.

There I stood, a Jew in the Jewish State of Israel, and neither a rabbi nor a policeman nor any other official bothered to watch or care that I seemed to be undergoing a Christian baptism. No moral police, no accusations of apostasy. Atheist, Baptist, Hindu, or JewBu, it did not matter to any Israeli official because my spiritual path was my own personal choice. I could have converted to Christianity on the spot and I still would have been free to worship at the tomb of the Hebrew King David or at any other Jewish holy site in the country.

On that same visit to Israel, David Weiss, another friend, went with me to visit the Western Wall, the last remaining remnant of the ancient Hebrew temple in Jerusalem. The temple was destroyed by the Romans nearly two thousand years ago. The Wall is the holiest site in Judaism. Worshippers can be seen standing reverently before it at all hours of the day, many of them from the Orthodox Hasidic sect, wearing their traditional black coats, black hats, and long beards and bowing and swaying as they softly chanted their Hebrew prayers.

Like my friend Suzanne, David had been born a Christian. He also began to meditate using mantras taken from Vedic scriptures, adopting the mystical teachings of both Hindus and Buddhists. David and I approached the Wall respectfully. While I stood quietly, feeling the deep inner silence amid a prayerful crowd, a Hasidic man standing next to David offered to say a prayer for his children. When David politely declined, the Hasid then asked whether he was married. David indicated that he was. "Then I'll pray that you should have children," the Hasid responded. "No, don't do that!" David insisted.

David had been married for years, but he and his wife had decided not to have children, and he wanted to keep it that way. "What's your name?" the Hasid asked, looking a bit confused. "David Weiss," he answered. "And you don't want children?" the Hasid persisted. Again, David shook his head no. David Weiss is a common Jewish name. The Hasid seemed somewhat flustered. It was only then that he asked, still a bit bewildered, "Are you Jewish?"

Most Jewish men want to raise a family, so the Hasid was puzzled. When David told him no, he wasn't Jewish, the Orthodox Hasidic Jew smiled warmly and went back to his own prayers. He continued to worship peacefully alongside David, who stood before the Wall with outstretched hands to feel its ancient energy, as if he were a Himalayan yogi witnessing a Sanskrit puja ceremony in front of a holy Hindu shrine. He stood in reverential stillness as the Orthodox Hasidic Jew next to him simply resumed singing his ancient Hebrew prayers and made no attempt to keep David from engaging in his own spiritual practice at the ancient Hebrew holy site. Spiritual freedom was more important to the Hasid than an enforced spiritual conformity.

Soon after we finished our visit to the Wall, Suzanne joined us. We all climbed up to the Dome of the Rock and the al-Aqsa Mosque that overlooked the Jewish temple below. Many devotees believe that the rock inside the dome is the place where Abraham brought his son Isaac and almost sacrificed him in accordance with God's instructions. We entered the dome and joined the crowd circling around the rock. I sensed a profound holiness that pulled me deeper into inner silence.

Next to the Dome of the Rock is the al-Aqsa Mosque, where Muslims believe the Prophet Muhammad ascended to heaven and received instructions regarding Islamic prayer before he returned to earth. Israel has granted Muslim religious authorities the exclusive right to administer the mosque. Al-Aqsa is the third holiest site in Islam, after Mecca and Medina in Saudi Arabia, where government officials have banned non-Muslims from entering either city.

As I stood outside the al-Aqsa Mosque, I became enthralled by its beauty. Orthodox Muslims believe that depictions of human beings encourage idolatry, so early Islamic designs are especially intricate to create a dazzling display of compelling visual artistry. I stood in quiet stillness, admiring the mosque's blue and gold mosaic, which covered the building in traditional Muslim geometric patterns.

As I was looking up at al-Aqsa in obvious reverence before this esteemed holy place, I was suddenly confronted by an angry Islamic official who shouted, "No praying! Only Muslims are allowed to pray at the mosque!" I was not praying, nor was I even walking into the mosque itself. I was outside, standing still, soaking up the silent spiritual presence within and staring upward to absorb al-Aqsa's beauty. But the official would not relent. For someone from another religion to pray before the sacred Muslim site was a sacrilege. Just sensing that I might be gazing up at the mosque while envisioning a god other than his was enough for the Islamic official to order me to stop looking with such veneration.

Not all Muslims agree with this approach. "Muhammad's work is with all people, without any difference between any religion," wrote Sidi Muhammad al-Jamal, a Sufi teacher from Jerusalem. "He leaves everybody to pray as they want, as long as they are facing God in their prayers." Bawa Muhaiyadden, a Sufi scholar from Sri Lanka, agrees with al-Jamal. "The Prophet taught us to love our neighbors, to let them follow any religion they wanted to, and to be free to worship any god they chose," he wrote. "If our neighbors wish to pray with us, then we must let them come." Although I knew that the liberal views of al-Jamal and Muhaiyadden are not the dominant ones among many of today's Muslims, the rigidity of the more radical Islamic tradition that I experienced at al-Aqsa was still startling.

We live in a democratic country where spiritual diversity is respected and legally protected, so our own cultural values often go unnoticed. Sometimes our preoccupation with universal values makes us less cognizant of our country's particular cultural values. We simply take it for granted that we have the right to pursue whatever spiritual path we choose. The traditions of a particular country and community frequently seem irrelevant to our spiritual quest. And to many spiritual seekers, a vigorous defense of our own culture's values reflects a primitive nationalistic mindset that divides people instead of uniting them.

Many spiritual seekers ask, "Who are we to judge one culture over another? Aren't we all united by our common humanity, with every country and community deserving equal respect? If we are truly devoted to the experience of inner silence and the spiritual harmony that it produces, does it really matter where we live? Why emphasize the differences between one form of government or one spiritual practice and another when it is political and religious differences that take so many countries to war?" Perhaps there are good reasons.

It is true that manipulative political leaders have cynically used the goal of spreading democracy as a political excuse to dominate other nations. Their armies have threatened other governments, practically declaring, "Democracy or else!" It seems reasonable that even if other countries do not embrace democracy and spiritual tolerance, we should still not try to impose our culture's values on them. All too often, a country's struggle to change another culture's system of government has really been a devious attempt to economically exploit a weaker nation.

Yet sometimes, when we celebrate our culture's democratic spirituality, rather than trying to convert or dominate, we might instead be simply showing our gratitude for being able to freely walk any path that deepens our spirituality, whether it be a Jew receiving a Christian baptism in the Jordan River, a Buddhist praying at the Jewish Temple Wall, a Hindu meditating inside a Catholic Church, or maybe even a non-Muslim standing in silent reverence before a grand and sacred Jerusalem mosque.

An aggressive loyalty to our own cultural values is frequently too narrow-minded and divisive. Blind patriotism can be too prideful, too arrogant. Yet doesn't our country's respect for spiritual diversity deserve praise? If so, isn't it worth defending?

The father of Barack Obama, the senator from Illinois, was a Muslim from Kenya who became an atheist. His mother, who was white, was born a Baptist, yet was skeptical of organized religion. Obama grew up without a sense of any religion until he became a practicing Christian as an adult.

Obama has eloquently defended his country's culture of spiritual diversity. "We need Christians on Capitol Hill, Jews on Capitol Hill and Muslims on Capitol Hill," he said during a speech to American lawmakers in Washington, D.C. Obama told his audience about the night he won an election after a tiring campaign, and how he decided to say a prayer. "It's a prayer I think I share with a lot of Americans," he said. "A hope that we can live with one another in a way that reconciles the beliefs of each with the good of all." More than an American prayer, Obama expressed the wish of all people everywhere who cherish democratic values and honor the right of every individual to freely walk the spiritual path of their choice or to choose no path at all.

If our culture's democratic spiritual values are worth honoring and even defending, we should do so with humility. After all, the heritage of many of today's democracies shows that these nations have not always been so tolerant. Our freedoms are a feature of modernism, the result of a long and often bloody political and religious evolution that over the centuries eventually gave rise to a remarkable embrace of spiritual diversity.

Prior to our modern era, many of us would not have fared so well in the spiritually intolerant cultures of the Western world. Four centuries ago, on November 30, 1554, Mary Tudor, the queen of England and a devout Catholic, had the English Parliament pass laws against heresy. She was determined to bring Protestant England back into the fold of Roman Catholicism and restore the pope's spiritual authority throughout the country. During her brief five-year reign, she became known as "Bloody Mary" for having 274 people killed for the crime of heresy. She ordered them burned at the stake, which is a particularly gruesome way to die.

John Foxe, a Protestant historian who wrote a history of persecution against Christians, detailed many of the executions instigated by Queen Mary, including the death of William Coberley, a tailor who was tried for preaching against the Catholic Church. Published in 1563, Foxe's account, which I have translated from the original Old English, reads, "At the stake for a long time as the wind was still, and after his body was scorched with fire, his left arm fell from him due to the violence of the fire, the flesh burnt to the white bone." Foxe continued, describing Coberley's horrible death, "After awhile, he stooped over with his chin drooping onto his chest, his right hand falling onto his breast, with blood and matter issuing out of his mouth. When they all thought he was dead, suddenly he rose right up, with his body in agony." Spiritual diversity, now guaranteed across Great Britain, had obviously not yet taken hold in sixteenth-century England.

The spiritual diversity we enjoy today took hundreds of years to achieve. During the Spanish Inquisition, which began in 1487, thousands of people, some say hundreds of thousands, were burned at the stake for holding beliefs contrary to those of the Catholic Church. In 1492, the year that the first Europeans landed in America on ships piloted by Christopher Columbus, the Jews of Spain were given a spiritually wrenching choice: either be baptized as Christians or leave the country. Muslims were also forced to convert or go into exile.

The Spanish Inquisition was brutal, lasting an astounding 354 years. The last execution took place in 1826, when Cayetano Ripoll, a poor Christian schoolteacher, was charged with promulgating beliefs that deviated from Catholic orthodoxy. Ripoll was found guilty of heresy and was publicly strangled to death. Today, the freedom to choose one's own spiritual path is guaranteed in Spain, but it took the sensibilities of our modern age to bring it about.

America, long considered to be a unique example of spiritual diversity, has its own history of narrow-minded spirituality. In 1641, Mary Latham, an eighteen-year-old girl, was living in Massachusetts. She had a troubled marriage with a much older man, and the frustrated, high-spirited girl was accused of having sex with several men. One of her lovers, James Britton, became haunted by a guilty conscience and eventually confessed to sleeping with the young girl, committing the crime of adultery.

John Winthrop, the first governor of the Massachusetts Bay Colony, explained in a diary entry that witnesses had seen Latham at her lover's house "and there continued drinking, till late in the night, and then Britton and the woman were seen upon the ground together." Both were found guilty of adultery. As recorded by Governor Winthrop, the man was "loathe to die, and petitioned the general court for his life," yet the young girl "attained to hope of pardon by the blood of Christ, and was willing to die in satisfaction to justice."

At the time, Massachusetts was practically a theocracy, adhering to the Puritan laws that strictly followed the biblical injunction "If a man commits adultery with another man's wife, the adulterer and the adulteress shall be put to death." On March 21, 1643, both Latham and Britton were hanged. Prior to her execution, Latham pleaded with "all young maids to be obedient to their parents, and to take heed of evil company." Those who might have held a less rigid interpretation of the Bible or even disagreed with its ancient codes of justice had little chance in early America's Massachusetts Bay Colony.

The Puritans, who fled to America on the *Mayflower* to escape religious persecution in England, did not hesitate to impose their own version of spirituality on others. Today, even though many Americans adhere to fundamentalist interpretations of the Bible that others believe are spiritually constricting, it is difficult to imagine that America's elected officials would ever put people to death merely because they had violated the official government view of spiritual purity.

As we look at the historical examples of spiritual intolerance, we might be prompted to say, "That was then! We're fine now." Yet are we?

In modern America, religion is still the basis for many conservative challenges to government policy, including support for prayer in public schools and opposition to gay rights, abortion, and the teaching of Charles Darwin's theory of evolution as fact, which is the overwhelming view of the scientific community. Yet beginning in the 1960s, the increasing expansion of civil rights for African Americans, women, and religious minorities has produced a generation of Americans that champions greater spiritual diversity.

True, the modern era of spiritual liberalism has taken hold in all of the world's democracies, especially during the last few decades. Still, cultural humility demands our acknowledgment that even in the modern era, complete spiritual freedom in many democracies is a relatively recent phenomenon.

When I was a young hippie, I spent a summer in Flagstaff, Arizona, a small city just north of Sedona that had a reputation for being a conservative cowboy town. I was planning to take classes at Northern Arizona University and was living with my girlfriend, who like me was a child of the sixties. Both of us were quite faithful to Timothy Leary's notorious appeal "Turn On, Tune In, Drop Out." We also shared the hippie creed "If it feels good, do it."

One day there was a knock on the door. "Police!" announced one of the Flagstaff officers. Figuring they were probably looking to arrest us for possession of marijuana, I quickly checked to make sure there was none on hand and then opened the door. The officer politely asked me my name, and after confirming that I was the one they were looking for, he then named my girlfriend, and asked whether she was also in the house. He said he just wanted us to come down to the station so we could answer a few questions. Staying calm and assuming it was probably all a mistake since they hadn't mentioned anything about illegal drugs, we obediently left the house, slid into the backseat of the police car, and sped away.

Upon arriving at police headquarters, we were quickly told that we were both under arrest. "For what?" I demanded. "Open and notorious cohabitation," I was told. "What's that?" I asked.

According to an old Arizona statute still on the books, it was illegal for adult couples to live together unless they were married. I suspected that conservative city officials might have been using the outdated law to try to force the hippies out of Flagstaff. My girlfriend and I were both jailed. No charges were filed and we were told we would be set free under the condition that one of us left town. Apparently, seventeenth-century puritanical religious attitudes were still alive and well in twentieth-century America.

We can see where the "open and notorious cohabitation" law came from. Several hundred years ago, the Puritans laid the groundwork in accordance with their concept of spirituality. Based on their fundamentalist interpretations of the Bible, between 1640 and 1685 the Puritans in just one Massachusetts county convicted more than a hundred women for having premarital sex. But this was Flagstaff in 1970, not 1670.

It wasn't until 2001 that the Arizona statute criminalizing "open and notorious cohabitation" was finally repealed. Although many Americans still believe premarital sex is a sin, no modern democracy would dare to make it illegal. Cultures that prosecute men and women for adultery and premarital sex claim that their laws are an expression of their spiritual views. Yet this view reflects more of a medieval mentality than a spiritual one.

During the Taliban's radical Islamist rule in Afghanistan, a medieval form of spirituality did dominate the country. On March 28, 1997, officials from the Department for the Promotion of Virtue and Prevention of Vice publicly stoned a woman to death. Her crime? She was found in the company of a man who was not one of her relatives.

There is a verse from Islamic scripture that some Muslim scholars claim endorses stoning as the penalty for adultery. And according to the Taliban, just being with someone of the opposite sex who is not a member of your family is enough to assume that you are having sex, making you guilty of adultery, with the prescribed stoning to follow.

It is difficult to believe that in today's world, someone would actually be stoned to death for adultery. Yet I have seen it done in a video that captured the ordeal of a woman who was wrapped in a white sheet from head to toe. She was dragged into a hole in the ground, just deep enough to cover her body up to her waist. Dirt was filled in so that she would be propped up, unable to move her legs, arms, shoulders, hands. With her head and face completely covered by the sheet, the stoning began. Crowds of enthusiastic onlookers picked up large rocks and hurled them at the helpless woman, one after another. I could see the blood oozing out from behind the sheet. After taking her last breath, the woman's head slumped forward.

In Leviticus, the Old Testament prescribes stoning if a virgin who is already engaged to be married has sex with another man. There have been numerous stonings in recent years for various kinds of illicit sex. Yet when an adulteress was brought before Jesus for possible stoning, he said, "Let the one of you who is without sin be the first to throw a stone at her." Perhaps those Taliban officials from Afghanistan's Department for the Promotion of Virtue and Prevention of Vice were all without sin.

In this modern era, who would apply a religious practice that took place centuries ago? Those who are still living a life rooted in an era that existed centuries ago.

"Every age has its scripture," the Koran says. Our modern age has embraced an approach to spirituality that is more tolerant, more diverse, and less violent than those that may have been suitable for societies that existed hundreds of years ago. Many nations have developed scriptures that encourage their own particular beliefs, yet they also respect spiritual diversity.

The differences between cultures that still stone people to death for having sex outside of marriage and those that do not have little to do with real differences in religion. They have more to do with the difference between a pre-modern age and the modern era. If your mentality, like that of the Taliban members in Afghanistan, is not attuned to the modern world, you adopt archaic approaches to spirituality, such as stoning. In societies that do this, the ability to follow your own spiritual path is difficult. We must accept this reality so that we might better support the political traditions that support spiritual freedom.

In modern democratic societies, hundreds of years of spiritual evolution have removed the last vestiges of religious intolerance, leaving us with cultures and countries that have an unprecedented respect for spiritual diversity, protected by both law and social practice. No one is stoned or hanged for having premarital sex or affairs. In the United States, Mormons who broke away into their own small sect to practice male polygamy, in defiance of the much larger mainstream Church of Latter-Day Saints, are forbidden by law to follow their religious teachings by marrying more than one wife. Such situations are extremely rare. In nearly every instance, Americans can live in the United States with whomever they want, however they want, anywhere they want, and follow any spiritual path they want.

Our political rights provide the foundation for our spiritual freedoms. It is nearly impossible to fathom that we could be executed because someone else's spiritual belief forbids us from spending time with a member of the opposite sex who is not a member of our own family. It is also difficult to imagine that we could be forced to go into hiding for attending a spiritual workshop or practicing a certain type of meditation because they are not officially sanctioned by the government.

We are lucky to be living in a tolerant, affluent culture. Our good fortune is obvious not only because of our professional and financial opportunities. We are lucky that our political culture also provides us with an abundance of spiritual opportunities.

The United States, like all other democracies, is host to numerous spiritual teachers from every country. In Northern California, an ashram was built for Sri Mata Amritanandamayi Devi, the Indian saint affectionately known as Amma, who travels the world literally hugging the devoted and the curious. She often stays up until dawn to make sure that every single visitor finds a home in her lap. I have visited her several times. It would be easy for the government to prevent me from doing so if I lived somewhere else.

At Amma's ashram in Kerala, India, it is not uncommon for crowds of a hundred thousand and more to wait in the sweltering sun for a distant glimpse of the smiling guru. Amma might sit for twenty hours straight without a break. Many have reported seeing Amma hug as many as twenty-five hundred people an hour. Yet at her ashram in Castro Valley, California, Amma will spend an entire day giving darshan to the same number of people. Unlike the devotees who sit outdoors for hours in the stifling Indian heat, I am able to fly to Amma's California ashram twice a year, where I spend my time comfortably meditating and chanting in the large indoor meeting hall. I make an occasional visit to the nearby chai tent for drinks and vegetarian snacks and later return to my air-conditioned room at the local Marriott Hotel for a bit of rest and room service. I even get to come back during the next couple of days for more of Amma's hugging darshan.

In the United States, Amma takes nearly six hours to do what she does in just a single hour back home in India. She even spends more time hugging each person in the United States. Otherwise, the people might feel cheated, Amma explained. "They would sue me!" She laughed. Amma gives us special attention not because we are necessarily more spiritually advanced or deserving, but simply because we are Americans or Germans or Italians or citizens of any of the other wealthy democratic countries where people might feel cheated because they are used to a certain standard of living and expect a certain level of comfort and spiritual attention. This national expectation impacts our spiritual development. Waiting amid thousands beneath a blazing hot sun might discourage us from following a spiritual path that would otherwise be beneficial. We are not used to these kind of difficulties, so we may find them unnecessary or too overwhelming. The culture into which we were born helps to define what is worth sacrificing for and what is not.

Spiritual realism recognizes the connection between spirituality and culture. It reminds us that the cultural values that enable us to pursue any spiritual tradition we choose is worth celebrating.

Our lives are blessed, as are the lives of all those living in free, affluent societies. We may not consider ourselves rich, but we are still among the world's wealthiest citizens. Some people feel guilty about this fact as if we are taking more than our fair share. Others might worry that if we extol our nation's economic achievements and our cultural freedoms, we run the risk of exchanging our appreciation of universal spiritual values for an excessive, flag-waving patriotism. Yet there are all kinds of pride and various types of patriotism.

Albert Einstein, the scientific genius who was a lifelong antiwar activist, denounced "the pestilent nonsense that goes by the name of patriotism." Yet he acknowledged the value of having "a communal purpose, without which we can neither live nor die in this hostile world." This common purpose can frequently grow into an aggressive nationalism that breeds intolerance and oppression, but Einstein was referring to "a nationalism whose aim is not power, but dignity and health." Spiritual realism embraces this kind of nationalism, one for which we can all be grateful and even proud.

Einstein understood that a collective consciousness that rallies around an allegiance to a single nation can be divisive. "If we did not have to live among intolerant, narrow-minded, and violent people,"

Einstein explained, "I should be the first to throw over all nationalism in favour of universal humanity." Most of us would join him in tossing nationalism overboard. But spiritual realists understand that we are indeed living among intolerant, narrow-minded, and violent people. It is not useful to let our loving spiritual impulses keep us from recognizing this reality.

There are intolerant and violent forces that reject our calls for a universal humanity. They openly challenge our right to express the acceptance, forgiveness, and compassion that flow from inner silence. This right has not always been applied in the United States and the world's other democracies, but it is an ideal that they cherish.

"We're hardly perfect," President Bill Clinton once told an audience in the Arab nation of Qatar. "We're still burdened with our haters and our dividers who use religion sometimes as an excuse to get and keep political power. We still are prone to be blinded by self-interest. Sometimes we're heedless of the feelings and views of others. On the other hand, for more than two hundred years now, America has become the longest-lasting democracy in human history because we kept stumbling in the right direction." Our spirituality can help America and all other free nations to continue moving in the right direction.

Often, a culture's spiritual evolution is guided by the ideals set forth in its infancy. There is a saying by the Greek philosopher Aristotle: "Well begun is half done." More than two hundred years ago in 1782, Charles Thomson designed the Great Seal of the United States, which featured a pyramid of strength with the eye of a divine destiny hovering over it. The design signified a new American consciousness, unified by a common respect for political freedom and spiritual diversity. Underneath the seal Thomson placed the Latin motto *Novus Ordo Seclorum* ("A New Order of the Ages"). The saying was derived from the Roman visionary poet Virgil, who wrote, *"Magnus ab integro seclorum nascitur ordo"* ("The great series of ages begins anew"). Our current new age that respects spiritual diversity was well begun, getting its start nearly two centuries ago. It has been a long evolutionary process to get us to where we are now. Aren't the economic, political, and spiritual benefits that we now enjoy worth honoring?

Although the world's cultures and countries still have a long way to go in the quest for universal peace and brotherhood, before we get too focused on our failures, perhaps it is wise to remind ourselves of how far we have come. This becomes even more apparent when we remember that not everyone envisions the same new age of spiritual freedom and diversity.

Not all national cultures undergo an auspicious rebirth. In 1942, Ayatollah Khomeini, the father of the 1979 Islamic revolution in Iran, expressed his own founding vision of a new era. "Those who study Islamic Holy War will understand why Islam wants to conquer the whole world," Khomeini predicted. "All the countries conquered by Islam or to be conquered in the future will be marked for everlasting salvation." Today, millions of people around the world still admire Khomeini. They are struggling to fulfill his dream of a spirituality where the entire world, conquered by a jihad of holy warriors, will be ruled by Islamic celestial law.

Khomeini, the leader who helped create the Islamic Republic of Iran, specifically and boldly called for spiritual intolerance. America's founders called for spiritual liberty. Is it too divisive to acknowledge which call resonates with us and which one repulses us?

Not all Muslims share Khomeini's view of jihad. "It is compassion that conquers," wrote Muhammad Raheem Bawa Muhaiyadden, the Sufi from Sri Lanka. "It is unity that conquers," he insisted. "It is this state that is called Islam. The sword doesn't conquer; love is sharper than the sword. Love is an exalted, gentle sword."

Compare this to Khomeini's call: "Kill all the unbelievers just as they would kill you all!" he urged. "Kill them, put them to the sword. People cannot be made obedient except with the sword!"

There is a culture of death on this planet that promotes itself as a culture of spirituality. Ignoring this does not make us more spiritual.

The German journalist Christoph Reuter described how many of Khomeini's followers see their very lives as swords, envisioning their own deaths as a path to an enlightened afterlife. The reporter wrote about the ten thousand Iranian children who were sent on a death march across minefields during Iran's war in 1979–1988 with Saddam Hussein's Iraq. Their mission was to detonate Iraq's buried explosives so that Iran's adult soldiers could safely make their way behind the young corpses. Each young child was armed with nothing but a small plastic key dangling from his neck. Ayatollah Khomeini explained that they were wearing keys to heaven, symbolizing the paradise that awaited the exploding children who had sacrificed their lives for the Iranian Islamic Republic.

The German reporter also saw a monument to Khomeini's adulation of death firsthand during a visit to Behesht-e Zahra, the largest cemetery in Iran. At the entrance, built during Khomeini's rule, is a structure called the Fountain of Blood, with red-colored liquid oozing out and cascading down a succession of marble steps. "The Tree of Islam can only grow if it's constantly fed with the blood of martyrs," Khomeini explained.

America's Declaration of Independence expresses a different view of spirituality. "We hold these truths to be self-evident," it declares, "that all men are created equal, that they are endowed by their Creator with certain unalienable Rights, that among these are Life, Liberty and the pursuit of Happiness." Would Khomeini's celestial law grant these same rights to Buddhists, Jews, Christians, and others? If not, should we ignore, acquiesce, or resist those who wish to impose it on us?

Often, it is only when our rights are directly threatened that we realize just how much spiritual freedom is linked to political freedom. My father was a kind, tolerant, compassionate man who deplored violence. When World War II erupted and his country was faced with a fascist challenge from Imperial Japan and Nazi Germany, he did not even wait to be drafted into the army. He quickly volunteered.

Albert Camus, the French writer and Nobel Prize winner, risked his life to join the resistance against the Nazis during their occupation of France in World War II. One of the reasons Camus fought fascism was because it threatened spiritual freedom. "When one knows of what man is capable, for better and for worse," Camus wrote, "one also knows that it is not the human being himself who must be protected but the possibilities he has within him—in other words, his freedom."

Our democratic culture's leaders often acknowledge the importance of spiritual diversity. President John F. Kennedy also fought the Fascists during World War II, winning a navy and marine corps medal for Gallantry in Action, the U.S. Navy's highest honor. Exactly twenty years later, Kennedy gave a 1963 speech at the University of California in Berkeley. "The wave of the future is not the conquest of the world by a single dogmatic creed," Kennedy said, "but the liberation of the diverse energies of free nations and free men."

Would Khomeini's celestial law protect the spiritual possibilities we have within us and allow for the liberation of the diverse energies of free nations? Would it give Amma the right to sit for hours in her Hindu ashram in Castro Valley and the one in Kerala, openly hugging and giving darshan to hundreds of thousands? Or do we have to ensure that the Khomeini-inspired fascist religious conquerors of today are somehow prevented from crossing the borders into the United States, India, Japan, Germany, and elsewhere?

Is the love of country and culture we need to protect our spiritual freedoms too nationalistic and narrow-minded for those of us who are wedded to the universal presence of inner silence? Every age, every culture, and every nation have their blessings and their shortcomings. We have a spiritual duty to honestly address the shortcomings of our modern age and the national culture in which we live. We also have an obligation to honor our new age culture and the political system that upholds our freedom to honor whatever we choose.

It is easier to expand our awareness of the peaceful quiet within when we live in a culture of spiritual freedom instead of political oppression. This is not misguided patriotism or crude flag-waving fanaticism. It is a realistic spirituality that recognizes the profound linkage between our own spiritual evolution and the collective consciousness around us.

Chapter 13

RESOLVING CONFLICT WITHIN
US AND AROUND US

Our spirituality is rooted in the silent calm within that enables us to make peace with the world. But what if the world does not want to make peace with us?

We have all faced emotional conflict, social conflict, family conflict, and even spiritual conflict. These are the ordinary clashes of everyday life: being rebuffed on a date, being unfairly criticized by a parent, dealing with fierce competition in the workplace, being torn between our devotion to a spiritual teacher and the realities of our own experience. These kinds of conflicts can be eased and often resolved through the expansion of inner silence and the compassionate love that it releases.

By increasing our awareness of the silent presence within, we gain a greater capacity to forgive because our forgiveness is less dependent on outside circumstances. We can love even if people do not love us back. Even if they reject us, even if they threaten us, we can remain peaceful and loving. The only thing that can keep us from loving is our own decision to stop loving.

Our awareness of silence, like our ability to love, cannot be threatened by anyone. Who can keep our awareness from moving into silence? Our awareness is like the wind, ever able to move freely. Trying to stop us from becoming aware of inner silence would be like trying to stop the air from moving around the planet. Even if our bodies are imprisoned, our awareness can never be. We can become aware of whatever we choose, wherever we are—unless someone is determined to make sure that we can no longer become aware of anything at all. Sometimes life's conflicts are not emotional, psychological, or spiritual. They are physical.

There are challenges that require more than good intentions and inner well-being. There are conflicts that threaten our freedoms, our lifestyles, our lives, and the lives of those around us. Then our inner stillness gives us more than inner peace. It can serve as an anchor to help bolster our resolve to defend what deserves defending. And it can also give us the ability to be compassionate toward those we must oppose.

For many of us, conflicts that involve physical force seem to be at odds with the spiritual values we hold so dear. Yet does spirituality require passivity when we are threatened by aggression? Must we acquiesce to violent repression? Should we surrender when the political freedoms that allow us to pursue whatever spiritual paths we choose are under attack by suicidal terrorists?

Many of us believe that these are questions we do not have to answer. We are not firefighters, who risk their lives when criminal arsonists strike, or police officers, who keep our streets safe while facing the possibility of being suddenly shot by a driver who is handed a traffic ticket. We are not soldiers or military planners who must decide whether, when, and where to deploy their troops. We are spiritual activists, not political activists. We are teachers, students, homemakers, office workers, artists, scientists, clerks, engineers, nurses, doctors, lawyers, or participants in any number of other nonviolent professions. Yet isn't it our spiritual duty to honor those firefighters, police officers, soldiers, and others who physically protect us?

Are we condoning violence when we support the local sheriff who might have to use force against criminals who want to steal, wound, rape, or kill us? Or do we recognize that it is not always violence itself that we abhor? Doesn't it depend on who is engaging in violence, who is the target of violence, and what is the purpose of violence? Spiritual realism upholds the dignity of all life. It rejects the use of force when love, humility, and understanding can bring peace. When they cannot, then spiritual realists recognize that there is nothing nonviolent about letting ourselves become the victims of someone else's violence.

Some might say that in this post-9/11 world, most of the rising concerns about physical safety are limited to the paranoid and the ignorant. They believe that goodwill is enough to protect us from those intending to murder us. They insist that spirituality is our shield, loving energy our sword. Is this reliance on the purity of our spirituality an insightful truth revealed by spiritual awakening? Or is it a spiritual delusion?

There are two main approaches to dealing with external conflict: the political and the spiritual. We often believe that we must choose one or the other. Many of us prefer the politics of consciousness rather than what often seems like the politically unconscionable. We frequently see physical force orchestrated by politicians as a failure of vision, a despicable path that relies on murdering others as a means of achieving an elusive national defense. Those adopting an exclusively spiritual approach urge that we all tap into our spirituality to transform others, thereby creating a powerful harmony that removes the need for a defense that relies on the use of force.

The divide between those favoring global change through spiritual evolution and others who call for a worldwide transformation through political change is a prominent feature of our modern culture. In many of today's democracies, this split between spirituality and politics can be traced back to the 1960s, when the hippie generation eventually coalesced into two main groups: political activists and spiritual seekers. In our post-9/11 world, the legacy of this divide has become increasingly apparent. How shall we respond to the al-Qaeda terrorists who have dedicated themselves to the destruction of our culture? Through the tolerance and the compassion that arise from a sincere spirituality, or through the armed threats and military strikes that govern international politics?

In the sixties, the Vietnam War was raging, the U.S. civil rights movement was struggling, and the world's persistent economic inequalities were being challenged. How did the solutions offered by political reformers and spiritual devotees differ? Perhaps these differences can teach us something about today's attempts to integrate spirituality with the political effort to create a more peaceful world.

I remember that when I was attending Maharishi's teacher training course, an agitated member of the audience stood up to ask a question. "How can you say that life is bliss when they are napalming babies in Vietnam?" he challenged. The chemical gel napalm was being dropped across the South Vietnamese countryside by U.S. planes targeting North Vietnamese fighters, but the incendiary weapons burned nearly everything in sight, civilians and combatants alike. The questioner was irate that someone could promote spiritual fulfillment as a solution to the horrors taking place in Vietnam. During the sixties, most people like him took a political approach to problem solving. Many of these young activists joined organizations like Tom Hayden's Students for a Democratic Society (SDS), Eldridge Cleaver's Black Panthers, César Chavez's Farm Workers Union, and Mario Savio's Free Speech Movement.

I once watched Tom Hayden give a compelling anti–Vietnam War speech alongside Jane Fonda, his then wife and a fellow activist. It was pure political activism, with more than a dose of near-religious fervor. Hayden, who later went on to become a California state representative, summarized his organization's purpose in 1962, when he was only twenty-two years old. Drafted in Michigan, it was called the Port Huron Statement of the Students for a Democratic Society. According to the SDS, politics should "be seen positively, as the art of collectively creating an acceptable pattern of social relations," the statement explained. "Politics has the function of bringing people out of isolation and into community, thus being a necessary, though not sufficient, means of finding meaning in personal life." Hayden's promise was that we could discover our spiritual purpose by taking a political path.

In 1964, Mario Savio hopped onto a police car during a campus protest against the political system that was responsible for the Vietnam War. Savio, just twenty-one years old at the time, delivered an impassioned speech. "There is a time when the operation of the machine becomes so odious, makes you so sick at heart, that you can't take part; you can't even passively take part, and you've got to put your bodies upon the gears and upon the wheels, upon the levers, upon all the apparatus, and you've got to make it stop!" The gathering crowd of Berkeley students cheered as Savio continued to shout, "You've got to indicate to the people who run it, to the people who own it, that unless you're free, the machine will be prevented from working at all!" Savio was signaling that the fulfillment of our spiritual purpose required living up to our political duty—which is to stop the machinery of injustice. He helped to pave the way for the campus antiwar protests that erupted across the United States until the war finally ended in 1975.

César Chavez, the California immigration rights activist, once spoke about his work in the sixties. He said he had been "driven by one dream, one goal, one vision: to overthrow a farm labor system in this nation which treats farm workers as if they were not important human beings." Chavez explained, "The only answer, the only hope, was in organizing. We had to register to vote. And people like me had to develop the skills it would take to organize, to educate, to help empower the Chicano people." For Chavez, improving the horrid conditions of exploited itinerant Mexican American farm workers not only needed a change of consciousness, it also required urgent political change.

In 1969, Eldridge Cleaver, the African American leader of the Black Panther Party, talked about his political agenda. "The party seeks to organize black people so they can move and take control of the life, the politics, and the destiny of the black community." Cleaver employed a combination of political activism and the threat of militant revolutionary violence to achieve his goals, which included a radical shift in the nation's collective consciousness that would ultimately empower African Americans and free them from the grip of institutional racism.

Cleaver, one of the most famous black militants in America, eventually dropped out of politics. Born a Baptist, he converted to Islam and then became a born-again Christian. "I used to think all our problems were economic and political. But at the end of the day I found out that our main problems are spiritual problems," Cleaver explained. "Because the connection between people and between Creation and the creator is not a political connection, it's not an economic connection, it's a spiritual connection."

People like Tom Hayden and César Chavez embodied the political movement that grew out of the 1960s. Others, such as Eldridge Cleaver, moved into a spirituality that replaced political action. Then there were those who almost from the beginning sought to solve social problems by taking a spiritual path that pushed politics into the background. This is the choice that many of us have made. People like Aldous Huxley and Baba Ram Dass epitomized the spiritual approach that emerged from the turbulent sixties. What was the rationale for their decision? Huxley and Ram Dass offered some reasons that might also explain our own.

In the 1960s, Aldous Huxley, the author and spiritual seeker, wrote a groundbreaking book, *The Doors of Perception*, that inspired me, Jim Morrison's rock group the Doors, and an entire generation to seek altered states of consciousness. Huxley's work introduced me to the notion that a change of consciousness could dramatically alter my perception of life and my concept of the meaning of life. Rather than focusing on changing the world, I would work to change myself. If I could become more peaceful on the inside, perhaps I might then be able to bring some peace to those around me.

Huxley took me through a door that led to a new world of mind-altering chemicals. But his book was more than merely a gateway to hallucinogenic drugs. Huxley's observations eventually prompted me to seek out spiritual techniques that produced natural, higher levels of awareness. Huxley was wary, if not outright disdainful, of politics. I soon found myself moving in the same direction. "One of the great attractions of patriotism—it fulfills our worst wishes," Huxley claimed. "In the person of our nation we are able, vicariously, to bully and cheat. Bully and cheat, what's more, with a feeling that we are profoundly virtuous." Huxley's spirituality left little room for politics. "I wanted to change the world," he explained. "But I have found that the only thing one can be sure of changing is oneself." Self-realization became my answer, too—not only to personal turmoil, but to global conflict as well.

Self-realization also became the aim of Richard Alpert, the Harvard University professor who was fired in 1963 for researching the use of psychedelic drugs as a vehicle for developing higher states of consciousness. Four years later, Alpert went to India where he met Maharajji Neem Karoli Baba. Alpert gave the Indian spiritual master a massive dose of LSD and waited to see his response. "My reaction was one of shock mixed with the fascination of a social scientist eager to see what would happen," Alpert recalled. What happened to the spiritual master who took LSD? "Nothing whatsoever. He just laughed at me," Alpert wrote. Alpert changed his name to Baba Ram Dass and renounced mind-altering drugs to follow the spiritual practices taught by his new guru, Neem Karoli Baba. Many others also made the same shift as Ram Dass, giving up drugs to follow a natural spiritual path to altered states.

Ram Dass spent the rest of his life devoted to spirituality, not politics. "Every advancement in man's condition has come about by someone becoming a little more conscious," Ram Dass told one interviewer. "War is the result of lack of consciousness. So is hunger. There's enough food to feed every human being that exists, but the consciousness of man is such that he says, It's my food, not yours." As for external threats, Ram Dass relied on inner spirituality. "No matter how much another person suppresses you, even if he crucifies you, it has nothing to do with your internal freedom," he explained. "These are the hardest things to accept—the relationship of the spirit to the external world." As Ram Dass said, our access to inner silence may indeed withstand the pain of impending death, through crucifixion or otherwise. There may be other realms where our consciousness survives, but the particular human experience of silence requires a human body. Once the human body dies, so does the human awareness of inner silence.

What does outlast our actual death? Belief in the afterlife is just that, a belief, not an experience. Those who might have the spiritual ability to perceive the existence of beings in other dimensions are still physically living on this planet, in human bodies that enable them to have those perceptions. And as long as we are living in this realm, our bodies deserve to be protected from disease and from violence.

Although there may be an afterlife, can we predict what the quality of that life might be? What will be the spiritual challenges that await us? Will there be only harmony and joy, or will there also be fear and conflict? Some may have the answers to these questions; others might not. What all of us can know is that the peace of inner silence is available now, in this lifetime. As for what comes next, it is not unreasonable to assume that our deaths will shift the experience of inner silence in some way. We will know the nature of that shift if and when it arrives. For now, our living human bodies guarantee that we can experience a peaceful stillness within at this very moment. The future will bring what it brings.

Some of us might believe that death is more like changing apartments. We simply move from one incarnation to another, and although the body dies, the spirit thrives. So does it really matter whether our physical existence on this planet continues or not? For those of us who answer yes, that living in this body does matter, then it is useful to try to understand the nature of the life-threatening challenges that exist in today's world. If we do not acknowledge these challenges, it is more difficult to engage them spiritually. If we care about our physical survival, then it might be wise for us to integrate, rather than separate, the spiritual protections that we have within us and the political defenses that are available to us. Our being spiritual does not mean that we can't use our hands to block someone else's fist.

Mainstream religions such as Christianity, Islam, and Hinduism have fundamentalist branches whose followers have merged spirituality and politics. Their approach to spirituality may not be rooted in the experience of inner silence, but they have tried to reconcile faith and political action. Yet since the 1960s, the separation between those who embrace a spirituality of expanded consciousness and the activists who call for greater political involvement appears to have widened.

Those who favor political action often criticize new age spirituality as a self-indulgent withdrawal from our culture's challenges. "After the political turmoil of the sixties, Americans have retreated to purely personal preoccupations," wrote the best-selling social critic Christopher Lasch. "Having no hope of improving their lives in any of the ways that matter, people have convinced themselves that what matters is psychic self-improvement: getting in touch with their feelings, eating health food, taking lessons in ballet or belly dancing, immersing themselves in the wisdom of the East, jogging, learning how to 'relate,' overcoming the 'fear of pleasure.' Harmless in themselves, these pursuits, elevated to a program and wrapped in the rhetoric of authenticity and awareness, signify a retreat from politics and a repudiation of the recent past."

Although Lasch's book *The Culture of Narcissism* was written more than twenty-five years ago, there are those who insist that it describes an ongoing self-indulgent aspect of modern culture. For these critics of the self-realization movement, Lasch had neatly summed up their complaint: "To live for the moment is the prevailing passion—to live for yourself, not for your predecessors or posterity." Yet many of us do look beyond the joy of our own individual self-realization. We do care about the traditions of the past and the happiness of future generations.

We can harness our inner silence to engage life's challenges, even the political ones, with greater calm and compassion. Our spiritual awakening does not necessarily mean that we must be politically unaware or indifferent. In this new era, spirituality and political responsibility can combine. We do not have to look away from the world's conflicts because we are strengthened by looking within. We are capable of experiencing our calming inner reality while also dealing with volatile, even threatening, external realities.

What are the external conflicts that threaten us? Environmental problems like global warming need urgent attention, as do the economic disparities between the rich and the poor that are increasing day by day. Meeting these challenges is difficult, but they can be resolved nonviolently. Unfortunately, this is not the case when dealing with suicidal terrorists who deliberately target defenseless men, women, and children. Spiritual fanatics, like those who perpetrated the attacks on 9/11, aim to kill innocent people who ride in airplanes, trains, cars, and buses and who go about their daily chores without malice in their hearts, with no wish to enslave others or deny anyone the right to worship as they please.

Is the threat of terrorism being exaggerated? It is unlikely that a group of terrorists could actually conquer today's democracies, whose economic and military power is unprecedented. But threats are not only a matter of territorial conquest. They can come from people living inside our borders who are determined to use terrorism to strip away our spiritual freedoms. Ultimately, suicide bombers might be incapable of conquering countries, but they nevertheless still hope to destroy the spiritual cultures of entire nations, and they are willing to destroy themselves in order to make it happen.

There have been numerous attacks against civilians since the 9/11 strikes that destroyed the World Trade Center hit the Pentagon, and killed the passengers who fought to keep their United Airlines plane from crashing into the White House or some other strategic target. The suicidal terrorists shouted, "Allah is the greatest!" as they plunged the airliner into an open field in Pennsylvania. The purpose of the attacks? To terrorize ordinary people like us— Christians, Jews, Buddhists, Hindus, as well as moderate Muslims—hoping to force us all to eventually succumb to their fanatical version of Islamic spirituality.

Is it something nefarious about the United States that provokes terrorist attacks? Shortly after 9/11, the Kennedy School of Government at Harvard University convened a meeting of faculty and staff to discuss the attacks. I sat and listened as several of my fellow students rose to declare that American arrogance was the true culprit behind the attacks. The Twin Towers, they claimed, located in the heart of Wall Street, represented U.S. military and economic imperialist aggression, like two giant domineering phallic symbols that had to be crushed. Yet as we have seen since 9/11, there have been numerous attacks across Europe, Asia, Africa, and the Middle East itself. It is not the opposition to U.S. hegemony that fuels al-Qaeda terrorism. It is any form of spiritual freedom, however vast or limited, that so infuriates these militant Muslim fanatics. If anything, America is merely the preeminent symbol of the expansive spiritual freedom that they abhor and work to destroy.

No one is spared from the Islamist terrorists' battle to force their brand of spirituality on the rest of us. Nationality exempts no one. On July 11, 2006, a commuter train in Bombay was attacked by radical Muslim terrorists. An explosion was detonated at 6:11 in the evening, deliberately timed to go off at the height of the rush hour when the trains were crowded with passengers returning from work. The aim was to kill and wound as many unarmed civilians as possible. Seven other blasts ripped through Bombay's trains and metro stations within the next eleven minutes. "There were people lying on the tracks with no clothes, there were dismembered bodies," reported Prashant Singh, one of the passengers, "scenes too gruesome to describe." Another passenger told of how his eye had been blasted out of its socket. Other wounded passengers had to be treated for severe burns and underwent painful amputations. Nearly two hundred people died; hundreds more were injured. The point of the attack? Islamic extremists are opposed to the rule of India, an overwhelmingly Hindu country, over Kashmir, which has a majority Muslim population. Their spiritual fanaticism has triggered a politics of terror. Not only in India and the United States, but in many more civilian locations throughout the world.

On March 11, 2004, four commuter trains were bombed in Madrid, also at the height of rush-hour traffic. The trains were packed with students, low-paid workers, and recent immigrants searching for a better life. "I saw a lot of smoke, people running all over, crying," one eyewitness told the *New York Times*. "I saw part of a hand up to the elbow and a body without a head face down on the ground." When a group of terrorist suspects were tracked down by Spanish police, one of them detonated a bomb in an act of collective suicide. The aim of the attack? Political analysts believe that the murder of innocent civilians by extremist Islamist terrorists was timed to influence Spain's upcoming parliamentary elections, which did result in the victory of Jose Luis Rodriguez Zapatero as prime minister. Zapatero had earlier pledged to withdraw Spanish troops from Iraq. This time, it was a savage spirituality that fueled a politics of terror.

"War is an extension of politics by other means," wrote Carl von Clausewitz, the legendary scholar who analyzed military strategy and political diplomacy in the early 1800s. For some, terrorism is also an extension of politics by other means, but the targets are not combatants on a battlefield. The intended victims are innocent commuters, office workers, restaurant patrons, and those who find themselves at almost any other locale among large crowds of unarmed men, women, and children. The aim of the Islamist terrorists' war is open-ended. Their violence won't cease when they force one or two countries to surrender. Islamist terrorists want to impose their spiritual views on every nation on earth and will commit suicide in order to do it.

There have been suicide bombings at restaurants in Israel, mosques in Iraq, pubs in Bali, a passenger ferry in the Philippines, a wedding reception in Jordan, and numerous other places around the world, nearly all of the strikes deliberately targeting people just like us. Some of the suicide bombers have been women who use their pregnancies to divert suspicion and hide explosive suicide belts under their maternity dresses. Islamist extremists have tried to invent other ingenious methods to spread terror, such as a device containing blood tainted with HIV that could infect people with AIDS during a terrorist attack. International terrorism is ongoing, as is the constant threat of future attacks. The violence is not enough to topple the United States or any of the world's other democracies. But if the countries that are training and equipping terrorists succeed in their drive to acquire nuclear weapons, terrorist violence could one day inflict hundreds of thousands of casualties. Then, instead of using pregnant women strapped with explosives and others rigged to spread HIV-infected blood, the terrorists will be able to use the ultimate weapon against us.

Is such a catastrophe likely? After the 9/11 attacks, George Bush repeatedly warned of a possible atomic "mushroom cloud" being detonated over a U.S. city by terrorists backed by the Iraqi dictator Saddam Hussein. Weren't these warnings discredited when U.S. inspectors failed to find any nuclear bomb-making materials or other Iraqi weapons of mass destruction following the American invasion that ousted Hussein? Many people still dismiss the threat of nuclear terrorism as an unfounded fear spread by trigger-happy right-wing politicians bent on increasing American domination over Middle East oil supplies. And, one might ask, even if terrorists did manage to obtain atomic weapons, wouldn't a nuclear strike against the major Western powers or any of their allies mean national suicide for the perpetrators? Countries that have their own huge arsenals of atomic weapons, such as the United States, Great Britain, and France, would likely retaliate against nations engaged in nuclear terrorism.

"The leaders of States who would use terrorist means against us, as well as those who would consider using, in one way or another, weapons of mass destruction, must understand that they would lay themselves open to a firm and adapted response on our part," cautioned Jacques Chirac, the former president of France. "This response could be a conventional one. It could also be of a different kind." Chirac warned that any nation that might equip terrorists with an atomic bomb should not "allow any doubts to persist about our determination and capacity to resort to our nuclear weapons." The former French president is not known for his pro-American sentiments. Chirac vigorously opposed the U.S. invasion of Iraq and was a stern critic of U.S. reliance on military power in its post-9/11 fight against terrorism, which made his statement especially note-worthy and ominous.

Surely, with the clear threat of total annihilation like the one uttered by President Chirac, no country would run the risk of sending terrorists on a nuclear-armed attack. But would their total annihilation matter to them? Would Islamist extremists be willing to commit collective suicide on a national scale? What if the fanat-ical Islamic rulers believed it would serve their spiritual mission, making them all martyrs and thereby eligible for a long-awaited heavenly afterlife?

During the cold war, the Soviet Union and the United States both had enough nuclear weapons to destroy each other in less than an hour. The conflict between the two rivals lasted for nearly half a century. What prevented them from attacking each other was the policy known as mutually assured destruction, often referred to as MAD in a bit of black humor. Rulers of each country knew that any attack on the other would bring about the certain destruction of their own nation. Not wanting to commit national suicide, they continued the nuclear standoff until the Soviet Union collapsed due to its own internal difficulties, ending the cold war.

These days, there are well-armed adversaries who either possess or are seeking nuclear weapons and who do not adhere to the logic of mutually assured destruction. Sharing the mentality of the suicide bombers whom they dispatch, these nuclear-armed terrorist governments might be willing to commit national suicide—if it meant destroying the non-Muslim "infidel" cultures that they oppose. "The global infidel front is a front against Allah and the Muslims," said Hassan Abasi, a senior spiritual adviser to the extremist leaders of the Islamic Republic of Iran, "and we must make use of everything we have at hand to strike at this front, by means of our suicide operations or by means of our missiles."

Even the certain death of hundreds of thousands of their own people does not appear to be enough of a deterrent to restrain these spiritual warriors. In a speech just a few months after the 9/11 attacks, Iran's former president Hashemi Rafsanjani talked about a possible nuclear exchange with Israel and the murderous calculation that might make it worthwhile. "The use of even one nuclear bomb inside Israel will destroy everything. However, it will only harm the Islamic world. It is not irrational to contemplate such an eventuality."

Does this mean that we must fear a country whose leaders announce their willingness to absorb a nuclear strike? Regimes do come and go. Prior to Iran's takeover by Muslim militants, it was one of the most pro-Western countries in the region and had unusually good relations with Israel. Former adversaries can become partners, as has been the case with Japan and Germany, who became two of the United States' closest allies in the aftermath of their deadly confrontation during World War II. Yet whether it be Iran or Iraq or any other country that is liable to risk a nuclear exchange, might the radical Islamist suicide terrorists who are not beholden to any nation actually attack us with atomic bombs? We cannot know. But isn't it our spiritual duty to try to make sure that they do not?

History does not offer much comfort when we try to assess future threats. In 1938, Great Britain's prime minister Neville Chamberlain arrived home from Munich, waving his recently signed agreement with Adolf Hitler. He declared that it would ensure "peace for our time," only to see its terms violated a year later, plunging the two countries into a war that subjected London to months of intense bombing by the Nazi air force. The Soviet Union's president Josef Stalin likewise saw his nonaggression pact with Hitler broken when German troops unexpectedly invaded and headed toward Moscow. The Japanese attack on Pearl Harbor was also a surprise, catching the United States off guard.

Predicting the likelihood and the severity of military threats is a dangerous business, but these inherent difficulties do not mean that we should shrink from the need to try to grapple with these issues. Our spiritual values do not require that we ignore political threats or cynically dismiss them. As the terrorist bombings in New York and Bombay and Madrid have shown, our innocence does not make us immune from attack.

Spirituality may not shield us from all physical dangers, yet our positive spiritual energies may be sufficient to transform ruthless leaders into willing peacemakers. Whether these energies will be enough cannot be predicted. We do know that physical force is not always necessary. Spiritual force has its own transformational power. Finding the right mix of spiritual and physical force remains the challenge of people of goodwill everywhere. Yet for many, renouncing the use of physical force under any circumstances is considered to be the purest form of spirituality. After all, they point out, didn't Mahatma Gandhi chase the British out of India without firing a shot?

"Religion does not teach us to fight with anyone," said Ghaffar Khan, a Pakistani Muslim tribal chieftain who became an unlikely ally of Gandhi, a devout Hindu. Khan was a member of the rugged Pushtun tribe, whose legendary fierce warriors have been feared for centuries. Khan, like Gandhi, was committed to the nonviolent overthrow of British rule in India. Yet on the Indian subcontinent, Hindus and Muslims were also engaged in a bitter and long-standing conflict. Both Khan and Gandhi pushed for an eventual reconciliation between Hindus and Muslims.

"You people must remove hate from your heart[s] and remove hate from the heart[s] of others as well and love each other," Khan told his fellow Muslims. "Because religion has always come in the world for teaching love." If Khan, the leader of a tribe steeped in a tradition of warfare, could appeal to his fellow Muslims, imploring them to resist the British colonialists without resorting to violence, then should we also take the same nonviolent approach when resisting suicidal Islamic fascists, even though they have declared their terrorist intentions to overthrow the world's democracies and replace them with a global Islamic theocracy?

George Orwell, the critically acclaimed author of *Animal Farm* and *1984*, expressed his respect for Gandhi's remarkable achievement. Yet Orwell also had his doubts about the wisdom of adopting non-violent resistance in all situations and every circumstance.

In 1949, five years after the defeat of Nazi Germany, Orwell gave his reasons for doubting the effectiveness of a strict adherence to nonviolent resistance. "The assumption, which served Gandhi so well in dealing with individuals, that all human beings are more or less approachable and will respond to a generous gesture, needs to be seriously questioned," Orwell wrote. "It is not necessarily true, for example, when you are dealing with lunatics. Then the question becomes: Who is sane? Was Hitler sane? And is it not possible for one whole culture to be insane by the standards of another? And, so far as one can gauge the feelings of whole nations, is there any apparent connection between a generous deed and a friendly response?" Are the Islamist terrorist leaders insane? Who knows? More important, will they react to our spiritual generosity by agreeing to live alongside of us in peace?

Will the power of our loving spirituality, which is nourished by our awareness of inner silence, be met with a nonviolent response from the militant Muslim fascists who use suicide bombers to try to eradicate our culture of religious and political freedom? Perhaps. Will our respect for spiritual diversity be able to pacify the Islamist terrorists who are bent on imposing their repressive, archaic spirituality on all of us? We can hope that it will. But is hope enough?

It was indeed the hope of two great minds from the twentieth century, Albert Einstein and Sigmund Freud, that violence be avoided through mutual understanding and compromise. They hoped that reason and compassion would finally put an end to the wars that have plagued humanity since time immemorial. In an open letter to Freud, the father of psychoanalysis, Einstein, the great physicist, sought to get Freud's insights on why nations continue to use violence against one another.

Einstein was a Jew living in Germany. Freud was also a Jew who lived in Austria, the birthplace of Adolf Hitler. Following the Nazi takeover of Germany, which would eventually spread to Austria and beyond, both Einstein and Freud were forced to flee their native countries. In 1932, just a few months after Hitler's victory in Germany's parliamentary elections, Freud responded to Einstein's inquiry about the psychology of war and the prospects for peace.

"Any effort to replace brute force by the might of an ideal is, under present conditions, doomed to fail. Our logic is at fault if we ignore the fact that right is founded on brute force and even today needs violence to maintain it," Freud wrote in his letter to Einstein. As his analysis proceeded, Freud cautioned: "The other indirect methods of preventing war are certainly more feasible, but entail no quick results. They conjure up an ugly picture of mills that grind so slowly that, before the flour is ready, men are dead of hunger." Freud's apparent mix of conviction and despair seems to be encapsulated in his final sentence to Einstein: "Should this exposé prove a disappointment to you, my sincere regrets."

Our spirituality may be able to slowly reduce the violent militancy of today's Islamist extremists. Yet before this slow, nonviolent spiritual transformation is completed, perhaps too many of us will die from extremist religious terrorism, just like the slowly grinding mill that is unable to produce flour fast enough to feed a waiting people dying of starvation. Is the risk of our relying on a slow-moving expansion of a higher global consciousness worth taking? Should we ignore the possibility that, tragically, we may also need physical force, along with spiritual force, to protect ourselves and those around us?

It may be difficult for those of us seeking the peace of inner silence to condone the use of physical force. Yet if we must, is there at least a way to wage war without hate? "Love your enemies and pray for those who persecute you, so that you may be sons of your father who is in heaven," Jesus told us. "Because he makes his sun rise on the evil and the good, and raise on the just and the unjust." But in order to love our enemies, we have to first know who our enemies are.

We can forgive those who persecute us, since the light of God's love shines upon all of us equally. But to pretend that there are no persecutors makes a mockery of forgiveness, for it implies that there is no one to forgive.

Is it possible to love our enemies and still use physical force to resist them? A loving parent must sometimes say no to a child. A child's disruptive behavior may even require a small degree of coercion, a time-out, a light punishment. At times, even the most sensitive parent might have to resort to mild physical restraint if the child poses a threat to himself or others. To allow our children to inflict harm is not love. It is ignorance, weakness, and moral neglect. A child who lacks the boundaries of an ethical path will just wander recklessly through a wilderness of unbounded selfishness and impulsive aggression. The same goes for grown-ups who harm others and who often wind up hurting themselves as well. Although we can love them, we must still stop them.

If we must say no to our spiritual adversaries, if restraint is necessary, then we can draw upon our spiritual strengths to pursue loving ways that might keep them from harming us. Yet even the most sensitive among us can also help to strengthen the collective political will needed to physically prevent our adversaries from terrorizing us or killing us. As David Ben-Gurion, the first prime minister of Israel, said, "While it is good that there be a world full of peace, fraternity, justice and honesty, it is even more important that we be in it."

Not everyone agrees with Ben-Gurion's view that survival trumps idealism. It's not that he thought that there was nothing worth dying for, merely that there were also causes worth killing for. Perhaps Ben-Gurion was driven by the fact that his people had barely managed to dodge total annihilation. For people such as Gandhi, where the complete and utter destruction of all of his countrymen was not even a remote possibility, survival is not necessarily preferable to idealistic purity.

"Hitler killed five million Jews," Gandhi said, referring to the Holocaust that actually killed six million. "It is the greatest crime of our time. But the Jews should have offered themselves to the butcher's knife. They should have thrown themselves into the sea from cliffs." When Gandhi's biographer Louis Fischer, himself a Jew, asked, "You mean that the Jews should have committed collective suicide?" Gandhi answered, "Yes, that would have been heroism." Yet, as I once heard Maharishi observe, submitting to such violence is not actually nonviolent. It is just swapping the prevention of someone else's violent death in exchange for our own violent death. We might want to ask ourselves whether it is spiritually responsible and morally just to engage in such a bargain.

Some of us are unwilling to let others kill us or murder our friends and families. We will not agree to a spiritual bargain that keeps ruthless terrorists alive and ready to impose their brutal rule upon us so that we can adhere to an idealistic concept of pure spirituality. Yet is deadly force really the only way to stop today's suicidal killers?

Military force is not enough to stop any enemy. A transformation in the collective consciousness of the cultures that produce such fanatical enemies is also needed. When the overwhelming majority of Muslim parents and grandparents and uncles and aunts and friends and lovers condemn Islamist suicide bombers rather than praise them, the terrorists will be marginalized, pushed to the outer fringes of Islamic culture. The social and spiritual stigma of having participated in terrorist atrocities will work as a powerful force capable of radically reducing and nearly eliminating the violence associated with religious intolerance. Ultimately, the long-term solution to militant Islam must come from moderate Muslims.

Compassionate love may one day persuade today's terrorists to disarm and to stop using their religious schools to raise another generation of suicide bombers. Their peace-loving coreligionists, in union with men and women of goodwill from all nations and religions, might one day manage to convince the Islamist extremists that their own spiritual fulfillment doesn't require the elimination of another person's approach to spirituality. Perhaps they may come to accept that peaceful coexistence is a worthy goal. Maybe al-Qaeda followers will come to realize that, in the words of the former Israeli prime minister Golda Meir, a crucial step on the journey toward peaceful coexistence requires that "they love their children more than they hate us."

A compassionate consciousness can help to transform the suicidal mentality of violent intolerance into an open-minded spirituality that honors life and respects diversity. After the Allied victory over fascist Nazi Germany and Imperial Japan in World War II, a consciousness of forgiveness helped to reconstruct both countries, creating demilitarized democratic cultures that honor racial and spiritual freedom. Likewise, in today's era, we cannot battle Islamist terrorists only with bombs and bullets, because we are not only being attacked by bombs and bullets.

A war is being waged on the level of consciousness, pitting a sensibility that respects spiritual diversity and prizes a love of enemies against a dark mentality that celebrates the death of everyone who is outside a closed circle of militant religious fanatics. "The great problem is that Al Qaeda has moved far beyond being a terrorist organization to being almost a state of mind," said Simon Reeve, a writer who has carefully studied Osama bin Laden and his followers. "That's terribly significant because it gives the movement a scope and longevity it didn't have before 9/11." Physical force may be needed to prevent terrorist attacks, but a toxic state of mind can be changed only by a healing state of mind.

To effectively use the healing power of our compassion, we must unhesitatingly look at the diseased mentality of a depraved spirituality. Understanding the nature of the consciousness we wish to elevate is often aided by giving a name to it. When psychologists speak of repression, denial, and the subconscious, this ability to parcel out aspects of the human personality and assign labels to them increases our understanding of who we are. If a terrorist believes that beheading an innocent man is a spiritual act, then calling such spirituality depraved helps us to grasp the nature of his mentality.

Name calling is not always just a cheap way to challenge someone's beliefs without having to seriously engage his or her ideas. In many instances, it helps to make apparent what may otherwise seem murky, which is why "calling a spade a spade" is a saying that has been around for centuries, with its roots going as far back as ancient Greece. To call a beheading the desperate act of a persecuted man, rather than the savage result of a twisted spirituality, does not help us. Such language is not the mark of a tolerant observer who avoids being judgmental but rather indicates someone who lacks judgment. Our own spirituality of tolerance does not mean that we should avoid identifying what is clearly intolerable.

Mislabeling the terrorist mentality or refusing to name it at all may prompt us into trying to use our compassion to address the political demands of terrorists, rather than showing them that we must all behave humanely regardless of the hardships we face. Spiritual realism means that we need not be afraid to take an unflinching, clear-eyed look at spiritual terrorism. It will give us the understanding we need to more effectively focus our compassion on that which needs healing. It will help us to identify what spiritual values are merely different and which ones are obviously depraved. And by shining a light on the depravity, we may be able to open someone's eyes to the value of kindness and may shift spiritual fascism into something more life affirming.

Even if we acknowledge the depravity of the terrorist mentality, aren't its dangers merely an exaggeration pushed by right-wing, warmongering, neoconservative politicians and fundamentalist preachers? Aren't these people steeped in a fundamentalist crusade of their own, determined to reshape the Middle East so that it conforms to their own flawed view of the Bible and to make huge profits from Middle Eastern oil in the process? Aren't they using fear to manipulate people into signing on to their own intolerant agenda? And aren't they smearing the entire Muslim religion in order to assert the superiority of their own Christian faith? Are those of us who support their actions spiritual realists or spiritual dupes?

A rejection of the extremist Christian fundamentalist views that are so prevalent among certain segments of our culture need not preclude us from publicly rejecting the views of Islamist extremists. Whatever the motives of those who cite or even exaggerate the dangers of terrorism, the message of the Muslim militants is clear: convert, submit, or die.

Our choice, as spiritual seekers, is not to arrogantly assert the superiority of our own culture. We know that our nation is filled with light and shadow. Most cultures also contain similar measures of lightness and darkness. Yet if we look around the world, every day we can see darkness emerging in one of its most virulent forms: merciless terrorist attacks, rampant child prostitution, forced starvation, along with a sad myriad of other daily atrocities. These are quite different from the dark failings found in democracies that strive, yet often do not live up to, the ideals of spiritual diversity and political tolerance.

The loving spirituality of expanded consciousness thrives in a democracy. And human dignity and spiritual freedom are under constant assault by spiritual dictators around the world. An article in the *International Herald Tribune* reported that in parts of southern Turkey, women "have been stoned to death, strangled, shot or buried alive." Why? "Their offenses ranged from stealing a glance at a boy to wearing a short skirt, wanting to go to the movies, being raped by a stranger or relative, or having consensual sex." Much of the area "is poor, rural and deeply influenced by conservative Islam," the newspaper explained. One seventeen-year-old girl who fell in love with a boy received a message from her brothers and uncles. "You have blackened our name," the message said. "Kill yourself and clean our shame or we will kill you first." The reason for these killings is to preserve the honor of family members who feel stigmatized for having a sister or a daughter who deviated from their primitive view of female virtue. The remedy is to have the girl put to death. Even rape can be construed as the fault of an unchaste woman.

Turkey has outlawed such honor killings. So now, rather than having their men found guilty for murdering their dishonored sisters and daughters, parents urge the girls to kill themselves instead. What kind of spiritual values make these practices prevalent in certain cultures and virtually unheard of in our own? Are they to be granted an equal measure of respect since our own culture's values are also flawed? Or is it better not to allow our humility to become an accomplice to someone else's brutality?

Worldwide, there are approximately five thousand honor killings a year. Although this practice is on the rise in Europe, primarily within the Turkish and the Pakistani immigrant communities, in any given year these murders represent less than five ten-thousandths of a percent of the entire Muslim population. There are millions and millions of Muslims who not only do not engage in honor killings, they abhor the practice. So, as horrible as it is, aren't we exaggerating the danger of a mentality that spiritualizes murder when it is perpetrated by only a tiny fraction of the world's population. Honor killings are just one example of the spiritual darkness spreading across this planet, one that would be rife in countries where Islamist extremists were able to succeed.

An al-Qaeda spokesman, Suleiman Abu Gheith, boasted about his commitment to a more widespread murderous ideology that seeks to smother us all in a blanket of religious fascism. "America is the head of heresy in our modern world, and it leads an infidel democratic regime that is based upon separation of religion and state." He condemned the United States for "legislating laws that contradict the way of Allah and permit what Allah has prohibited." What did Gheith recommend as a penalty for our having the audacity to separate religion from government and to enact laws based on the outcome of democratic elections? "We have the right to kill 4 million Americans—2 million of them children—and to exile twice as many and wound and cripple hundreds of thousands," Gheith declared.

Like the United States, every democratic culture in the world separates church and state in order to maximize spiritual freedom. This divide not only keeps governments from establishing one state religion, but it also keeps them from adopting laws that interfere with the right to freely practice any particular religion. Freedom of religion is what al-Qaeda and its fascist Islamist fellow travelers condemn as heresy.

What they brand as heresy was the pride of America's founding fathers. "I fully and conscientiously believe, that it is the will of the Almighty, that there should be a diversity of religious opinions among us," Thomas Paine wrote in *Common Sense*, the work that inspired a generation of democratic revolutionaries to forge a new nation called America. "I look on the various denominations among us, to be like children of the same family." This spiritual diversity, championed by Paine and his fellow visionaries, is the very thing that the Islamist fascists so deeply detest.

"They hate what is best in America," wrote Bernard-Henry Levy in his study of the Islamist extremist mentality. "What they hate is democracy." Following his investigation into the beheading of the American journalist Daniel Pearl by Islamist terrorists, the noted French philosopher concluded, "They hate sexual freedom and the rights of women. They hate tolerance. They hate the separation of religion and state. They hate modernity." And, as Levy explained, "they hate it all in the name of their own purity."

The dangers of their hatred are clearly evident. We are reminded of them every time we take our shoes off before walking through a metal detector at the airport. Yet still, must the Islamist militant's hate of our spiritual diversity be met with such harsh denunciations? Can't we defend ourselves without having to condemn them? Or maybe we can even ignore them. Perhaps their declarations are mostly the hateful words of a small fringe group that is unlikely to ever garner enough followers to seriously threaten us. More people die on the highways every year than are killed in terrorist attacks, so maybe each new bold declaration of hate is just overblown dramatic rhetoric uttered by fanatics who have no real popular backing. Perhaps their hatred is a mentality without teeth, a fanciful impotent culture of death and revenge, confined to a small band of religious zealots who are incapable of seriously challenging our own spiritual freedoms. If so, why should we take their hatred seriously?

Nonie Darwish is the daughter of a famed Palestinian fighter who made cross-border raids into Israel. Her father killed nearly four hundred Israelis and wounded more than nine hundred others. After Darwish's father was killed during one of his attacks, Egypt's president Gamal Nasser honored him as a national hero and asked Darwish and her siblings a simple question: "Which one of you will avenge your father's death by killing Jews?" Darwish was just eight years old at the time. She and the other children in her family were stunned. As Darwish grew out of the culture of vengeance and death, she looked back over the years. "I witnessed honour killings of girls, oppression of women, female genital mutilation, polygamy and its devastating effect on family relations," Darwish wrote. "All of this is destroying the Muslim faith from within." More than forty years later, such official backing for the implantation of a violent and repressive spiritual mentality at such a young age is not only still with us, it is thriving. It is more prevalent than ever.

Thousands and thousands of children are attending extremist religious schools where they are being taught to loathe spiritual diversity and honor spiritualized murder to force the world into submitting to a spirituality of terror and intolerance. We cannot know how this indoctrination will affect future generations, but taking its possible consequences seriously makes it more likely that our own spirituality of kindness and compassion might find its way into the hearts of these child victims of spiritual abuse.

Many of these terrorist schools are able to proliferate so easily because even the more mainstream education throughout much of the Middle East is often limited to a set of core traditions and beliefs that are frequently unable to absorb the enormous social and political changes that are taking place in today's world.

Much of the success of extremist Islamic teachings can be traced back to the Arab world's relative isolation from the influences of modern liberal cultures. According to a *United Nations Arab Development Report*, the Arab world translates only about three hundred books a year, which is a fifth of what Greece alone translates annually. Amazingly, the entire number of books translated in the Arab world during the last eleven hundred years has only been about ten thousand, the UN reports, "almost the average that Spain translates in one year."

Without easy access to the ideas and the practices of the world's leading democracies and a true understanding of the spiritual traditions of other nations, centuries-old superstitions and beliefs often remain untouched by the moderating sensibilities of the modern age. A legacy of authoritarian rule, passed down from tribal chiefs and religious leaders, leaves little room for a free and informed debate on topics ranging from the role of women to the presence of competing faiths in an era of increasing globalization.

Is this critical view simply Arab bashing, a despicable prejudice against an entire culture, and an unfair demonization of one of the world's most popular religions? Or is it a simple reality? Such failings are not limited to any one race, nation, or religion. We in the United States have enslaved others, burned people at the stake, cheered at public hangings, and scalped our enemies. Today's terrorism may primarily be an Arab-Muslim phenomenon, but our own cultures were steeped in yesterday's terror. Perhaps they will one day be the engine of tomorrow's terror.

Yet for now, our nation's spiritual culture has evolved so that we no longer stone adulterers or practice slavery. Our spirituality is attuned to the particular circumstances of the modern age, allowing us to honor traditions while also reforming them to suit new realities. We no longer let caste, race, and gender play such significant roles in determining who gets access to spiritual masters, who can receive certain spiritual techniques, and who can teach others how to develop their own spiritual potential. We follow female priests and rabbis, divine mothers and female gurus. We see Christians meditating in Hindu ashrams and Buddhists worshipping in Jewish synagogues, not only accepting our shared spirituality but encouraging it.

There are numerous Islamic reformers working to bring ultra-conservative Muslims into the modern era. They are trying to move the Islamic worldview away from morbid and divisive teachings about the Muslim faith into a more modern understanding of the benefits of religious diversity and a shared spirituality. "Any text, including those that are Islamic, provides possibilities for meaning, not inevitabilities," wrote Professor Khaled Abou El Fadl. "If the

reader is intolerant, hateful, or oppressive, so will be the interpretation of the text. It would be disingenuous to deny that the Qur'an
and other Islamic sources offer possibilities of intolerant interpretation. Clearly these possibilities are exploited by the contemporary
puritans and supremacists. But the text does not command such
intolerant readings." Neither the Koran nor any other spiritual text
interpreted by someone steeped in our modern culture's liberal view
of spirituality would sanction the ancient brutalities championed by
today's Islamist extremists. The conflict is not with Islam itself but
with those militant extremists who seek to apply a brutish, archaic,
and distorted version of Islam.

When we are deeply settled into the quiet stillness within, it can
be jolting to think and speak about the dangers of religious dis-
tortion, bigotry, and cruelty. In our peaceful inner silence, we are
often overwhelmed by feelings of generosity, acceptance, and serenity. This contentment can even lead us into championing tolerance
of the intolerant. But spiritual realism keeps us connected to the
outer world. Should we really be tolerant of people like Abu Musab
al-Zarqawi?

An al-Qaeda leader in Iraq, Zarqawi is believed to have personally
beheaded twenty-six-year-old Nicholas Berg with a large butcher
knife. Zarqawi later released a videotape of Berg's death screams as
his knife sawed across Berg's neck so that he could publicly brag
about the beheading. Viewers were shown Berg's decapitated
head being triumphantly held aloft like a grisly trophy. His was
just one of many more similar beheadings to come. Zarqawi boasted
that "God honored us and so we harvested their heads and tore their
bodies in many places." Contrast his savage killing of the innocent
young telecommunications worker with the Old Testament proverb
"If your enemy falls, do not exult. If he trips, let your heart not
rejoice." This is the motto of nearly all those who adhere to the
liberal values of the modern age. And proud videotaped displays of
harvested heads are the flags of al-Qaeda's primitive spiritual
terrorists.

When we become accustomed to being immersed in the comfort of inner silence, it is not always so easy for us to acknowledge that fellow seekers can be dangerous adversaries. How can people who are so committed to following God's will be so deadly? Western history has shown us the numerous cruelties of the Crusaders and the Inquisition that were perpetrated in the name of religion. But to read about the religiously inspired tormentors of the past is not the same as recognizing that such people are still among us. Haven't today's seekers, regardless of the path they are on, learned by now that competing religions need not be enemies of one another? Don't they know that we would never use our own spiritual beliefs as an excuse to dominate those who do not share them, even if they tried to dominate us? Perhaps we would be wise to follow the advice of Yossi Halevi, the Israeli journalist: "Never do to others what was done to you, and never underestimate the intentions of your enemy."

Even if we have more spiritual adversaries than we care to admit, what could possibly be their ultimate intentions? Do they really despise us because our spiritual sensibility differs from theirs? Isn't there some other political or economic reason for their wrath? "Every Muslim, from the moment they realize the distinction in their hearts, hates Americans, hates Jews, and hates Christians," Osama bin Laden explained. "This is a part of our belief and our religion."

Bin Laden does not speak for all Muslims. Yet calling his cohorts Islamist fascists and terrorists is rejected by people who insist that the use of such labels is inaccurate or even racist. They charge that such terms imply that Islam itself is fascist or militant when it is merely a peaceful religion that has been hijacked by crazed extremists. Whatever we choose to call them and however twisted their view of Islam, the jihadists themselves believe that their Muslim faith is the source of their zeal and the reason for their terror.

Bin Laden boldly declared that the United States is "the worst civilization witnessed in the history of mankind." He singled out the

United States for special condemnation for not following the sharia, the Islamic law whose interpretation bin Laden reserves for himself and his fanatical allies. Bin Laden rejects the United States as a "nation who, rather than ruling by the sharia of God in its Constitution and Laws, chooses to invent your own laws as you will and desire." He extols a spirituality that embraces a death-obsessed consciousness: "Being killed for God's cause is a great honor achieved by only those who are the elite of the nation. We love this kind of death for God's cause as much as you like to live. We have nothing to fear for. It is something we wish for." Bin Laden's suicidal Muslim terrorists might have nothing to fear, but do we?

Muhammad Taqui Partovi Sabzevari was an eminent Iranian cleric who offered spiritual inspiration for the Islamic Revolutionary Guard Corps, the military wing that provides weapons and training for the Lebanese terrorist group Hezbollah. "The Almighty has promised us that the day will come when the whole of mankind will live united under the banner of Islam, when the sign of the Crescent, the symbol of Muhammad, will be supreme everywhere," Sabzevari proclaimed. "But that day must be hastened through our jihad, through our readiness to offer our lives and to shed the unclean blood of those who do not see the light brought from the heavens by Muhammad in his divinely-inspired vision. . . . It is Allah who puts the gun in our hand. But we cannot expect him to pull the trigger as well simply because we are faint-hearted." According to Sabzevari and his militant Muslim partners, it is the blood of people like you and me that is unclean, so being murdered by Islamic terrorists is the fate we deserve. In this post-9/11 era, is it smart to ignore the spiritual sickness that arises from such zealotry? Spiritual awareness can heal, but we must first realize that there is a disease in need of a cure.

We may think that our own move away from mainstream religion makes it less likely that we would be targets of today's religious warriors. After all, our spirituality transcends the distinctions that define traditional religions. There is no need to compete with us because we don't compete with anyone. Our spirituality embraces everyone, excludes no one, and welcomes all seekers, regardless of their particular faith and background. We know that the core of all religions makes us all spiritual brothers and sisters: Catholic, Protestant, Buddhist, Jew, Muslim, Mormon, Baha'i, Hindu, Sikh, whatever. Why would a religious man or woman, however moderate or militant, want to attack people who openly declare that their faith is as true as the next?

There is a popular saying among Middle Eastern Islamic extremists, "First the Saturday people, then the Sunday people." Friday is the Muslim Sabbath, Saturday is the Jewish Sabbath, Sunday is the Christian Sabbath. Muslim militants strive to first drive the Jews into submission or worse; then afterward, to do the same to Christians. Other faiths are also targets of these spiritual warlords, as witnessed by Afghanistan's Muslim fundamentalist Taliban leaders who took twenty days to destroy two giant Buddhist statues that had been carved into a cliff and that had managed to survive for nearly two thousand years before finally being felled by these religious warriors.

"The breaking of statues is an Islamic order," explained Mullah Mohammad Omar, the Taliban's supreme leader, as his acolytes carried out his religious edict to destroy the towering sacred Buddhist images. "Only Allah the Almighty deserves to be worshipped, not anyone or anything else. The statues are insulting to Islam." What of the Hindu statues of Krishna and Kali, the carved Catholic icons of Mary, or even the depictions of Jesus Christ on the cross? Apparently, spiritual diversity is an insult to Mullah Omar's perverse view of Islam. Will such people really make room for us in the spiritual universe that they inhabit?

The war cries of Islamic fascists often drown out the voices of Muslims who do believe there is room in this world for people of all faiths, whether they follow mainstream religious paths or a spirituality that transcends them. Those like the Sufi mystic Bawa Muhaiyadden work hard to show the world a more enlightened

Islam. "We are not Muslims if we discard someone saying, 'He holds another belief. He belongs to a different religion,'" he taught. "None of that matters. What we need is to be one." As for the claim that Allah puts the gun in a Muslim's hands, Muhaiyadden said, "Don't carry a sword, carry God's qualities. Don't carry a knife or a cannon, carry a heart of truth filled with God's beauty." This wisdom is the Muslim light that we can all embrace.

Muhaiyadden knows that people of God honor all paths to God. We need no protection from Muslim moderates like Bawa Muhaiyadden. It is easy to love him. We can also love bin Laden, although he boasts of a spirituality that loves death more than we love life. We can love Sabzevari, the Iranian spiritual leader, even though he urges his followers to shed the blood of non-Muslims. We can love them, but we can also resist them.

Our resistance to violent spiritual oppression does not require that we overlook our own culture's intolerance and arrogance. We do not have to be saints in order to denounce evil. No nation is perfect, including our own. Contrasting light and dark is a relative judgment. We are not pitting total purity against complete depravity. As Tony Blair, the former British prime minister, admitted when he had to reluctantly but firmly resist Islamist oppression, "In this dilemma, no choice is perfect, no cause ideal." We can acknowledge our imperfections, yet spiritual realism understands the need to resist those who threaten our evolution toward greater perfectibility. Without freedom, there can be no progress. This is not only a political reality; it is a spiritual one as well. How far would you get if you were unable to follow a spiritual path that you believed in?

Our resistance to spiritual terrorism does not mean that we have to accept whatever policies our governments might adopt. We can resist Islamist terrorism while also opposing the U.S. invasion of Iraq or any other nation that we do not believe warrants attack. We can condone the use of force to stop suicide bombings while simultaneously condemning the treatment of terrorist suspects at the

American prison in Guantanamo. We can recognize the threats posed by violent spiritual fascists and still denounce the abuses of captured fighters at the Abu Ghraib U.S. prison in Iraq. We can criticize the tapping of civilian phone calls and the surveillance of e-mails as unnecessary violations of our right to privacy without calling for the dismantling of all intelligence activities that might one day prevent another deadly terrorist attack. Although we may disagree over how best to resist Islamist terrorism, our differences need not prevent us from helping to create a collective consciousness that recognizes that some type of resistance is needed.

There are consequences for all of us when we refuse to support the resistance against spiritual fascism. Today's spiritual terrorists do not merely threaten our physical survival. They are determined to eliminate the spirituality that helps to define who we are. And if our spirituality is not worth protecting, then why is it worth pursuing?

Leon Wieseltier is an author and a literary critic who has explored the problem of determining when a war is just and why it should be fought. "Wars are not won by surviving, but by surviving as you are," he wrote. "But to survive as you are, you must believe in what you are. You must believe that you have something to lose. The hatred of all things military is a sign that you do not." For many spiritual seekers, merely surviving is not enough. It is also essential that our spirituality can thrive.

Our ability to survive physically so that we can experience the spirituality of inner silence is something that we do not want to lose. Within the boundaries of mercy and forgiveness, we may have to do what is necessary to defend ourselves. Loving kindness and firm resistance are not contradictory. When we feel secure, physically and spiritually, we can express a compassion that values restraint even in battle. Not every weapon needs to be used, not every enemy must be slain. In victory, the defeated can be shown mercy. This compassion is the hallmark of the deep-seated humanity that is expressed by all those who share our spiritual purpose, whether they be soldiers or seekers.

What is needed to ensure that both our physical and our spiritual lives can survive the onslaught by those determined to destroy them? Emotional clarity, not wishful thinking. Spiritual realism acknowledges the need to be emotionally and spiritually strong enough to accept the tragic reality that we must confront oppressive forces of darkness.

Can we be complacent in the face of our culture's continuing confrontation with spiritual darkness? "Don't you see that all these Osama bin Ladens consider themselves authorized to kill you and your children?" warned the Italian journalist Oriana Fallaci. "Because you drink alcohol, because you don't grow the long beard and use the chador or the burkah, because you go to the theatre and to the movies. Because you love music and sing a song, because you dance and watch television, because you wear the miniskirt or the shorts, because on the beach and by the swimming pool you sunbathe almost naked or naked, because you make love when you want and with whom you want." This emotional and intellectual clarity can help us develop the spiritual courage that will shake us out of a spirituality of complacency and make us strong enough to resist spiritual fascism.

What form should our resistance take? Everyone must make his or her own choice. Expanding our awareness of inner silence, coupled with our focused awareness of external tragedy, might be a powerful force capable of ushering in greater cultural understanding and spiritual harmony. Not everyone is destined to become a soldier. Yet the collective consciousness of our unified resistance to religious terrorism is enough to support both the battlefield fighter and the spiritual seeker who preaches nonviolence.

Mahatma Gandhi was a great spiritual leader. Yet he also acknowledged the purity of a soldier fighting for a just cause. When writing about the violence that most of us abhor, he spoke of moksha, which is enlightenment; the rishis, who are teachers; and the plight of Arjuna in the Bhagavad Gita.

Arjuna, a righteous warrior, was reluctant to fight against an opposing army that included members of his own clan. He pleaded with Krishna to give him guidance. "If anyone, deceiving himself, commits violence in the name of nonviolence, of course he would not attain moksha," Gandhi wrote. Yet, he explained, "It would not be right for Arjuna to think of retiring to a forest." Gandhi did not consider pacifism the highest ideal of spiritual life. "His duty was to fight and kill. Retiring to a forest may be the right course for a rishi; it was not so for Arjuna." Defending righteousness is also a spiritual act. "There is a possibility of moksha for one who commits violence," Gandhi said.

Even Gandhi, the most famous nonviolent warrior in modern history, acknowledged that committing violence for a righteous cause may sometimes be necessary when fulfilling our spiritual duty. When a soldier uses violence as a shield to protect the innocent and restore justice, then it is duty, not deception.

Gandhi's views about nonviolence were more complex than they might seem. When Gandhi said that it would have been better for the millions of Jews killed in Hitler's concentration camps to walk willingly into the gas chambers, he was calling for the renunciation of violence even if it is the only way to save ourselves. But his call for collective suicide was reserved for those who would ordinarily be unwilling to sacrifice their own lives in service of the ideal of total nonviolence. For this reason, he suggested that Jews willingly submit to their death to avoid having to kill others. When the issue was not about personal sacrifice but instead involved saving the lives of others, Gandhi's nonviolent ideal gave way to an even higher one. He believed that we should not insist that others willingly submit to death. If the innocent and the weak choose life, then it is our duty to protect them. Perhaps there should have been a more vigorous call by Gandhi's followers to protect the millions of helpless concentration camp inmates who were obliterated in the ovens of Auschwitz, Dachau, Treblinka, and the numerous other Nazi killing factories across Europe. The same for the millions who have been the victims of genocide in Cambodia, Rwanda, and Dharfur, in other times and places, then and now.

Apparently, Gandhi would have sanctioned the use of force by concentration camp inmates trying to protect the lives of Jewish children who were incapable of making an informed choice about life and death and the lives of other innocent men and women who were unwilling to embrace their march into Hitler's gas chambers. Actually, almost none of Europe's Jews used violence to defend either themselves or others from their Nazi tormentors. Only after discovering the uselessness of such restraint did the death camp survivors decide to seek refuge in their ancient homeland, where they would indeed take up arms to protect both themselves and their fellow Jews from yet another attempt at annihilation, this time in the alleyways of Jerusalem and Tel Aviv instead of the streets of Germany and Poland. Yet however nuanced the formulation, choosing which circumstances justify violence and which do not remains a challenge for all of us.

Gandhi believed that for some people, violence in service of a just war is not only necessary, it is mandatory. "Under certain circumstances," he wrote, "war may have to be resorted to as a necessary evil." Although nonviolence is the preference of gurus and saints, sometimes there is no choice. "Even if we believe in nonviolence, it would not be proper for us to refuse, through cowardice, to protect the weak," Gandhi explained. "I might be ready to embrace a snake, but, if one comes to bite you, I should kill it and protect you."

If the poisonous snakes of a toxic spirituality are coming to bite us, and if we are not soldiers like Arjuna, whose duty is to fight on the battlefield, then can't we at least offer our spiritual support to those who are willing to protect us and our families, friends, and neighbors?

Maharishi also cites the Bhagavad Gita to explain why our spiritual duty sometimes compels us to support the use of physical force. "The event of war is a natural phenomenon," he wrote. "It is a process of restoring the balance between the negative and positive forces of nature. To rise to the call of a war to establish righteousness is to respond to the cosmic purpose." Maharishi acknowledged that it is not everyone's role to become a soldier, a kshatriya, for whom fighting is just and natural. Establishing "righteousness for the good of the world is the most glorious and justifiable way of fulfilling the life of a kshatriya," Maharishi insisted. "The kshatriya who does not accept a just fight wavers from this natural stream of evolution."

All fighters may see their cause as just, especially the militant Muslim terrorists who are willing to commit suicide to impose their harsh version of extremist Islam on all of us. We must look into our own hearts to determine whether our cause is just. Although, like our adversaries, we are not perfect, the question remains: are our aims righteous? If they are, we must decide what our spiritual duty is to help ensure that they are fulfilled.

When faced with the task of restoring balance between the negative and the positive forces in nature, we must decide whether we are willing to use our spiritual power to help resist negativity and whether we are ready to support those who are prepared to use military power to protect us and to risk their lives while doing so.

The decision to support the use of military force to settle disputes is a painful one. "Weapons are the tools of fear; a decent man will avoid them except in the direst necessity and, if compelled, will use them only with the utmost restraint," the *Tao Te Ching* tells us. The righteous soldier knows that peace is the ideal, and that he must have compassion for the foes of peace even if he is forced to fight them. "His enemies are not demons, but human beings like himself. He doesn't wish them personal harm. Nor does he rejoice in victory. How could he rejoice in victory and delight in the slaughter of men? He enters a battle gravely, with sorrow and with great compassion as if he were attending a funeral." Spiritual realism dictates that we, too, must enter all battles reluctantly and with great sorrow, always remembering that our enemies are not demons, and that our love for them keeps us from rejoicing in our victories and their deaths.

Our willingness to love those who wish to harm us makes us reluctant warriors. Our compassionate spirituality makes us eager to use any option, other than military force, that might realistically protect our spiritual diversity and our existence as a free people.

Theodore Roosevelt, the tough American president who won the U.S. Congressional Medal of Honor for his battlefield bravery and who was also awarded the Nobel Peace Prize, is known for the saying "Speak softly, but carry a big stick." Sometimes, when spiritual force is not a viable option, the mere threat of physical force is enough to keep the peace. Yet whether we actually use force or threaten to use force, the spiritual calm and confidence that arise from inner silence allow us to resist our enemies without having to hate our enemies.

Can we really passionately resist our adversaries without drawing upon our hatred of them? Aren't rage and revulsion the ingredients we need to sanction the use of force? During a frightening encounter in Shanghai, I saw that we can love our enemies without having to deny that indeed they are our enemies. And I learned how it was possible to resist them without hating them.

One day, as I was walking along a Shanghai main street dotted with exclusive hotels and expensive shops, I was approached by a well-dressed Chinese man who asked me to visit his new nightclub to see whether it would appeal to American tourists. It was in the middle of the afternoon, so my guard was down. Nevertheless, I told him no several times, explaining that I rarely visited nightclubs so I would be of little use in assessing their appeal to American tourists or anyone else. The man persisted, hurriedly following me and talking quickly, imploring me to take a fast look inside his club. I continued walking, shaking my head no, heading for the Shanghai waterfront.

When he pointed out his club, which was across the street from a luxury hotel, I figured it was a safe neighborhood, so I gave in and agreed to check it out for a few minutes. I walked into a beautifully decorated dining room, with a vast area filled with small tables. Even though it was supposed to be a nightclub, the room was packed with Chinese businessmen eating lunch and chatting with associates. My host led me into a side room, sliding open the traditional Chinese rice paper doors painted with red figures, exotic birds, and colorful flowers. I entered the small room and sat down comfortably on a large cushioned sofa. There was an ornate brown coffee table just in front of the couch. Chinese artwork had been tastefully hung along the walls. At the other end of the room was a television set connected to speakers, with a microphone sitting on top.

My host politely asked whether I would like something to drink. "Just a Coke," I told him. He quickly returned with the drink, along with a large platter of cashews, almonds, sunflower seeds, and tiny pretzels, delivered by a pretty young Chinese waitress. My host quickly left. The waitress sat down beside me on the couch, asking in broken English whether I would care for another drink or more snacks. She made small talk as I impatiently waited for my host to return. After waiting for quite a while, I began to get even more restless and asked the waitress several times to find out when he was coming back. She just sat there politely, then suddenly asked whether I liked karaoke. "I guess so," I shrugged, wondering why she had asked, yet still eager to leave and continue my afternoon walk along Nanjing Road to the Shanghai waterfront.

The young waitress turned on the television, picked up the microphone, and knelt on the floor close beside me. She began to sing an innocent love song in a lovely voice as beautiful images of the Chinese countryside slowly floated across the TV screen. She then snuggled closer and began rubbing my thighs. Realizing where this was going, I stood up and told her I really had to leave. "No," she said nervously. "Please." She was obviously afraid of something. "You don't want to stay with me?" she asked pleadingly. "No, that's alright," I answered. "You are a pretty girl, but I have to leave now." Her fear intensified. "Will you tell them you stayed with me?" I told her that she was attractive and spoke English quite well, and that I was sure she could get a job working for an American company in Shanghai as a receptionist or a translator. "You will tell them you were with me?" she persisted. I warned that she was in a dangerous business, that there was a risk of getting AIDS, and that she should be careful. My paternal instincts were aroused as her fear deepened.

Finally, my host returned. I stood up and told him that I had to go. "Yes," he replied crisply. "I will get check." A few moments later, he walked back into the room and handed me a bill for more than $2,000. I laughed. "This is the most expensive Coke I have ever had," I joked, assuming the bill was actually 20.00 Chinese yuan, which would have been worth only about $2.50, not $2,000.

No, my host insisted. "It is two thousand American dollars!" I stood up abruptly. "I have to go," I said, walking toward the door. "Here is all you get." I stuck five dollars in his hand as I got closer to the door. Suddenly, a couple of men entered. Then a third one came up behind them and pushed his way toward me, blocking my exit. He was a large, powerful man, nothing like the typical small-framed Chinese men whom I usually encountered. "You pay!" the big one said, practically shoving up against me as he stared menacingly into my eyes. "This is not right," I insisted. "I am not paying two thousand dollars!" Obviously the club's bouncer, the big guy edged even closer and looked straight down at me. Clenching his teeth and almost raising his fist, he demanded, "You pay!"

I sat back down and explained that I was a professor, not a businessman, and that I didn't carry that much cash with me. "You can come to my hotel," I suggested. "I can give it to you there." They were too smart for that flimsy ploy, knowing that hotel security would apprehend them. After I showed them my open wallet, which had only about $40 in it, the bouncer seemed furious. After much haggling and increasing threats, I pulled some bills from my shoe, which was my customary hiding place to avoid getting pick-pocketed when traveling through certain foreign countries. "This is all I have," I said, reluctantly handing the ringleader about $200. Seeing me pull the bills from my shoe, he believed that I was not carrying any more cash, which was almost true. I also had a few bills hidden in my socks, just in case. Paranoia or precaution? This time the answer was obvious.

The bouncer pushed me out the back door. The chief thug in charge handed me a couple of dollars for cab fare. A taxi was already waiting in the alleyway with the engine running. They pushed me into the car and the taxi sped away. After traveling a few blocks, I demanded that the driver stop and let me out. He refused. As he slowed down to make a turn, I opened the door and jumped out. I then hurried back toward the club, stopping at the front entrance. There was a policeman directing traffic right outside. I was soon approached by a man who asked, "You want girl?" He pointed to a group of young prostitutes lingering half a block away from me. I shook my head no. "You want two girls?" he asked. Again, I declined. "Three girls?" he offered. "I never take less than a dozen," I joked. I then got serious. "Do you know who owns that club?" I asked, pointing to the entrance behind me. "No," he insisted. "I not know." I looked at my watch. "Then it's too bad for him," I said. "Because if he doesn't come out in five minutes, I go to state security."

In China, there are two levels of law enforcement: the regular police and the much-feared state security officers. "I am a guest of the Party," I told him, referring to the Communist officials who had invited me to discuss a possible educational joint venture. "I don't go to him," I said, pointing to the policeman directing traffic. "I go to state security." I held my hand like a gun, pointing my finger to my head and then wiggling my thumb as if pulling the trigger. "Bullet in the back of the head. Not him," I repeated, looking at the traffic cop. "I go to state security." I looked at my watch. "The owner has five minutes. I am a guest of the Party. I will go to state security." I again used my hand to imitate a gun pointing at my head.

Chinese state security will execute someone not only for the crime of trying to challenge Communist Party rule. They will shoot a prisoner merely for embezzling funds, making an example of him to root out corruption. The families of those killed by a gunshot to the head are often charged for the cost of the bullet.

When I threatened to report the nightclub owner to state security, cell phones started ringing on the street. The pimp who assured me that he did not know who the nightclub owner was suddenly began talking nervously on the phone. He looked up at me, and I looked back down at my watch. "Five minutes!" I shouted. "Then I go to state security." I figured that since the club owner dared to rob me in the middle of the day, with a policeman standing right outside the club, the traffic cop could not be trusted. Maybe he was being paid off by the owner to look the other way. Plus, the man was illegally pimping his hookers in plain sight. The policeman could not be trusted, and state security offered me the ultimate threat.

A man soon emerged from the club, surrounded by an entourage of shady characters. I guessed that he was the club manager. My original host was not with them; he was probably out prowling for another victim. "What is problem?" he asked in broken English. "I want my money back," I demanded. "No money," he claimed. "Then I go to state security," I replied. "Come inside club and I give you money," he promised. I was not about to go back into the place. I pointed to a McDonald's across the street. "Bring my money and I'll meet you in the McDonald's," I told him. "Okay, okay, okay," he stammered, walking back toward the club. "And bring the girl!" I shouted. "Why you want girl?" he wondered. "Just bring my money and the girl, or I go to state security," I demanded. "Okay, okay," he said. "I bring girl."

I waited at the McDonald's. The club manager arrived quickly with a colleague, along with the girl who had sung karaoke while propositioning me. She could not have been much older than twenty, if that old. We all sat down. The manager asked how much money had been taken from me. "More than four hundred dollars," I told him. It was closer to $200, but I suspected there would be some bargaining. I was right. "Too much," he said. "I give fifty dollars." I shook my head. "No," I insisted, "four hundred dollars." He become edgy, frustrated. I smiled. "You steal from me, and now you want to negotiate about how much you want to give me back."

After some more haggling, we settled for somewhere around $180, just shy of what was stolen from me. "And I want the girl," I told him. "Why you want girl?" he asked, somewhat shocked. I then leaned over to the young girl and looked closely into her eyes. "If you want to go away from this place, I will take you," I promised. "They won't hurt you." "Yes," she said, starting to cry. "I want to go. I did not know they are bad man. I come from small village. I work for tuition, for school. I did not know they bad man."

As I got up to leave, the two thieves laughed and asked me whether I wanted to go drinking and dancing with them at some nightclubs. "We like you," the manager said sincerely. "We like you," his compatriot agreed. "We have good time together," the manager promised. "We show you town, many clubs." I laughed. "I don't think so," I said. "Why?" the manager asked, as if startled. "You steal from me and then you want to go drinking with me?" I said with obvious amusement. I then told them that they had a nice club, and that there was no need to steal from customers. "Many Americans will want to go to your club. You don't have to steal from them. If you don't steal, you will make more profit."

I then left McDonald's with the girl and we walked down the street, almost arm in arm. "I from small town," she told me again, still upset. "I not know they bad man. I work for tuition." I asked whether she had some place to stay. She said she had a brother who had just arrived in Shanghai. He was staying at a hotel not far from where we were. "I will take you there," I said. As we walked toward the hotel, I offered to pay her tuition, not knowing whether anything she had told me was even true. "No," she said. "You good man. I no want money. You good man." I tried to convince her to let me pay for her tuition, but she kept refusing.

"Is there anything I can give you?" I asked the girl. "I want to help you." She stopped and looked at me thoughtfully. "You send me fashion magazine," she shyly suggested. "Fashion magazine from America." She jotted down her address and handed it to me. I was struck by her declining the money in favor of a *Cosmopolitan* or *Vogue* magazine. This reduced my suspicions. However, I was still unsure about what awaited me when we arrived at her brother's hotel. Sure enough, when we did arrive, her brother happened to be standing outside the hotel. He greeted his sister with a big smile and a bigger hug. After several more embraces, she began to speak in Chinese. She must have told him how I helped her because the brother soon began vigorously shaking my hand, nodding his head yes several times to convey his gratitude.

I then walked back to my hotel, pleased that I had threatened to use force to retrieve my money and release the young girl from forced prostitution. All the while, I had had little disdain for my adversaries, although they had to be stopped. I felt that their offer to tour the local nightclub scene and party with them was actually sincere, though bizarre. They could see that my determination to seek justice and to threaten them with violence in order to get it did not prevent me from relating to their humanity. Perhaps it was easier since it would have been China's state security imprisoning them and not myself. It might have been easier for me to forgive since I would not have been the one who was forced to strike them. And the danger I faced was nothing like those on a battlefield, during a police raid to stop an armed robbery, or during an operation by undercover agents to foil a terrorist plot. Perhaps hate is necessary in those instances. I couldn't know.

I wondered whether it was possible to personally wound or kill an enemy without having to hate him. Was my confrontation in Shanghai tense? Absolutely. Did I feel physically threatened? Certainly. Was I really willing to ask state security to use force to set things right? Probably not. I did not want the thugs to wind up shot in the back of their heads. But I did want to see justice done. I was eager to use coercion to ensure that it was achieved and to see physical force used if it was needed to free that helpless young girl.

I realized that threatening to have others do the wounding or the killing might have made it easier for me to leave room in my heart for compassion and understanding. Can we really love our enemies even when we might have to personally use physical force to resist them? I hoped so, but I was not sure—until Eliyahu McLean introduced me to Yoav, one of his friends in Israel. Yoav is a spiritual seeker who believes in the stabilizing peace that inner silence offers. Yet Yoav had also served his country as a tough army solder in the Israeli Defense Forces. He was willing to take the lives of enemies threatening to take his own and to destroy those around him.

Yoav was also a committed environmentalist. When driving across Israel, he insisted that I boycott the most direct roads in protest against his government's defacement of the pristine desert. Yoav embraced a spirituality that revolves around the attainment of higher states of consciousness. He attended the Friday night gatherings at the Tel Aviv beach, where throngs of meditators and spiritual seekers danced to the beat of traditional Indian drums. They chanted and celebrated under the evening sky in honor of the profound healing consciousness that they so fervently desired after living in a country that has seen nothing but war for more than sixty years.

As we drove through the Israeli countryside, I asked Yoav whether he was able to fight his enemies without having to hate them. He recalled how he had been assigned to the volatile Israeli occupied territories on the West Bank, patrolling the cramped alleyways to root out Palestinian suicide bombers who tried to cross the border into Israel proper. The terrorists were on their way to blow themselves up on buses and in hotel lobbies, restaurants, train stations, and wherever else large gatherings of helpless unarmed civilians might be found.

Sometimes he had to shoot, Yoav confessed. To do that, he needed to hate them. He needed his hate so that he could feel the rage he needed in order to shoot. I asked Yoav whether there was no alternative. He explained that once the threat is over, you do not have to keep the hate inside of you. You should let it go. Then you can return to the love you have for everyone, including your enemy.

"Fear and joy, it's like a circle," Yoav said. "Both contraction and expansion, like the beating of a heart, are needed. To only have expansion is not life. The key is not to get stuck in the contraction, in the fear, or the expansion, the joy. Instead, keep them moving, flowing, like a circle." This circle represents the flow of thought, emotion, and action in the external world. "We can also be aware of the still point in the center of the circle," Yoav said. This center is the silent stillness of our inner world that transcends all movement.

Expansion and contraction, they are the natural cycles of everyday life. Some of us may even have to contract with fear, so that we can draw upon the energy that comes from rage, which gives us the strength to physically protect our lives. "Don't let the fear stop you. Be careful," an Israeli taxi driver had told me, referring to the suicide bombers who attacked Israeli buses, stores, and cafes. "But travel on the buses, go to the cafes. Don't let them stop you, don't change your plans." The strength of his anger rose, along with his courage. "You win by living." His rage gave him strength, although it appeared that his hatred was a constant. Instead of moving into compassion when the immediate danger passed, it seemed as if he always felt at risk, so his anger and resentment rarely gave way to tolerance and understanding. A return to inner silence is what can give us the inner calm that allows us to let go of past fears and lingering hate.

This determination to continue living an ordinary life despite the fear was also shared by Ya'qub Ibn Yusuf, the owner of Olam Qatan, the largest New Age bookstore in Jerusalem. Ya'qub, however, was clearly someone who managed to move between compassion and resistance in a cycle of contraction and expansion.

After I bought some books at his store, Ya'qub invited me to lunch. We went right next door, to Café Hillel. As we talked about fear and spirituality, he mentioned to me that we were sitting in the same café that had been attacked by a suicide bomber the previous summer, killing seven people and wounding more than fifty others. Among the dead were Dr. David Appelbaum, the head of the emergency room at Shaare Tzedek Hospital, and his twenty-year-old daughter, Nava, who was to be married the following day. Ya'qub was careful, but, like the taxi driver, he, too, was not going to let fear stop him from living a normal life, which included having his lunch at the usual place just next to his bookstore, the site of a recent suicide bombing.

As I ate with Ya'qub at the Café Hillel, I felt a bit unnerved. I reassured myself that most likely, lightning would not strike twice in the same spot. If the café had already been bombed once, what were the odds that the same place would be struck again? A few years later, my logic proved flawed. At Falafel Rosh Ha'ir, a popular falafel stand in Tel Aviv, suicide bombers attacked twice in four months.

In Israel, almost no one appeared fearful. Nearly everyone seemed to be going about his or her business with a dignified, defiant normalcy. Yet I sensed a subtle fear lurking beneath the surface. Even when I was strolling along the Tel Aviv beachfront on a sunny afternoon, fear lingered in the warm summer air. One day I stopped by a tiny fast-food place just a few yards from the beach to grab a Coke. As I was about to enter, I was immediately blocked by a young security guard. He was lounging out front but was quick enough to check beach bags and purses to prevent a suicide bomber from carrying explosives inside.

The country's overarching fear is enough to make people see potential enemies even when they are in the midst of the most innocent situations. Suspecting that the odd loner might be planning an attack rather than just lingering to enjoy the ocean breeze, the young guard, who seemed to be lazily hanging out at the fast-food doorway, was ever vigilant. I felt my heart contract as he eyed me suspiciously. As I settled into the country, I became even more careful, avoiding buses because I could and making sure that in the middle of large crowds, there were no unattended packages that might be holding bombs instead of gifts. The Israelis, though, insisted on normalcy. At one dance club I attended, the young crowd refused to post the usual security guards out front. The kids almost seemed to be daring the terrorists to keep them from living their lives freely and innocently.

As Yoav had explained, when the fear is over, we can let joy and love flow back in. And while the fear and joy ebb and flow, the enduring stillness within centers us. It is what enables us to make peace with the changing cycles of positive and negative energies. Inner silence is also what calmed me as I continued to sip Cokes at sidewalk cafés and dance at places that were frequently targeted by people intent on terror.

Love, fear, joy, rage, compassion—the cycles of life. These are the circular movements of the outer world, like the natural cycles of the inner world, where distractions take us out of silence, and our expanding awareness brings us back into silence. And so it goes, as Kurt Vonnegut would say.

Aaron Wolf, an American serving in the Israeli army, described a similar experience of the cycles of anger and compassion. "When you are attacked, you think of nothing," he wrote. "Then I strike hard. But at night, when I can think about what happened, it bothers me." As the *Tao Te Ching* explained, a righteous warrior does not rejoice in victory. "How could he rejoice in victory and delight in the slaughter of men?" After the battle ends, whether in victory or defeat, the rage he needed to fight subsides, allowing for love and compassion to reappear.

"There are the times when matters become so tangled that war is unavoidable," wrote Pandit Rajman Tigunai, a spiritual leader from the Himalayan Institute whose teachings come from a five-thousand-year-old lineage of spiritual masters. "Winning the war is only part of the mission. After the victory, it is crucial to find a way to restore harmony and justice." The way to restore harmony is through spiritual love. And our ability to love and to forgive is strengthened when we return to the peaceful silence within us all.

What if the world does not want to make peace with us? Sometimes force or the threat of force is needed to save lives. There is no contradiction. Just as there are times when a surgeon must cut off a limb to save a patient, there are times when we must use force to end the use of force. It is a tragic reality, worthy of our despair. But our spiritual realism must be strong enough to resist oppression and resilient enough to return us to compassionate acceptance once our resistance has ended.

There may be conflict between light and dark on this planet. Yet in our despair we can also rejoice, for light is more powerful than darkness, and love outlasts hate.

Chapter 14

SHIFTING INTO AN ACTIVE
ENLIGHTENMENT

L ight is more powerful than darkness. Silence is more powerful than light. Love is more powerful than silence. An active awakening is more powerful than a passive awakening. What is a passive awakening? It is the personal immersion in inner silence, to the exclusion of almost everything else. What is an active awakening? It is the application of inner silence in everyday life, which fulfills the purpose of enlightenment.

The purpose of our enlightenment is more than just the presence of inner silence. There is a saying in politics, "Peace is more than the absence of war." Once the shooting stops, new political realities can be created. Former adversaries can start to trade with one another, exchanging ideas as well as products and developing new alliances. The peace that follows war can create more constructive interactions among different cultures, making the world more harmonious and political life more fulfilling. Our awakening is more than the absence of our personal suffering. It can help to reduce the suffering of others as well.

Once we become awakened, new spiritual energies can be activated, which can make the world around us more harmonious and our spiritual lives more fulfilling. Just experiencing silence itself does not create anything new, other than our own personal pleasure. When we are passively immersed in inner silence, we can peacefully pass the time remaining silent and still, with no need to do or even say anything. Perfect monks in a perfect world. Yet the world is not peaceful, and we have no choice other than to live amid the conflict. Actively taking our silence into the world can create moments of quiet understanding that can help to reduce the conflict.

Khalid Abu Osama, the Palestinian taxi driver who took me to his home on the West Bank of the Jordan River, knows something about conflict. Apart from whatever spiritual stillness he might manage to experience, physical threats and humiliations are still a daily reality for him. Our passive awakening does little to help make his life less frightening. Yet our active awakening can help to make him feel more encouraged.

Khalid's life is a struggle because his hometown of Bethlehem, the birthplace of Jesus, was the home of numerous suicidal terrorists. Their terrorism, directed at unarmed Israeli men, women, and children, prompted Israel to create a circle of security that has often made this sacred place a virtual prison. Virtually nothing could move in or out of the city without having to pass an Israeli checkpoint manned by tough, cynical soldiers armed with clubs, tear gas, and guns. They were ready to target anyone who might have the slightest resemblance to an enemy. And for these Israelis, many Palestinians on the West Bank fit that description. It is difficult and tragic because many West Bank residents are potential enemies.

Apparently harmless young women may turn out to be lethal, such as twenty-one-year old Andalib Suleiman al-Taqatiqah, who was reported to have been pregnant when she blew herself up to kill

Israelis. Even elderly grandmothers can be killers in disguise, such as sixty-four-year-old Fatma Omar An-Najar, who strapped explosives under her dress for detonation in an Israeli city. Without knowing who is deadly and who is not, Israelis often see their innocent Palestinian neighbors as potential suicidal murderers, making peaceful coexistence nearly impossible.

So the average hardworking Palestinian family man like Khalid, who spends his days in a city under siege, may wind up seeking desperate refuge in the brutally defiant Islamist terrorist group Hamas, lured by promises of liberation and relief. Nearly all Jews become his enemy, turning a local conflict into a larger religious war. This religious clash has metastasized into a global one, pitting Islamist extremists like al-Qaeda and their Hamas sympathizers against all non-Muslims and even against other fellow Muslims whose version of Islam they oppose.

Yet when our awakening is active, then our own experience of inner silence is carried into this troubled world, helping us to make heartfelt connections with potential enemies like Khalid and generate a shared calm that may one day expand into a generation of peace. A deep pervading silence is more than a luxury solely experienced in spiritual workshops and remote hilltop ashrams and living rooms. It can be activated so that even a proud and pained Muslim man like Khalid can reveal his humanity to someone like me, a Jew in the midst of Arab Palestine, as we ride together through the streets of Christian Bethlehem.

After I ate lunch at his home and we visited King Herod's ancient fortress, Khalid drove me through the streets of Bethlehem toward the Israeli security checkpoint that would lead me out of town. The language between us was just a smattering of broken English, yet the soothing silence we shared was palpable, as if it could be held in our hands, as if the stillness we experienced in that remote ancient desert ruin had followed us back into the world.

When we turned onto the main road, Khalid quietly drove past dozens of shops bolted shut in the once-thriving city made a ghost town by pilgrims and tourists too afraid to visit. Then, suddenly, a throng of young Palestinians broke through our silence, nearly throwing themselves onto the windshield. They ran alongside the slowing car, flailing their hands through my open window as they dangled beads and plastic icons of the Virgin Mary and an assortment of cheap Bethlehem souvenirs, yelling at me, pleading with me, urging me to buy a few things, anything, something.

Unrelenting, these Palestinian youngsters continued to run alongside the car as Khalid carefully drove by them. Some were barely out of their teens and many others were already in their twenties, perhaps even older. They poked and wagged and shouted out their paltry prices, continually bargaining while I gave no sign of buying. As I kept shaking my head no, their smiles gave way to frustration and then their faces quickly returned to cheerfulness. They had been well trained in the art of selling, in which you refuse to let the gloom of repeated rejection stop you from trying to close a deal.

No longer able to let this poor mass of humanity move past me without a sale, I reached into my pocket and began to hand out bills. I felt uncomfortable, as if I were some grand poohbah dispensing alms. I declined to take their trinkets in return for my cash, having neither need nor desire to accumulate brass saints and key-chained crosses and unwilling to turn the poignant moment into a business transaction.

The dozens of outstretched hands were left behind as Khalid slowly drove the car out of the city. We sat in silence. Not an awkward silence, but a warm, soothing silence. Although I still felt somewhat glum, I was comforted by my act of charity. As I lingered in my gratification, I looked over at Khalid, expecting an appreciative nod at my having done a good deed. Instead, I saw tears in his eyes.

I said nothing, letting Khalid have his quiet weep. There was no self-pity, not a hint of anger in him. His cry was pure. He was entitled to his tears. Khalid wiped his eyes, shook his head slightly, then turned toward me. "What we've become," he sighed. "Like beggars." He dried his eyes with a flick of his wrist. This tough Bedouin, an heir to generations of proud desert tribesmen, tilted his head and looked toward his bleak horizon.

In our shared silence and through his tears, Khalid had confided in me. In that profoundly silent moment, we were both just present. We shared a truth, its sorrow, and perhaps even some hope. The hope that comes when silence is active, enabling us to connect to each other. Khalid and I were strangers separated by land, religion, income, race, and centuries of tradition, yet our sinking into silence slowed time and bridged differences. In the quiet stillness beyond words, there we sat, both connected to the same life that can weigh all of us down, yet experiencing the same silence that lifts us all up.

The openness that we were able to share in the midst of a city brimming with terrorist anger and defensive aggression came from a simple experience of silence—not the passive kind that emerges only when we are comforted by the security of loving teachers and safe places, but an active silence that is present even when we are surrounded by the clamor of conflict.

Spirituality is not about detachment or separation from the unpleasant and the painful. Awareness of the silent presence within doesn't require withdrawal. The beauty of inner silence is that its calming stillness helps to connect us to everything and everyone, in every place. We can make peace with the world because we are in it and not hiding from it. We can even help the world become a little more peaceful because we are actively bringing our peace into it.

Detaching ourselves from the world is a form of maya. The Sanskrit term *maya* is commonly used to describe the illusions that veil spiritual truths. It is a state of mind that mistakes a changing superficial reality for a more profound one that does not change. Those in maya do not realize that the only thing that does not change is silence.

Typically, maya refers to the condition where people link their self-images to the changing circumstances of their lives—money, status, beauty, power, success—not realizing that these are fleeting. A liberated self-image comes from the realization that we are more than the changing circumstances that we find ourselves in. The core of our being is the spiritual stillness within and the loving kindness that emerges from this inner silence. Those in maya see their worldly accomplishments as lasting achievements that can give their lives true meaning. Yet since all of these feats are impermanent, ever subject to change, and always shifting, those of us who are fooled by maya frequently become lost in a swirl of disappointment and despair. Maya is the illusion that life's external circumstances can offer us permanent happiness. Yet maya can also be something else.

Believing that happiness comes from detaching ourselves from external circumstances is also a form of maya. An active awakening embraces all of life, both inner and outer. The maya of a passive awakening sees the external world as a reality that we should ignore because it is always changing, thus not worth getting too involved in. This vision of spiritual detachment is an illusion created by a spirituality of denial.

Although the peaceful silence within us cannot be changed, when we can actively carry our silence into the outside world, with eyes open, we help to change that which can be changed. Life around us can be made more peaceful because we are more at peace.

When we break through the maya that believes that developing a higher state of consciousness requires us to detach ourselves from the world, we awaken to the fullness of a life that values all of existence: the inner world of silence and the external world that can be nourished by silence. Inspired by silence, we speak. Anchored in stillness, we act.

What acts are most inspired by silence? The cosmic mission of our awakening is to love more fully. Rather than confining ourselves to the passive experience of silence, when we actively take our calming inner silence out into the world, our quiet loving kindness unlocks hearts naturally, without effort, fulfilling what the gurus call dharma—the purpose of our lives.

An active awakening that gives to others is dynamic, purposeful, healing. How much can we really give to the world? If our awakening is passive, not much, since our spiritual life is also passive, uninvolved, almost uncaring. When we sit back and do nothing but experience inner stillness, nothing much changes on the outside. Satisfied with our own inner lives, we add little else to the lives of others. Afraid of humanity's dark side, we retreat into a preoccupation with the supposedly perpetual pleasures of spiritual perfection and justify our passivity by calling it enlightened detachment.

Even the enlightened recluse does something. Actively awakened people use inner silence to offer kindness to all living things. The inner spiritual peace that they experience makes them less dependent on others and more giving. They need nothing but their love to survive, and sharing that love is joyful. Although they may be secluded in remote jungles, their awakening is active. They quietly walk the land, radiating the harmonious energies that emanate from their inner silence. At peace with the world, they still work to bring peace to the world. They may spend most of their time living away from this world of conflict, yet they often serve others by regularly welcoming seekers, making pilgrimages through sacred lands, appearing at holy places, generously calming whomever they pass, reassuring the fearful, empowering the helpless, and loving the loveless. They are saints because they behave in a saintly manner.

Spiritual love is what makes our awakening worth attaining. Our contact with inner silence frees us to love more freely, more often, whether we are facing tragedy or not. Our wealth and health may waver, our belief systems may change, all things come and go, yet our spiritual love remains. As St. Paul explained, "Love never ends. As for prophecies, they will pass away. As for tongues, they will cease. As for knowledge, it will pass away." Our love does not pass away. It can survive each generation. The love that we express can continue to exist, as long as human beings continue to exist.

Our spiritual love, activated by our own awakening and uniquely expressed by each of us, can affect future generations. The people we love pass along their feelings to their children, and to their children's children, and onward. "Is it true, that your love traveled alone through the ages and worlds in search of me?" wrote the Indian poet Rabindranath Tagore. "That when you found me at last, your age-long desire found utter peace in my gentle speech?" The profound spiritual love that human beings express can move across the universe, through the infinity of time and space, influencing others in a chain reaction of loving kindness that is passed along from one person to the next in each subsequent generation. The love my parents felt was given to me, which I passed along to my children, who will give it to theirs. Our loving energies, fueled by our awareness of inner silence, flow across the planet, bringing peace and happiness to whomever they reach.

The active expression of spiritual love makes us worthy of our awakening. Isn't love the one unique thing that we can add to a world of endless change? Civilizations rise and fall, today's inventions are replaced by tomorrow's discoveries, people die as others are born. Yet had we not lived, we would not have been able to contribute our unique expression of love to this creation. Love is our spiritual legacy, fulfilling the purpose of our awakening.

We are here to love one another. The peaceful confidence we feel from the silence within enables us to be more giving. We are more fully able to support, teach, guide, create, reassure, and inspire others. When our awakening becomes more active, we can bring our generous spirit into the world and help to change lives. "As a rule there are in everyone all sorts of good ideas, ready like tinder," wrote Albert Schweitzer, the great humanitarian doctor who spent years healing the suffering victims of disease throughout Africa. "But much of this tinder catches fire, or catches it successfully, only when it meets some flame or spark from outside, i.e., from some other person. Often, too, our own light goes out, and is rekindled by some experience we go through with a fellow-man. Thus we have each of us cause to think with deep gratitude of those who have lighted the flames within us."

Silence exists with or without us, but love cannot exist unless we express it. Love needs to be shown, given, felt. Like inner silence, love can always be accessed. The nature of love is compassion. And we can choose to be compassionate anywhere at any time. For this reason, startling acts of kindness can be found in unexpected places.

The unexpected once took place in Istanbul, Turkey, where conflicts among Kurds, Turks, Armenians, Jews, and Muslims have periodically erupted in bloody violence. A few years ago, a twenty-two-year-old member of a terrorist cell called the Great Eastern Islamic Raiders' Front joined a fellow suicide bomber in an attack against two synagogues, killing more than twenty people and wounding hundreds of others. The *New York Times* columnist Thomas Friedman reported that unlike other families who frequently honor their suicide bombers as holy martyrs destined for a heavenly afterlife, the father of the twenty-two-year-old attacker was devastated. "We are a respectful family who love our nation, flag and the Koran," the father said. "But we cannot understand why this child had done the thing he had done." The suicide bomber's father then made a striking appeal. "First, let us meet with the chief rabbi of our Jewish brothers," he offered. "Let me hug him. Let me kiss his hands and flowing robe. Let me apologize in the name of my son and offer my condolences. We will be damned if we do not reconcile with them."

The world is filled with similar unexpected acts of compassion that reveal the power of a love that is actively engaged in the world. In the Middle East, a twelve-year-old Palestinian boy was mistakenly shot in the head and the chest by Israeli soldiers. The soldiers thought the toy gun he was carrying was a real one. Two days later, the boy died of his wounds. Amazingly, the parents decided to donate his organs to Israeli children. "We want to send a message of peace to Israeli society, to the Defense Ministry and the Israeli parliament," the boy's father said. "They killed my son, who was healthy, and we want to give his organs to those who need them." "Violence against violence is worthless," the boy's mother added. "Maybe this will reach the ears of the whole world so they can distinguish between just and unjust."

The twelve-year-old Arab boy's heart was transplanted into a twelve-year-old Israeli Arab girl. A Jewish teenager received the boy's lungs. Portions of the boy's liver were given to a seven-month-old Jewish girl and a fifty-eight-year-old mother of two. One of the boy's kidneys went to a three-year-old Jewish girl. The other kidney was transplanted into a five-year-old Arab Bedouin girl. The boy's father was thankful that his son "had entered the heart of every Israeli." While nations fight, its citizens can still show compassion for one another. Compassion is the love that does not exist until it is expressed.

Our contact with inner silence can generate a compassion that feels almost unlimited. Almost. Sometimes, however, even our compassion is not strong enough for us to embrace those who seem unworthy of loving. The unworthy will still confound us and repulse us. Light may be more powerful than darkness, but it is not bright enough to completely eliminate darkness.

Despite the loving kindness that our awakening unleashes, it can still be difficult for us to forgive what seems to be unforgivable. Like love, the unforgivable has also been with us throughout the ages, in the present and in the distant past, in modern societies and traditional cultures. The Aztec Indians were thought to have offered little resistance to the Spanish conquerors who arrived in their lands nearly five centuries ago. Then archaeologists discovered remains that showed that residents of one Aztec village had imprisoned more than five hundred Spanish women, children, and soldiers. The Spaniards were kept in cages. Each of the condemned had to listen to the cries of the others who were dragged to a ritual death, one by one, over a period of six months, until the last remaining survivor was finally slaughtered. The ritual sacrifices were carried out on the temple steps by priests and town elders who "sometimes ate their victims raw." One report described how the religious leaders ate the "bloody hearts or cooked flesh from their arms and legs once it dropped off the boiling bones." Our compassion is with the victims of this horrible plight. Little is left for their torturers.

Our devotion to spirituality seems to call upon us to love without conditions. We even try to make room for those who eat hearts that are still beating. Yet although we are no way near as violent, we can still be hurtful in our own way. So, in our humility, we recognize that despite our own kind of cruelties, we, too, seek unconditional love. When we are nurtured by the presence of inner silence, we are inspired to love as we want to be loved, without judgment, without conditions. It becomes harder to judge the failings of others.

In *Unforgiven*, a Clint Eastwood movie, a young sidekick kills a cowboy who ruthlessly scarred the face of a prostitute with a knife. Shaken by the experience, the boy boasts with tentative pride that the man "ain't gonna breathe again, ever." Eastwood's character, a seasoned veteran of too many shootouts, says, "It's a hell of a thing killing a man. You take away all he's got and all he's ever gonna have." Trying to calm himself, the quivering young shooter answers, "Well, I guess he had it coming." Eastwood replies, "We all have it coming, kid."

When it comes to judging others, we all have it coming, so we want forgiveness, and we want to forgive. We may come to believe that the awareness of the fulfilling stillness within gives us a plat-form to forgive because we need so little from others. Emboldened by our inner peace, we can look compassionately upon those who issue threats and commit crimes, knowing that our inner tranquil silence cannot be threatened. Yet the world's madness often pushes our compassion to its limits. Even when the peaceful presence within opens our hearts to all, we still can find ourselves raging against some people.

Every day, our newspapers detail the human madness that can challenge a complacent spirituality, one that accepts all things as part of a larger divine plan. Eventually, the complacency may be forced to give way to a healthy outrage that demands that we unashamedly make judgments about good and bad. The world is a mix of positive and negative, cruelty and mercy. Yet we are human, and our humanity cries out for us to condemn what is negative, to reject what is unkind.

There are unbelievable tortures occurring right now. Spiritual love does not mean that we must refrain from denouncing them and those who perpetrate them. Sometimes these madmen seem to be reveling in a chaotic frenzy of wanton cruelty without purpose, and there is little that we can do but unequivocally revile them. "There is nothing that you can't do to someone in the Middle East today," and there is no leader who can "put a stop to the madness," Thomas Freidman wrote in one of his *New York Times* columns. "We've seen Sunni Muslims in Iraq suicide-bomb a Shiite mosque. We've seen Shiite militiamen torture Sunnis in Iraq by drilling holes in their heads with power tools." Spiritual realism requires that we refrain from coddling these terrorists with misplaced compassion, as if our loving kindness should keep us from condemning them. We may all have it coming, but some of us more so than others.

Sometimes it is easier to judge people when their madness is more subtle than the straightforward horrors of unbridled violence. The crimes that are less deadly are often the ones that make us most judgmental. Inner silence does not preclude us from being outraged by these less violent but still insidious crimes, such as the kind that take place every month, every week, and every day in parts of Cambodia. In a village near the Cambodian capital of Phnom Penh, child prostitutes are provided to adult American men in search of sex with children. Chris Hansen, an NBC News reporter, told how he was approached by a pimp who offered to provide him with very young girls. The pimp was only fifteen years old. His prostitutes were even younger. "Despite all we've seen," Hansen reported, "we're stunned at just how young he says they are—eight-year-olds."

Many young girls in Cambodia and elsewhere are forced into prostitution by poor parents who are desperate to earn some money. "We meet dozens of children," Hansen reported. "One girl says she's nine. She's joined by another who says she's ten." Traveling with Hansen was the chief investigator for the International Justice Mission. The NBC correspondent reported the investigator's reaction. "In twenty years as a cop," Hansen explained, "he's never seen anything like this." Inner silence enables us to make peace with the world. Yet does this mean that we no longer care about what happens in this world? Shall we strive for an awakening that gives us a type of nonjudgmental compassion that stops us from rejecting those who traffic in eight-year-old sexual slaves? Our compassion may prompt us to weep for both the perpetrator and the victim, but our spiritual realism requires that we embrace one and vigorously scorn the other.

Negativity will also be with us, but as human beings is it not our duty to rail against it? We are all outraged by the horrors of war. Doesn't this outrage reinforce our commitment to prevent it, even if we have little choice but to live with it? "Wars will be with us for a long time, perhaps forever," Hermann Hesse wrote. "Nevertheless, the elimination of war remains our noblest goal." We may not be able to make everyone peaceful, but we can always try to create more peace. We may compassionately open our hearts to those who want to cut out our hearts; we can still try reaching out to them, again and again. But we must always be prepared to denounce them and stop them. To restrict ourselves in the name of compassion is to delude ourselves into thinking tolerance can make all things more tolerable.

I have seen how others have managed to reach out again and again to those who seem unreachable, without having any illusions about their despicable crimes. When I was traveling on the West Bank, I visited Rabbi Menachem Froman, a Hasidic rabbi who lives in Tekoa. Religious communities like Tekoa are among the most controversial Jewish settlements on the West Bank. To millions of Muslims everywhere and especially to the Palestinians who claim these lands as their own, these communities are symbols of an unfair religious domination by Jews and an unjust military occupation by Israelis. The residents of Tekoa are loathed by the vast majority of the world's Muslims and are the targets of a fierce Palestinian hatred. Being the object of Muslim hatred has not thwarted Froman's eagerness to bring his love to the Muslim world.

Rabbi Froman is not only a critic of Islamist extremism, he is also extremely critical of what he says are the material and sexual excesses that are undermining American culture. After he lectured me for a while about the sins of my country, I jokingly told him to be patient, that the United States is a young nation and that we may eventually grow out of our adolescent debauchery. He laughed, without agreeing. I touted the blessings of our liberal American culture. He smiled in disagreement.

Surprisingly, the rabbi suggested that we meditate together. He did not ask me to meditate in any particular manner, Jewish or otherwise. We both just sat there with our eyes closed, experiencing our silent spiritual companionship. He knew the transcendent value of inner silence. I then asked Rabbi Froman how it felt to be the object of so much hatred. "Our suffering is a tunnel," the rabbi said. "The depths of our tragedies can be a path that leads us toward a greater compassion." "Why is there so much tragedy?" I asked. "How should I know?" he asked with a shrug. "This is the question that all the great sages have been trying to answer." I had mistakenly asked the cosmic "why" question, when our real task is to discover how to best soothe the victims of tragedy.

Rabbi Froman spends his days teaching and praying in the modest hilltop settlement. He knows all too well that tragedy can strike at any time, challenging our ability to tunnel into the depths of our compassion. In 2001, two fourteen-year-old boys who lived in Tekoa were discovered inside a nearby cave. Palestinian terrorists had smashed their heads in with rocks, killing them both. Rabbi

Froman took me down to the cave where the bodies of the two murdered teens had been found. The innocent energy of these young boys was clearly present, pulling me down into an aching sorrow and not into any deep compassion for their killers.

The tragedy at Tekoa did not prevent Rabbi Froman from reaching out to one of his most hateful adversaries. He sought a meeting with Sheikh Yassin, the founder of Hamas who had orchestrated the numerous suicide bombings that took the lives of so many innocent Jews, and whose unnerving picture I saw on the wall of the Bedouin taxi driver's home in Bethlehem.

Rabbi Froman hoped that Sheikh Yassin would relate to him as one devout believer to another. "We talked for many long hours. I spoke with Yassin about a truce on a religious basis," Froman wrote. "We Jews believe in our vision of the future, and you Muslims believe in your vision of the future," the rabbi told Yassin. "All believers know who runs the world. Why not leave something to Him?"

The rabbi had appealed to their shared belief that only God rules, and thus we can express the humility and infinite compassion that God has given us. Sheikh Yassin did not respond to Rabbi Froman's appeal. Still, despite the horrible murders at Tekoa, the rabbi searched for a way to understand his enemy and went through the tunnel that took him to a place where he could also love his enemy. His spiritual duty is to create more love. How others respond is up to them.

Many of his fellow Israelis accused the rabbi of being too naive. How could Froman sit down with a man who sends suicide bombers to carry out terrorist attacks against him and his neighbors? Froman's defense against violence is realistic; it does rely on politicians and soldiers. But it doesn't rely only on them. He also tries to protect his loved ones with the straightforward simplicity of compassion. Froman's spirituality is pure in its intent and inspiringly optimistic. I could understand the reasoning of the rabbi's critics. His love did seem a bit naive. Almost playfully defiant, he exuded a simple, innocent love similar to the kind we experience as children, before the cynicism of the adult world begins to close in on us. Yet he never forgot the harsh reality of terrorist hate, especially since he was living in a place where he was a particularly visible target of it.

A six-year-old girl once suggested, "If you want to learn to love better, you should start with a friend who you hate." Perhaps that's what Rabbi Froman did when he reached out to Sheikh Yassin. And when I went to the Tekoa cave where the two teenage boys had been murdered by terrorists, the rabbi did not use the moment to express his rage against their killers, nor did he talk about seeking vengeance for the killings. He just let me cry. And I felt as if the world was crying with me.

Sometimes all we can do is weep. Making judgments about others seems pointless. Children experience this phenomenon more often than adults do. They frequently resort to tears when they are forced to accept hurtful situations without being given the opportunity to change them. A four-year-old boy once went next door to an old man whose wife had just died. He saw the man crying in his backyard, so he walked over and sat on the man's lap. After watching the boy sit for a while, his mother later asked what he had said to the man. "Nothing," the boy answered. "I just helped him cry."

Sometimes compassion leaves us speechless. Even though our silence is active, all we can do is share a moment of stillness together. When I attended sessions with Mother Meera, I watched how the Indian spiritual leader did not speak to any of the many seekers who came to visit her. Not a word. Her spiritual work is done in complete silence. The people simply wait in line, and when it is their turn, they kneel down in front of her, and Mother Meera looks into their eyes. Each encounter offers the seeker a glance into her maternal silent presence. Yet Mother Meera's awakening stays active because she actively brings her loving silence into the world. She doesn't sit alone, absorbed in nothing but her own inner silence.

"Everyone must work," Mother Meera explained. "I am working. Everyone must do what they can. This is not a time for people to withdraw from the world. It is a time for people to work with the power of love of the Divine in the world." This is an active awakening.

"People should go on living their ordinary lives," Mother Meera teaches. "I want people to be strong, self-reliant, unselfish, and to contribute to the world with whatever skills and gifts they have. I want them to work. All the old separation between 'holy' and 'worldly' are not real. Everything is divine. Everything. All this is God."

People everywhere are working to bring the divine into this world. In a narrow winding side street in Arab Jerusalem, bustling with Palestinian children who peered out at me, bewildered by my presence, I was welcomed into the home of Sheikh Abdul Aziz Bukhari, who for nearly forty years has been quietly working to bridge the separation between the holy and the worldly. Sheikh Bukhari's home is often a peaceful meeting place for Muslims and Jews, where spiritual unity replaces the raw tension of political animosity.

At a remote desert temple, I experienced the same healing unity that I had felt when I was in Sheikh Bukhari's Jerusalem home. Nebi Musa is an Islamic stone shrine on the West Bank, built in the Judean Desert near the road to Jericho. Muslims believe that Moses is buried inside the tomb at Nebi Musa. As do Christians and Jews, Muslims also revere Moses as a prophet.

When I arrived at Nebi Musa, the only building in a vast stretch of yellow desert, I was greeted by Sheikh Muhammad Usta, a hearty man with a large beard who was one of the caretakers of the mosque. He told me how the shrine had been built as a holy site for Muslim pilgrims traveling between Mecca in Arabia and the al-Aqsa Mosque in Jerusalem.

Obviously proud of his Islamic heritage, Sheikh Usta agreed to chant an Islamic prayer. He stopped occasionally to explain the meaning of some of the sacred Arabic phrases. As the sheikh's resonant voice filled the silence of the remote desert mosque, my eyes filled with tears. I wept at the reality of a common spirituality that had not yet been experienced by so many of us.

Sheikh Usta's quiet work at Nebi Musa helps to narrow the divide between worldly conflict and spiritual harmony. He works alone in the desert at a secluded holy site. Every spring, nearly a hundred thousand Muslim worshippers visit the site. He quietly offers his spiritual love and Islamic prayers to all who pass his way, Arabs and Jews alike, sharing Mother Meera's vision that everything and everyone is divine.

Is spiritual love, such as the kind offered by Sheikh Usta, effective only with spiritual seekers? Or can those who seek political change also be changed by our spirituality?

When I visited Haifa, a mixed Arab-Jewish city in Israel, I saw how political action can be influenced by spiritual compassion. I attended a meeting of Arab Israelis and Jewish Israelis seeking reconciliation. One of the participants was Eliyahu McLean, the same peacemaker who helped me journey into Arab Bethlehem.

During the gathering in Haifa, the Israelis respectfully listened to the Palestinian narrative, in which they depicted themselves as political victims of a historical injustice. They insisted that European colonial powers took their land and gave it to the Jews in a ploy to maintain control of the Middle East and its oil. The Palestinians listened carefully to the Israeli narrative, which saw the Jews' history as a two-thousand-year struggle to survive. This narrative insisted that Jews had finally grown weary of living in too many anti-Semitic cultures that had been committed to their subjugation, even their annihilation, and that Israel was their final refuge. Underlying the clash of the Palestinian and Israeli narratives, and the subsequent political arguments and bitter accusations that followed, was extraordinary compassion. It was a deeply spiritual compassion that expressed itself through the determination to find a political accommodation and even create a true friendship among former adversaries.

The experience in Haifa reminded me of my encounter with an elderly Palestinian shopkeeper who was hawking his wares in the souk, the open-air market in the Arab sector of Old Jerusalem.

When the shopkeeper learned that I was an American, he soon began to complain about President Bush, the U.S. war in Iraq, and the U.S. policy toward Muslims. It did not take long for compassion to overcome political conflict. "Look in my eyes," I told him. "There is peace between us. We are the same." He warmly agreed and invited me to dinner.

During another gathering of Jewish Israelis and Arab Muslims, Eliyahu, a religious Jew, and Ghassan Manasrah, an Islamic Sufi teacher, brought people together to work for political peace through interreligious dialogue and worship. Manasrah led a *zikr* ritual where we slowly walked around the perimeter of the room, moving to the rhythm of a hand-held drum, as the Islamic Sufi chant bound all of us together, Arab and Jew, in a loving circle.

Afterward, Eliyahu lit the Friday night candles that celebrated the arrival of the Jewish Sabbath. Muslims and Jews stood side by side, listening reverently as Eliyahu sung the Hebrew prayers. The room was blessed by the compassion that arose from an active group awakening.

Moments like this one are all too rare. More often, there are times when the world's injustices seem so great that our compassion is simply not enough to comfort us. We may even feel compelled to denounce God for creating a planet where, throughout the ages, unimaginable cruelties have continued to flourish everywhere.

When confronting such cruelties, how can we react with anything other than outrage? How can our awakening generate a compassion that is always accepting, when even the compassion of God Himself has its limits? His compassion for us does not prevent Him from allowing the darkest cruelties to haunt humanity. We might declare that it is not God Who allows cruelty, it is humanity that chooses to behave cruelly. But does our free will really depend on other human beings having the ability and the desire to torture others? Is this the best our omnipotent God can do? Even the innocent among us, who have never chosen to harm others, are not spared from the deadly choices of humanity's free will. Where was God's compassion when he forced Jesus to die an excruciating physical death just so that the rest of us could find spiritual salvation?

"From a God who is a loving father, who is actually Love itself, one would expect understanding and forgiveness," the pioneering psychotherapist Carl Jung wrote. "So it comes as a nasty shock when this supremely good God only allows the purchase of such an act of grace through a human sacrifice, and, what is worse, through the killing of his own son. One should keep before one's eyes the strange fact that the God of goodness is so unforgiving that he can only be appeased by a human sacrifice!" Even when our awakening actively creates more love and expresses increasing compassion, can we always be compassionate when God is not? Despite the glory of resurrection, must we also accept the painful reality of crucifixion? Should we not be outraged by it?

It is not only our own imperfections that must be forgiven. Perhaps the imperfections of a Creator Who allows innocents to die and the helpless to suffer also requires our forgiveness. When we forgive the world for its sins as we ask forgiveness for our own, and when we forgive the Creator Who gave us too many things to forgive, we push our compassion to an even higher level.

Yom Kippur is a day of atonement, when Jewish worshippers traditionally reflect upon their own imperfections and pray for God's forgiveness. Should we not also lament the sinful imperfections of life that are not of our own making? "I think that Yom Kippur is a dual process," wrote Elie Wiesel, the Holocaust survivor who witnessed firsthand humanity's confounding potential for depravity. "I will forgive the Creator and He will forgive me," Wiesel explained, carrying out his own profound version of the Yom Kippur ritual.

Perhaps our active awakening may one day fill us with such a powerful compassion that it can extend to all beings, including the Creator of all things. Our constant return to inner silence may give us the strength to hold on to our compassion, even when the world's criminality tries to steal our loving kindness. Yet for now, even our compassionate understanding must give way to outrage.

Is it more compassionate to accept life's cruelties than to be outraged by them? Are we being compassionate when we fail to condemn the life force that brings pain to others? Are we being spiritually compassionate when we hide behind the pretense of a lofty understanding that embraces all things equally, even if they are cruel and hateful?

When we do bring our inner silence into this world, we can feel both compassion and outrage simultaneously. Our inner silence gives us the strength to have compassion for those who inflict suffering even as we condemn them for it. "Clear and sweet is my soul, and clear and sweet is all that is not by soul," Walt Whitman wrote. An active awakening helps us love others the way we love ourselves. But it does not keep us from being outraged by others who behave in brutal ways that we would not. Souls are sweet, but they do not always act sweetly. Silence connects us to that joyful sweetness, while our conscience moans over life's bitterness.

Although we are spiritually realistic, our inner silence inspires us with hope. The fulfilling quiet presence within unleashes a powerful positive energy that is unafraid, almost indifferent to failure, resilient enough to keep us loving the world even though there is much in the world that is unlovable. We are optimists, not because we are unrealistic, but because the reality of our own quiet tranquility makes us more confident that even if there are some people who may not be able to experience inner peace, there are millions of others who can. This energetic optimism keeps our hopes alive, even when things appear hopeless.

There is no failure in trying to bring happiness to a world that will always have suffering. We are indifferent to our failings when the effort is noble. "It is we men of the spirit, we poets, seers, fools, and dreamers, who plant trees for later," Hermann Hesse wrote. "Many of our trees will not thrive, many of our seeds will be sterile, many of our dreams will turn out to be mistakes, delusions, and false hopes. Where is the harm in that?"

It is through our love and compassion that we can hope to uplift the world. Does it make any sense to try to change a world that seems beyond our ability to change? Maybe not. But spiritual love is mystical, beyond reason. We can take the peace of our inner silence out into the world, as if this might help to enlighten the world, even though the world may only be able to enlighten itself.

Even when inner silence seems to have vanished, we can still love this life. Amid the clamor of cruelties and our loud protests against them, we can continue to carry our inner stillness into this world and quietly connect with one another, soothing those who need healing, bringing joy to those who crave it.

As spiritual realists, we are never afraid to engage the world as it is. Inner silence gives us the strength to see things clearly, to judge what needs to be judged, even as we continue to calm those who wish us harm. Our spirituality gives us the power to actively try to make this troubled world a bit more livable and lovable. Our spirituality is not weak, fanciful, or fleeting. Our spiritual fulfillment is real, lively, and dynamic.

An active awakening is more powerful than a passive one. Our inner light is more powerful than the surrounding darkness. Our spiritual love, which arises when we are awake to the peaceful stillness of this moment, is the most powerful of all.

Hallelujah. Jai Guru Dev. Namaste. Inshallah. Shalom. Peace. Silence.

INDEX